MODERNISM IN POETRY

Studies in Twentieth-Century Literature

Series Editor:
Stan Smith, Professor of English, University of Dundee

Published Titles:
Rainer Emig, *Modernism in Poetry: Motivation, Structures and Limits*

Modernism in Poetry: Motivations, Structures and Limits

Rainer Emig

Longman
London and New York

Longman Group Limited,
Longman House, Burnt Mill,
Harlow, Essex CM20 2JE, England
and Associated Companies throughout the world.

*Published in the United States of America
by Longman Publishing, New York*

First published 1995

ISBN 0 582 23919 2 CSD
ISBN 0 582 23920 6 PPR

British Library Cataloguing-in-Publication Data

A catalogue record for this book is
available from the British Library

Library of Congress Cataloging-in-Publication Data

Emig, Rainer, 1964–
Modernism in poetry : motivation, structures, and limits / Rainer Emig.
p. cm. — (Studies in twentieth century literature)
Includes bibliographical reference and index.
ISBN 0–582–23919–2. — ISBN 0–582–23920–6 (pbk.)
1. American poetry—20th century—History and criticism. 2. Modernism (Literature)—United States. 3. Hopkins, Gerard Manley, 1844–1889—Criticism and interpretation. 4. Yeats, W. B. (William Butler), 1865–1839—Criticism and interpretation. 5. Eliot, T. S. (Thomas Stearns), 1888–1965—Criticism and interpretation. 6. Pound, Ezra, 1885–1972—Criticism and interpretation. 7. English poetry—History and criticism. 8. Modernism (Literature)—Great Britain. I. Title. II. Series: Studies in twentieth century literature (Longman (Firm))
PS310.M57E45 1996
821′.91091—dc20 95–7334
CIP

Set by 5 in 10/12 Bembo
Produced by Longman Singapore Publishers (Pte) Ltd
Printed in Singapore

Contents

Foreword

Literary movements usually come into being by slaying their immediate precursors. In the case of modernism, however, the slaughter of the fathers was counterbalanced by a resurrection of the grandfathers. Ezra Pound and T.S. Eliot, for instance, disavowed their Romantic inheritance in order to assert their roots in an earlier tradition trumpeted as 'Classicism'. Pound's slogan, 'make it new', was in practice a demand to 'make it old', to kick out last year's words in favour of the year's before.

Many modernists perceived their works as a defence against, rather than a celebration of modernity. Rejecting the fad-swept world of modern culture, which Eliot condemned as a 'vast panorama of futility and anarchy', they strove to colonise the future with the spectres of the past. The notorious difficulty of assigning dates to modernism (1907–25 is Frank Kermode's suggested timespan, 1910–30 Peter Faulkner's, while other critics place the movement's origins much earlier and its ends much later) reflects the temporal discomfort of the modernists themselves, their sense of being 'posthumous' or 'out of key' with time. Works like *The Waste Land*, *The Cantos*, and *Ulysses*, with their dizzying catapults through time, bespeak their authors' sense of homelessness in history.

Thus the question as to just how modern modernism was – or is – continues to provoke controversy. Were the modernists true revolutionaries, or were they just – in Yeat's words – the last Romantics? Undoubtedly the modernists were steeped in the Romantic tradition they so noisily denied; yet in many ways their aspirations are beyond us still, newer than now, more modern than modernity. Criticism is still trying to catch up with the innovations of the early decades of the century; it is arguable that the recent explosion of literary theory represents a delayed reaction to modernism, which happened, like an infantile trauma, too early to be understood. Thus modernism, in spite of its reversion to the past, preempts the future, rendering all later works revisions of its visions.

The latest defence against the afterlife of modernism is post-modernism. Like modernism, postmodernism asserts its novelty by trampling on its antecedents; in fact, postmodernism travesties modernism in much the same terms that modernism travestied Romanticism. According to its pundits, postmodernism revels in absence, whereas modernism strove for presence; postmodernism opens up the realm of chance, whereas modernism insisted on determination. Where modernism synthesised, postmodernism disperses, breaking up the 'grand narratives' of the West in favour of a multitude of local and competing narratives. So forced are many of these oppositions as to justify the cynical suspicion that postmodernism is merely modernism in new packaging: a marketing device concocted to create new books, new jobs, new stars in a profession always starved for novelty. More charitably, however, postmodernism has been right to challenge the academic canon of modernism, traditionally dominated by conservatives like Pound and Eliot to the exclusion of the feminist and leftist countercurrents of the period.

Even the canonical figures, however, are too complex to be relegated to the obsolete. The value of Rainer Emig's book, especially in the present climate, is the discernment with which it brings those complexities to light. In close analyses of Hopkins, Yeats, Eliot, and Pound, Emig shows how modernist poetics grappled with questions of signification, authenticity, and responsibility which postmodernism tends to shrug aside, in a glib celebration of the simulated and the second-hand. Modernism, by contrast, insisted on the artwork's debts to the world, the poet, and the past, while also acknowledging its flight from all those creditors. In any case, reports of the death of modernism are greatly exaggerated; there is too much life left in its dilemmas to lay the modernist inheritance to rest.

Maud Ellman
March, 1995

Acknowledgements

The present book derives from a D.Phil. thesis written under the hospitable roof of Christ Church, Oxford, between October 1989 and January 1992. The research was made possible by generous scholarships awarded by Cusanuswerk (the academic sponsorship scheme of the Catholic bishops of Germany) and the British Academy. The revisions for the final version were helped by the relative freedom of my position as research fellow of the Graduiertenkolleg am Fachbereich 3, the Graduate School of Literary and Communication Studies, at the University of Siegen, Germany.

My initial thanks go to John Fuller who patiently supervised a project that was certainly not always his cup of tea – and a student who was sometimes rather reluctant to be supervised. His sound knowledge and common sense have helped the project a great deal.

I also have to express my gratitude to Terry Eagleton and Maud Ellmann who read and examined the thesis and, despite the constraints of the academic ritual, managed to pass on helpful criticism. Robert Young was kind enough to have a look at the chapter on psychoanalysis. His remarks made me realise that I was on the right track and helped me integrate the theoretical section of my study with the rest.

Various fellow students and friends of mine took the time to read drafts of parts of my work. Their criticism has made me clarify many points and drop some others. These were Beate Rosskopf, Sabine Roth, Jean Long and Jonathan Hope.

Stan Smith proved a rigorous reader of the drafts of the book, and his suggestions have shaped the final result. Together with my publisher, Longman, he continued to believe in the relevance of what I have to say – and the possibility of making it accessible to readers.

I would also like to thank those people whose friendship, advice, and hospitality made my research a much more enjoyable time than it would otherwise have been. These were José Luis González Medina, Sveinn Haraldsson and Michaela Giebelhausen in Oxford, and Gerald Carlin, Harjit Kaur Khaira, Karin Littau and Iain Hamilton Grant at Warwick. Of my Siegen colleagues Sabine Boscheinen has been especially supportive.

My special thanks are due to Gerald Siegmund, not only for being my friend for so many years, but also for reading my revisions for the eventual book and suggesting clarifications when he was very busy with his own demanding research.

My final thanks are to Edward Larrissy who suggested I undertake research on modernism in the first place. Together with Michael Bell he made me realise that I might not be in the wrong place in English Studies while I was working on my MA at Warwick University. In this respect, I am also indebted to Norbert K. Buchta and Verena Lobsien at Johann Wolfgang Goethe-Universität Frankfurt am Main who pushed me in the right direction and encouraged and supported my rather undirected progress whenever possible.

The remaining weaknesses and errors of the present book are entirely my own.

Publisher's Acknowledgements

We are grateful to the following for permission to reproduce copyright material:

The Ezra Pound Literary Property Trust and Faber & Faber Ltd/New Directions Publishing Corp. for the poem 'Histrion' from *A Quinzaine for this Yule* by Ezra Pound, Copyright © 1995 by The Trustees of the Ezra Pound Literary Property Trust; extracts from *A Guide to Kulcher* by Ezra Pound and *The Spirit of Romance* by Ezra Pound, Copyright © 1968 by Ezra Pound; and 'As for Imagism' from *The New Age, XVI/The Literary Essays of Ezra Pound*, Copyright © 1935 by Ezra Pound. Faber & Faber Ltd/Harcourt Brace & Co for extracts from the poems 'The Love Song of J Alfred Prufrock', 'Hysteria', 'The Hollow Men', 'Journey of the Magi', 'Song for Simeon', 'Whispers of Immortality', 'Portrait of a Lady', and 'Ash Wednesday' from *Collected Poems 1909–1962* by T S Eliot (Faber & Faber, 1974), Copyright © 1936 by Harcourt Brace & Company, Copyright © 1964, 1963 by T S Eliot; and an extract from *Selected Prose of T S Eliot* ed. Frank Kermode (Faber & Faber, 1975), Copyright © 1975 by Valerie Eliot. Faber & Faber Ltd/Harcourt Brace & Co for extracts from the poems 'Little Gidding' and 'Burnt Norton' from *Collected Poems 1909–1962* by T S Eliot (Faber & Faber 1974)/*Four Quartets*, Copyright 1943 by T S Eliot and renewed 1971 by Esme Valerie Eliot. Faber & Faber Ltd/New Directions Publishing Corp. for the poem 'On His Own Face in a Glass', extracts from the poems 'La Fraisne', 'Cino', 'The Picture', 'Erat Hora', 'The River Song', 'Papyrus', 'L'Art, 1910', 'In a Station of the Metro', 'Hugh Selwyn Mauberley', 'An Object', 'Portrait d'une Femme', 'Apparuit', and 'Silet' from *Collected Shorter Poems* by Ezra Pound

(Faber & Faber, 1984)/*Personae* (New Directions), Copyright © 1926 by Ezra Pound; extracts from *The Literary Essays of Ezra Pound* ed. T S Eliot (1954), extracts from the poems 'Canto XXXIX', 'Notes for CXVII et seq.', 'Canto XC' and the poem 'Fragment (1966)' from *The Cantos* by Ezra Pound (Faber & Faber, 1987)/*The Cantos of Ezra Pound* (New Directions), Copyright © 1934, 1948 Ezra Pound; and an extract from *Selected Prose 1909–1965* by Ezra Pound edited with an introduction by William Cookson, Copyright © 1973 by The Estate of Ezra Pound. Simon & Schuster, Inc for the poems 'The Song of the Happy Shepherd', 'To the Rose Upon the Rood of Time' and 'The Lover Tells of the Rose in His Heart' from *The Poems of W B Yeats: A New Edition*, ed. Richard J Finneran (New York: Macmillan 1983).

Introduction

'Modernism' has become a familiar term in the last decades. It is common knowledge that it summarises artistic tendencies from roughly the turn of the century until the Second World War. The products of these tendencies are characterised by abstraction, obscurity and a multiplicity of perspectives which, when combined, leave both the established forms of realism and the unreal, but still coherent, imagery of symbolism behind. In terms of literature, unexplained allusions, obscure and often 'non-literary' language and the disintegration of coherent narratives and settings into startling and apparently unrelated images are considered reliable indicators.[1]

Yet while the historic location of modernism and descriptions of its surface features are easy to come by, it is much more difficult to point out the internal characteristics of a modernist work. When taken out of its historic and artistic framework, its context, what is it that makes a work a modernist one? The question is not merely an academic pastime, as the recent debates about the validity of the concept of 'postmodernism' demonstrate. If there is such a thing as postmodernism, then modernism must arrive at some limits. What are they and how can they be described in structural terms? If there is no such thing as postmodernism, and modernism merely continues in a slightly altered shape, then what is its 'original' shape, and what do the alterations look like? The difficulty of answering these important questions points towards a critical neglect that has left modernism hovering uneasily between two related concepts, those of modernity and avant-garde.

The term modernity describes the results of the period of philosophical, scientific and political upheavals commonly known as the Enlightenment. Drawing on the humanistic ideas of the Renaissance, the thorough destabilisation of religion through the Reformation, and the rationalistic philosophical systems of the seventeenth century (with Thomas Hobbes and John Locke as their most important English representatives), the eighteenth century combined these to attack in a radical way what were perceived as insults to human freedom and reason: the theological view of the world and its justification of the feudal political order expressed in absolutist monarchy. Isaac Newton's mechanistic view of the universe and the French Revolution as the attempt to put into practice the rational ideas of contemporary philosophers about society can be regarded as the most powerful expressions of the new era.

When taken out of the established theological framework, however, man is forced to define his role and actions himself. (The exclusive use of the masuline form is intentional: the subject of Enlightenment is generally imagined as a male one – a bias that reappears in modernism.) Both history, and subjectivity as the concept that describes what man *is*, now become problematic areas, while nature and objective reality (whose rules are gradually unveiled) are often seen as separated from the human sphere. In particular, the effects of the Industrial Revolution (which followed in the footsteps of the Enlightenment and is the important materialist aspect of modernity) force man to reconsider his position in a world which seems simultaneously at his disposal and utterly inaccessible. Romanticism is an expression of this attempt, but as will become evident in the present study, modernism, too, can be interpreted as a late endeavour to come to terms with the rifts that were thrown open by modernity.

'Avant-garde', on the other hand, appears to be connected with art only, and therefore alien to the universal concept of modernity. Innovation, originality, and the undermining of established artistic norms are its major characteristics. Yet a look at their theoretical bases reveals that these endeavours only make sense when the creative subject behind them is considered liberated from metaphysical and religious master-plans as well as the servility to rulers who determine what art is. A proof of this is the *Querelle des anciens et des modernes* which started as a debate between philosophers, artists and writers in France in the late seventeenth century and quickly infiltrated the rest of Europe. Traditional values and achievements (especially those of antiquity, i.e. the ancient Greeks and Romans) were held up as norms by the *anciens*, while the *modernes* insisted that standards in life and art had to be developed out of contemporary positions.

It is evident that the struggle would have been groundless without the awareness that the present was radically different from the past.

The conviction that man is autonomous from supreme schemes outside his domain is necessary for the belief in the possibility of originality. Inside a system of belief that sees man merely as the tool of a Divine plan, for instance, artistic originality would be impossible or even blasphemous. Within an intellectual framework based on human autonomy, originality becomes the benchmark of human quality. Thus the cult of the original and the genius that the Romantics propagated. Thus also the many modernist avant-garde movements which continually declared radical breaks and new beginnings.[2] The inflation of these gestures hints at some problems within the avant-garde position which will be touched on by this study.

Somewhere between the achievements of modernity (or perhaps at its very end) and the radical gestures of the avant-garde is the place of modernism. Yet despite some attempts at describing this location adequately,[3] modernism has remained an annoyingly opaque concept in art and literature, a term that seems both too general and too ill-defined to be of much use. The deficit becomes most apparent when 'modernism' is used as 'classical modernism' in the description of an established canon of writers and artists. The impression is that the adjective 'modernist' has too rapidly been transformed from a critical (and usually negative) term of description to a safe theoretical category to be filled with much content.

The gap between general concepts and artistic practice becomes most irritating in the analysis of modernist works, especially in the field where artistic construct and the underlying theories, the aesthetics of modernism, display the closest affinities. If the German theorist Wolfgang Iser is correct and poetry is indeed a paradigm, a model of the pattern, of modernism,[4] then it becomes essential to find out what this means in terms of the structure of poems. What goes on in poems that makes them modernist ones?

This question describes in shorthand the aim of the present study. The approach should procure insights for the analysis of texts which are a necessary supplement to 'external' approaches trying to define literary modernism by outlining the cultural, social and economic conditions of the late nineteenth and early twentieth century which form the background of their production. These undoubtedly shape the texts, yet not in a direct mimetic way which would make the works merely a plaster cast of the time of their creation. When this is naïvely assumed (and both conservative and Marxist critics sometimes have the tendency to do so) modernism is denied the relative autonomy gained in the arts much earlier, i.e. the growing independence from direct responses to their environment. Modernism is then treated as if it were in fact not modern.

The 'internal' approach of this study will try to demonstrate the particular set-up of modernist poems, yet also the – often problematic – theoretical premises of rhetorical figures such as symbols, metaphors and metonymies which feature crucially in them. These figures are usually called tropes. If this study prefers to describe them as structures, it does so in pursuit of one of its aims which is to show the internal connections at work between these constructs, interrelations triggered off by important underlying problems which lead to strategies of coping with them. The three most crucial areas of modernist poetry's struggle will be unveiled as, firstly, the concept of a self, a controlling force within the texts; secondly, the idea of a reality which is external to the poems and with which they interact; and finally its own mechanisms of interchange between subjective inside and objective outside.

All these areas are experienced by modernist poems as inextricably linked with language. Therefore, in order to arrive at a complete picture, the analysis has to start with one of the basic meaningful units within language, the sign. The crucial role of the sign in relation to reality will be presented as the offspring of modernism, yet also as the reason for its limitations. The analysis will then proceed through more complex entities – which will be described as variants of the sign – up to the largest structure, myth. The analysis of myth, which also appears as a fictional origin of modernist poems, will display the circularity inherent in modernist aesthetics.

The justification of this structural approach is to be found in the simple yet decisive insight of the Russian theorist Yuri Lotman who claims that language is the material of poetry (Lotman 1976: 17–21). While this seems to be self-evident on one level, taking it seriously for a critical approach often appears to be a problem, especially for Anglo-Saxon scholars raised on theories which foreground complex issues, such as feeling, truth, and life in general, while neglecting or even obscuring the means with which texts tackle these issues. The present study will therefore concentrate on crucial features in the works of four poets which exhibit the central structural shifts within modernism very clearly. Gerard Manley Hopkins's poems will be scrutinised for their attitude towards the sign. William Butler Yeats's poetry stands as an informative example of the uses and difficulties of the symbol. T.S. Eliot's poems will demonstrate the offspring and multiple functions of metaphor and metonymy. Ezra Pound's works will help to shed some light on modernist poetry's ambivalent attitude towards myth. It is to be hoped that – as a welcome by-product – these readings will also shed some new light on established poems.

At this point, a problem of method must be admitted. If a structural description of modernism is to be developed, then the choice of examples is already a determining factor. Which is to say that even the attempt to distance oneself from an established canon of authors only ever leads to the creation of a new one. In fact, the problem cannot be solved. Yet, as will become evident, this study shares Paul de Man's conviction that modernism is not so much the feature of one historic era as a recurring element within literature itself. In his words:

> The appeal of modernity haunts all literature. It is revealed in numberless images and emblems that appear at all periods – in the obsession with a *tabula rasa*, with new beginnings – that finds recurrent expression in all forms of writing. No true account of literature can bypass this persistent temptation of literature to fulfill itself in a single moment.[5]

The reasons why these modernist tendencies feature more crucially in some historic periods and locations than others are explained by studies of the historic and intellectual climate of modernism.[6] The authors selected for the present investigation are in fact established members of the critical canon – with the possible exception of Hopkins.[7] Their varying positions with regard to the evasive concept of modernism will be outlined in the following analyses. In these, Hopkins will be situated on the threshold, Yeats half in, half outside, Eliot fully immersed, and Pound already on the way out. The aspects highlighted by their works should help to draw the sometimes far from stable demarcations, the boundaries of the modernist 'project' in poetry.

This first half of the present study may be read separately as a structural description of modernist poetry. Its individual chapters can be used as analyses of central aspects in the works of the discussed authors as well as concise introductions to the sign, symbol, metaphor, metonymy and myth.

Showing the borderlines, the limits of modernism in English poetry is not only necessary for a complete structural picture, but also essential for an understanding of the internal motivations which bring modernist poetry into being in the first place. While there are critics and theorists who believe that modernism does not come to an end, that it can perpetuate itself endlessly in an internal process of productive self-criticism, a dialectic,[8] the present study is convinced that endings of various kinds are an important feature of modernist works. As will be shown, modernist poems often present themselves as both generated out of themselves (i.e. without an external point of origin) and as potentially timeless and immortal. 'End' thus becomes a central issue in modernist poems. It appears as fascinating fetish and shunned taboo, as silences and alternatively dissolutions which almost magically attract the texts, yet at the same time as something (or 'nothing') that the poems fight, against which they erect aesthetic barricades of various types.

The three areas in which ends and limits in modernist poetry become most poignant are the mentioned aspects of subjective interior, objective outside, and the interchange between the two. Modernist poetry's attempt to present itself as generated out of itself exposes its quarrel with its internal mechanisms of control, its concepts of a self of the texts. Its endeavours to present itself as timeless, independent of its historical location as well as potentially immortal, hint at its problems with its exterior. Finally, its difficulties as an evaluating principle capable of making artistic and moral judgements, one of poetry's traditional functions, shows that modernist poetry finds it impossible to control the interchange of the texts and their exterior. More than that, modernist poems ultimately fail to award themselves the value that literature had hitherto been granted as a matter of course.

In order to achieve more than a mere description of these impasses, as an attempt to understand them in the larger frame of the 'modernist project', the second half of the present enquiry is needed. It broadens the view and permits an analysis of modernist poetry as one facet, one discourse of modernism, whose features reappear, sometimes more easily discernible, in neighbouring or indeed overlapping disciplines. A structural outline of modernist poetry can present an apparently complete picture. But this is exactly where its problem lies. It too easily falls prey to modernism's tendency of self-effacement, of hiding behind its own mechanisms, which grants it seemingly unrestricted control within its own sphere.

This dubious autonomy of modernism – which also finds its expression in the very idea of a 'project' – will be criticised in this study. This explains the recurring emphasis on impasses and paradoxes. This should not be confused with an anti-modernist position, one that is hostile to modernism. Indeed, the approach tries to honour modernism exactly because of its internal tensions, its attempts at creation even when forced to be a reaction. The dangers resulting from these internal problems, however, must not be ignored by any proper evaluation of modernism.

The three areas of tension where limits become apparent determine the structure of the second half of the present study. The problems of the constitution of the subject are pursued in the analysis of modernist poems through the theories of psychoanalysis. In the terminology of this project, identity is that which controls the poems while being created by them. It is therefore the equivalent of the psyche in psychoanalytic theories. The structures of this textual identity are connected with assumptions concerning subjectivity – which is ultimately a philosophical concept. This identity is expressed in, misrepresented by and the controlling force behind voices, personae, and characters in the poems. It is part of the texts. Therefore simple equations of either voice or identity or subjectivity with the authors of the poems must be avoided.

The interaction of this subject (or its absence or mutilation) with its outside (imaginary or real) and the effects of this relation on the texts will be discussed in terms of textual economy. 'Economy' will be used in a metaphorical sense as a governing principle within texts – and not in its more traditional meaning as a description of the relation of capital and labour. The problems of exchange and value will be in the centre of this section – and, again, the dangers or opportunities of limits: retention or dissolution, frozen assets or unlimited expense, so to speak. This seemingly abstract enquiry will be linked with an issue that is both central to modernist poems and visibly on their surface: their relation to literary and poetic tradition.

The final section of the second half of the present study will then try to define more clearly what the problematic outside of modernist poems looks like. It will outline (in an admittedly condensed way) some radical philosophical attitudes towards language and its capacity to grasp reality and even truth. The nineteenth-century philosopher Friedrich Nietzsche will provide the prologue to a discussion which then moves on to two radically different philosophies of language: Ludwig Wittgenstein's drastic reduction of its potentials in his early treatise *Tractatus logico-philosophicus* and Martin Heidegger's seemingly opposed view of language as the very origin of Being. Sketches of their argument will be related to similar concepts in modernist poetry. The impasses of philosophical reasoning will present themselves as compatible with the limits of modernism in English poetry.

As with the first half of the present study, the second half can be read on its own as a more theoretical evaluation of modernist poetry. The chapters on psychoanalysis, economy and language philosophy can also be taken out of context as approaches to these fields of study from the related area of literary studies.

The concluding summary and evaluation will be a final act of expansion while at the same time returning to the starting position. Theodor W. Adorno's *Aesthetic theory* and related writings will help to place the characteristics of modernism as detected by Paul de Man, its internal ruptures and self-destructive tendencies, into a larger framework. In this expanded frame of reference, a very fundamental, but unusual variant of the question concerning the possible limits of modernism, the truth or falsity of modernist poems, will be the issue. Yet it will not be examined in a traditional way that relies on external norms of right and wrong, but in a once more 'internal' assessment starting from the ruptures within the poems' interior logic, their own notions of truth. The question will thus be the one cunningly asked by the narrator of Thomas Mann's fictional exploration of modernist art, *Doctor Faustus*:

> In a work there is much seeming and sham, one could go further and say that as 'a work' it is seeming in and for itself. Its ambition is to make one believe that it is not made, but born, like Pallas Athene in full fig and embossed armour from Jupiter's head. But that is a delusion. Never did a work come like that. It is work: art-work for appearance's sake – and now the question is whether at the present stage of our consciousness, our knowledge, our sense of truth, this little game is still permissible, still intellectually possible, still to be taken seriously; whether the work as such, the construction, self-sufficing, harmonically complete in itself, still stands in any legitimate relation to the complete insecurity, problematic conditions, and lack of harmony of our social conditions; whether all seeming, even the most beautiful, even precisely the beautiful, has not today become a lie.
>
> (Mann 1968: 175–6)

NOTES

1. I am using a list of characteristics employed to describe Eliot's poetry in Carpenter 1981: 57.
2. For a discussion of modernist avant-garde movements see Bürger 1984.
3. The most successful recent studies are Schwartz 1985 and, even more convincing, Eysteinsson 1990. Eysteinsson demonstrates the links between Anglo-American, French and German modernism. The

theoretical background of his study also covers Anglo-American, French, and German thinkers.

4. Iser 1966. The German *Moderne* is used both for modernity and modernism, but the textual examples in the volume show that modernism is the target of investigation.
5. De Man 1983: 142–65 (152). Paul de Man uses the term 'modernity', but describes the features that this study will consider those of modernism.
6. The best studies are still Bradbury and McFarlane 1976 and Bell 1980.
7. Although called a 'proto-modernist' in Bergonzi 1977: 177, there is indeed a clear distance between his works and the modernism of the early twentieth century. The posthumous publication of Hopkins's poems in 1918 coincided with the first vogue for modernist poems, so his first critical reception was indeed both too enthusiastic and too naïve. Yet this does not exclude the possibility of structural links between his works and the later ones analysed in this study, links which explain his outsider status in Victorian poetry.
8. An important contribution to the debate concerning the limits of modernity (and thus modernism) is the essay by the German philosopher Jürgen Habermas: 'Modernity – An Incomplete Project', reprinted in translation in Foster 1985: 3–15.

CHAPTER ONE

Problems of the Sign: Gerard Manley Hopkins (1844–89)

1. THE CHANGING CONCEPTS OF THE SIGN

Throughout history the concept of the sign has not been as stable as our seemingly unproblematic everyday use of the term suggests. When we talk of 'signs' in ordinary communication, we tend to assume that a sign is something (a signal, word or gesture) which stands for or points at something else (a warning, direction, or message, for example). Yet the relation between the sign and the reality it is meant to represent have been defined in very different ways. From antiquity until the Renaissance, for instance, the concept was commonly a tripartite one that consisted of the three entities *signifier* (the element that represents – either as a material artefact, writing for instance, or a sound, gesture, etc.), the *signified* (the reality it stands for), and the third element of *similarity* which related the two others. These three entities were imagined as concrete and real.

Around the seventeenth century, 'similarity' became integrated into signifier and signified and part of each, while disappearing as an external reference point. The sign was thus transformed into a binary concept while still retaining a linking element between its two parts. An example of the result of this process is the allegory which combines representation and represented reality in one figure of speech or visual representation. The famous drawing of the French king Louis XIV as the sun (he was both known as *Le Roi-Soleil* (the Sun King) and brought the absolutist concept of kingship to a sun-like zenith) is a perfect illustration.

During the nineteenth century, the linking element of similarity disappears.[1] The reasons for this are complex. Yet it would not be wrong to assume that scientific advances, such as Darwin's theory of evolution, together with the ever-intensifying effect of the Industrial Revolution shook the belief in a predetermined order of things – which could be expressed in a stable concept of similarity. Instead, both objects and human subjects were granted individual power – and so were signs. This created gaps between human subjectivity and nature, for example, which paved the way for Romanticism. It also spawned a more problematic concept of the sign, one that still consisted of signifier and signified, yet had greater trouble holding those two parts together. While the effects of this changed concept of the sign were felt in literature as early as the middle of the nineteenth century, it took half a century more for it to be expressed in theory by the Swiss linguist Ferdinand de Saussure.

The starting point of Saussure's linguistic theories is the definition of the sign, the smallest unit in the semantic network of meaning, as 'the combination of a concept and a sound pattern'.[2] He exemplifies this by using the sign for 'tree' as an example. The concept of the tree (which he regards as a psychological phenomenon) is somehow similar to the universalist concept which includes all trees in their 'treeness'. It can only become a linguistic phenomenon by its relation with a sound pattern (a physical phenomenon), i.e. in English the sound [tri:] (Saussure 1983: 67).[3] Like the two sides of a single sheet of paper, psychological concept and linguistic phenomenon cannot exist separately.

Both concept and sound pattern gain their distinction by difference. The concept 'tree' is not that of 'horse'; the sound pattern of the word 'tree' is neither that of 'free' nor 'three' (102).[4] The interaction of differences produces something that is 'positive in its own domain. A linguistic system is a series of phonetic differences matched with a series of conceptual differences' (118). Yet, '*the contact between them gives rise to a form, not a substance*' (111). This means that Saussure's concept does not know an outside of language, a referent (i.e. a real object or entity) that language relates to. His theory is one of articulation, not of representation. For Saussure the function of language can be described while remaining entirely inside the boundaries of language. This closed nature of language will become a central issue and the most important problem of modernism.

According to Saussure, the link between signifier and signified is arbitrary. That does not mean that the sign is subject to the free choice of the speaker, but that it is ultimately unmotivated. There is no intrinsic reason why the word 'tree' should signify the concept of tree. French has a different word for it and so has every other language. Only the conventions of the 'linguistic community', a term that is not clearly defined by Saussure and could refer to speakers of the same language as well as to distinct dialect and social groups, govern its choice (67–9).

Yet there is the possibility of reaching some form of motivation: '*The sign may be motivated to a certain extent*', Saussure claims, but concludes that this motivation can only ever be achieved within the network of signs. His example: the arbitrary French *vingt* (twenty) versus the internally motivated *dix-neuf* (nineteen) which consists of two arbitrary signs (nine and ten) gaining motivation only by their mathematical relation (130).

The following section will demonstrate that Hopkins's poems are indeed motivated by discoveries similar to Saussure's. Yet far from admitting an ultimate lack of motivation at the very basis of language, Hopkins's poems struggle to overcome this arbitrariness. The motivation of this struggle is ultimately a religious one which aims at preserving a belief in a Divine harmony of things – which includes language, too. Yet it is also a struggle that will be shown as central to the aesthetics of modernist poetry as its attempt to bridge the gap between reality and language. Hopkins's radical failure to reunite the two poles of his poems propels him from his Victorian roots into the no man's land of modernism.

2. A POETRY OF STRUGGLE

Hopkins's poetry is characterised by a series of contradictions which appear on – and between – all its levels. Its imagery is essentially Victorian in his nature poems in which a reverence for natural phenomena untainted by human interference is linked with an almost aggressive condemnation of the effects of industrialisation (as in 'Binsey Poplars'). All the same, the deeply religious premises which visibly structure his works with their militant Catholic flavour are understandably alien in the context of the still predominantly anti-Catholic British culture of the late nineteenth century.

The shape of his poems is traditional. There is no hint at *vers libre*, free verse, or any of the avant-garde techniques that were to dominate English poetry only a few decades later. All of his lyric poems are rhymed, in most cases using simple rhyme-schemes. Yet within this unadventurous form a lot of formal exploration takes place. There are numerous internal rhymes, alliteration and assonance in abundance. Together with the often radically inverted and condensed syntax, the unusual sentence order that is also characteristic of Hopkins's verse, this frequently turns the poems into almost illegible formal knots. Their difficulty is not at all reduced by being topped with Hopkins's peculiar concept of stressing syllables, his 'sprung rhythm'. Influences are the Milton of *Samson Agonistes* and Hopkins's studies of a form of Welsh poetry, the *cynghanedd*.[5] An example of this formal overcharge is the beginning of 'The Leaden Echo and the Golden Echo':[6]

> How to kéep – is there ány any, is there none such, nowhere
> known some, bow or brooch or braid or brace, láce, latch or
> catch or key to keep
> Back beauty, keep it, beauty, beauty, beauty, . . . from
> vanishing away?
> Ó is there no frowning of these wrinkles, rankèd wrinkles
> deep,
> Dówn? no waving off of these most mournful messengers,
> still messengers, sad and stealing messengers of grey? –
>
> (Hopkins 1970: 91)

The effect of this artifice, an endeavour that W.H. Gardner rightly calls leading 'poetry forward by taking it back – to its primal linguistic origins' (Hopkins 1953: xiv), is twofold. It creates an impression of precision through the introduction of manifold structural relations within a controlled form. On the other hand this formal precision is not at all mirrored by a simultaneous semantic exactness, a definable meaning. On the contrary, the tension of formal overcharge in Hopkins's poems creates blind spots of meaning, indeterminacies that the most ingenious interpretations have not been able to clarify.[7]

For this analysis, the problem of signification, more precisely that of the sign which seems to be so dominant in Hopkins's works, will be of particular importance. The insights procured by this approach should then be checked concerning their applicability to a general poetics of modernism.

3. SIGNIFICATION AS APPROPRIATION: 'INSCAPE'

Hopkins's poems are expressions of a desperate struggle for adequate expression. The experiments undertaken in them, the radicalisation of accepted poetic standards, such as inversion (the violation of accepted sentence order), neologisms (the introduction of new words), and stress, drive his works towards such an extreme departure from the norms – not only of everyday language, but also of Victorian poetry – as to make them almost incomprehensible in parts. Yet it is questionable whether this is a desired effect of Hopkins's techniques. Experiment in his poems is never undertaken for its own sake. Hopkins is not an exponent of the *l'art pour l'art* position which, in seeking art for art's sake, refuses to take its interaction with everyday life into consideration. As his painstakingly developed concept of 'inscape' shows, the belief that every object of Divine creation is characterised by a particular inherent quality which also shapes its outward appearance is central to his ideas and a determining force of his poetry. A journal entry of 10 August 1872 demonstrates his attempts to capture even the smallest features of natural phenomena:

> I was looking at the high waves. The breakers always are parallel to the coast and shape themselves to it except where the curve is sharp however the wind blows. They are rolled out by the shallowing shore just as a piece of putty between the palms whatever its shape runs into a long roll. The slant ruck or crease one sees in them shows the way of the wind. The regularity of the barrels surprised and charmed the eye; the edge behind the comb or crest was as smooth and bright as glass. It may be noticed to be green behind and silver white in front: the silver marks where the air begins, the pure white is foam, the green/solid water. Then looked at to the right or left they are scrolled over like mouldboards or feathers or jibsails seen by the edge. It is pretty to see the hollow of the barrel disappearing as the white combs on each side run along the wave gaining ground till the two meet at a pitch and crush and overlap each other.
>
> (Hopkins 1980: 56)

Hopkins was very much aware, though, that the close adherence to the differentiation visible in nature often resulted in awkward poems. In a letter to his friend Robert Bridges in 1879 he remarks:

> No doubt my poetry errs on the side of oddness. I hope in time to have a more balanced and Miltonic style. But as air, melody, is what strikes me most of all in music and design in painting, so design, pattern or what I am in the habit of calling 'inscape' is what I above all aim at in poetry. Now it is the virtue of design, pattern, or inscape to be distinctive and it is the virtue of distinctiveness to become queer. This vice I cannot have escaped . . . .
>
> (Hopkins 1980: 77)

The origin of Hopkins's concept of 'inscape' is commonly sought in Duns Scotus's concept of *haecceitas* ('thisness'), an impression prompted by Hopkins's professed admiration of the twelfth-century philosopher.[8] Indeed in a journal entry of 19 July 1872, Hopkins writes: 'But just then when I took in any inscape of the sky or sea I thought of Scotus . . .' (Hopkins 1980: 56). Recent critical approaches, however, stress the emergence of differentiation or particularisation from the eighteenth through the nineteenth century. It is regarded as a concentration of power within subject and objects and becomes a common feature in the discussion of the autonomy of the self (Ong 1986: 18; Robinson 1985: 8). It is apparent that this differentiation also informs Saussure's concept of the structure of signification as the matching of two layers of differentiation: conceptual differentiation and differentiation articulated in signs.

Hopkins's central concept is therefore linked with contemporary aesthetic ideas which ultimately lead from Romanticism through Victorianism to the aesthetics of modernism. Jerome Bump stresses Hopkins's transition from a Keatsian regard for nature as beautiful surface to the conviction that intense observation and contemplation can reveal the unity within natural phenomena (including human beings). This in turn is closely linked with John Ruskin's concept of the 'imagination penetrative' which can be discovered in one 'fountain-like impulse' (Bump 1982: 30). In Hopkins's terminology the equivalent of this impulse is 'instress'. It describes the effect of the 'inscape' of natural phenomena on the human percipient, as in the case of primroses, for instance: 'Take a *few* primroses in a glass and the instress of – brilliancy, sort of starriness: I have not the right word – so simple a flower gives is remarkable. It is, I think, due to the strong swell given by the deeper yellow middle' (Hopkins 1980: 50).

What are the particular effects of the concept of 'inscape' on the signifying efforts of Hopkins's poems? How do they respond to the demanding task of creating a sensible representation of natural objects, of respecting their individual essence? The short admission in the quoted journal entry, 'I have not the right word', already hints at problems it causes in attempts at poetic descriptions. Two – seemingly contradictory – reactions of Hopkins's poems to the demands to 'inscape' and 'instress' are easily perceptible: differentiation and fusion. The first stanza of 'Pied Beauty' illustrates these features:

Glory be to God for dappled things –
  For skies of couple-colour as a brinded cow;
    For rose-moles all in stipple upon trout that swim;

Fresh-firecoal chestnut-falls; finches' wings;
Landscape plotted and pieced – fold, fallow, and plough;
And áll trádes, their gear and tackle and trim.

(69)

The general argument of the poem, that beauty is to be found even (or particularly) in heterogeneous things, is illustrated by carefully chosen images. Directly or allusively, all the four elements are mentioned (air, water, fire, earth) as well as their inhabitants (finches, trout, the coal, the cow). The stanza closes in typical Victorian fashion mentioning human beings (and again, implicitly, men) in charge of all creation, their endeavours and tools. Careful differentiation creates a well-organised imaginary map. The poem charts its signifying territory. A first act of appropriation of reality has taken place.

A look at the adjectives of the text and an examination of the way the stanza relates its elements reveal the same characteristic. The poem tries to connect and fuse dissimilar images. Its most prominent descriptive elements are compounds ('couple-colour', 'rose-moles', 'fresh-firecoal chestnut-falls') which attract attention because they are neologisms, newly coined terms, but even more so because they join elements which are not commonly regarded as related, words belonging to unrelated paradigms (i.e. fields of meaning). Their relation can be logically explained ('rose-moles', for instance, refers to the colour of the moles; 'fresh-firecoal chestnut-falls' to the resemblance of freshly fallen chestnuts to coals), but it is evident that the poetic fusion has taken away the steps preceding it. The effect of this condensed imagery is paradoxical. It is striking and original, but it is also alienating and disturbing. It creates the impression of precision, but the neological status of the images prevents their integration into established units of meaning and creates an uncertainty that defeats the precision while creating it.

The tensions detected within the signifiers of the stanza are paralleled by those created by the relations of its elements. There are three mechanisms of relating at work in the stanza: comparison, preposition, and parataxis. The comparison relates couple-coloured skies *to* a brinded cow; the preposition places rose-moles *in* stipple upon trouts. Parataxis eventually sums up the stanza's attitude of collecting and combining elements indiscriminately.

Already on the level of their basic elements, signs, Hopkins's poems display internal tensions. His concept of 'inscape' sets demanding rules for the creation of art. Language is no longer freely available for mere ornamental descriptions of reality. On the contrary, the way in which this reality is perceived, its Divine originality in even the smallest of its features, demands a new language, one that is utterly original and specially created for every object it is meant to represent. The application of a theologically motivated concept of 'inscape' – which still believes strongly in a linking element of similarity between reality and language – to a language that has lost this link causes the problems within Hopkins's images. Together with another concept, that of 'selving', i.e. achieving the closest possible identity with one's self, the predetermined character given by God to every object and creature in the act of creation (in Hopkins's religious framework of thought), it makes poetic creation an almost impossible task. In his works, the unusual verb 'to selve' appears prominently yet cryptically encoded in a poem which discusses the natural order of all things in the form of a meditation, 'As kingfishers catch fire, dragonflies draw flame':

> Each mortal thing does one thing and the same:
>   Deals out that being indoors each one dwells;
>   Selves – goes itself; *myself* it speaks and spells,
> Crying *What I do is me: for that I came.*
>
> (90)

The role of the poem in Hopkins's concept can therefore not simply be mimetic representation, the imitation of an external reality. This would neither meet the demand of 'inscape' nor that of 'selving'. The poems must gain an 'inscape', an individual essence, of their own, one that in its ideal form would be identical with that which the poem describes, its 'content'. This demand, however, generates severe problems. On the theological level, a poetry capable of creating its own 'inscape' would indeed take the Divine act of creation into its own hands. Hopkins shuns this apparent case of artistic hubris as much as his poetic precursor George Herbert did. Not only are Hopkins's years of poetic silence after joining the Jesuits telling; the seduction inherent in human capacities (especially artistic ones) are directly mentioned in his poems. 'Morning, Midday, and Evening Sacrifice' is a discussion of the proper use and appreciation of the beauty of body and mind:

> The dappled die-away
> Cheek and the wimpled lip,
> The gold-wisp, the airy-grey
> Eye, all in fellowship –
> This, all this beauty blooming,
> This, all this freshness fuming,
> Give God while worth consuming.

Both thought and thew now bolder
And told by Nature: Tower;
Head, heart, hand, heel, and shoulder
That beat and breathe in power –
This pride of prime's enjoyment
Take as for tool, not toy meant
And hold at Christ's employment.

The vault and scope and schooling
And mastery in the mind,
In silk-ash kept from cooling,
And ripest under rind –
What death half lifts the latch of,
What hell hopes soon the snatch of,
Your offering, with despatch, of!

(84)

But not only the creative aspect of poetry turns out to be troublesome. Its aesthetic autonomy, the independence of the final work from its model in reality, becomes a problem, too. The aesthetic qualities of the poems themselves, so necessary to achieve 'inscape', can entangle their reader. Poetry therefore easily achieves the opposite of what it should do – according to Hopkins's belief. Rather than alerting its percipient to the beauty of Divine creation, it can eclipse this original creation with its own secondary – and thus lower-grade – one. This is not merely a problem of faulty artistic judgement. After all, in Christian doctrine the attempt of a Divine creation to outclass its Creator is the reason for the downfall of the angels around Lucifer. In human terms, the entanglement in surface beauty (and this entanglement can also be an erotic one) distracts from the origin of all beauty, God. The beginning of 'To what serves Mortal Beauty?' illustrates this problem:

To what serves mortal beauty ' – dangerous; does set danc-
ing blood – the O-seal-that-so ' feature, flung prouder form
Than Purcell tune lets tread to? ' See: it does this: keeps warm
Men's wits to the things that are; ' what good means – where a
glance
Master more may than gaze, ' gaze out of countenance.

(98)

On the level of signification, the tension is again that of referentiality. Hopkins's poems indicate an overwhelming interest in phenomena outside the text. These need not be objects only; they can also be abstractions, such as Divine love, grace, etc. The existence of these phenomena seems unquestioned. They are – through their 'inscapes' – the driving force behind the creation of the poems. Yet the material quality of these phenomena appears to be very different from that of the texts. Hopkins's poems show an awareness that they are constructed of signs, because they constantly stress the discrepancy between their texture and that of their 'content'. Signs cannot achieve the factuality of phenomena – unless, of course, these phenomena are themselves only aesthetic fabrications.

This leads to a point that is rarely discussed in analyses of Hopkins's poetry, yet so central when one questions the purpose of his poems and the origin of their complexity, their tortured language. Is it so irrefutable that there are no doubts concerning the objective reality of nature in his poems? Are the poems discussing a struggle with faith always based on a firm belief, or are they not rather the offspring of, the defence against, if one likes, severe doubts? These uncertainties can be related to the very nature of writing.

The technical difficulties of Hopkins's poems which often bring them close to a semantic breakdown, a collapse of meaning, act as a safety-net. The poems know and discuss the dangers and pitfalls of signification, especially its aspect of appropriation. By naming, the texts take possession of phenomena, gather them in their own autonomy, and thus exercise their own act of creation which mocks the Divine one, because it is always subjective, personal, and thus inevitably egoistic. Read under these assumptions, a poem like 'Peace' gains rather different dimensions:

> When will you ever, Peace, wild wooddove, shy wings shut,
> Your round me roaming end, and under be my boughs?
> When, when, Peace, will you, Peace? – I'll not play hypocrite
>
> To own my heart: I yield you do come sometimes; but
> That piecemeal peace is poor peace. What pure peace allows
> Alarms of wars, the daunting wars, the death of it?
>
> O surely, reaving Peace, my Lord should leave in lieu
> Some good! And so he does leave Patience exquisite,
> That plumes to Peace thereafter. And when Peace here does
>   house
> He comes with work to do, he does not come to coo,
>   He comes to brood and sit.
>
> (85)

The poem goes beyond merely describing peace or the desire to attain it. It tries to conjure up peace inside its own sphere – very much like a magic spell, with all the characteristics of the latter, most notably the continual repetition of the desired thing. This is the perilous and blasphemous aspect of appropriation within signification.

Yet, dangerous as it presents itself, signification is the only possible approach not only to natural objects, but also to the crucial aspects of faith. The sacramental element that, according to Jeffrey Loomis, permeates the whole of Hopkins's poetry calls for actual signs. These would be both representation and the actual thing, signs which merge with the mysteries of faith (Loomis 1988). A poem like 'The Blessed Virgin compared to the Air we Breathe' is a fairly harmless illustration of this desire for 'objective signification' which is ultimately a desire for reference. Its double edge is stressed in a more complex text, 'Spelt from Sibyl's Leaves'. This poem is concerned with language and its influence on the perception of reality on all its levels, from the title to the very last line. It consists of various paratactic conglomerations, unconnected lists of adjectives and nouns, which are so dominant as to eclipse the terms they are connected with completely. The first one is already a good example: 'Earnest, earthless, equal, attuneable, ' vaulty, voluminous, . . . stupendous'; adjectives meant to describe 'Evening' which, once it has been mentioned, is instantly replaced by 'tíme's vást, ' womb-of-all, home-of-all, hearse-of-all night' (97).

The sheer dominance of the substitutions over the innocent term 'Evening' shows that not so much *a* description is in the focus of the poem, but the very act of describing, signification. Indeed, once let loose, the temptation of signification seems to become uncontrollable:

> Waste; her earliest stars, earlstars, ' stárs principal, overbend
> us,
> Fíre-féaturing heaven. For earth ' her being has unbound; her
> dapple is at an end, as-
> tray or aswarm, all throughther, in throngs; ' self ín self
> steepèd and páshed – qúite
> Disremembering, dísmémbering ' áll now. Heart, you round
> me right
> With: Óur évening is over us; óur night ' whélms, whélms,
> ánd will end us.
>
> (97)

The effect of this anarchy on the human subject represented by the speaker of the poem is catastrophic: the lines illustrate its dissolution.

Paradoxically, the only defence left to the subject is to take part in the orgy of signification, to jump on the train hurrying towards complete annihilation and then to take – at least limited – control. How? By signification.

Only the beakleaved boughs dragonish ' damask the tool-smooth
    bleak light; black,
Ever so black on it. Óur tale, O óur oracle! ' Lét life, wáned,
    ah lét life wínd
Off hér once skéined stained véined variety ' upon, áll on twó
    spools; párt, pen, páck
Now her áll in twó flocks, twó folds – black, white; ' ríght,
    wrong; reckon but, reck but, mind
But thése two; wáre of a wórld where bút these ' twó tell, each
    off the óther; of a rack
Where, selfwrung, selfstrung, sheathe- and shelterless, ' thóughts
    agaínst thoughts ín groans grínd.

(98)

What may be read as a rather Manichean[9] division of the world into good and evil, the saved and the damned, can also be interpreted as a description of writing. Its symbols black and white are linked with other give-aways, such as 'tale', 'skéined stained véined', all of which relate to the appearance of writing on the page.

This would explain the unorthodox equation black, white / right, wrong. Usually, black and wrong, white and right are associated. Here, white stands for the anarchic chaos preceding signification, the empty page which permits everything, because it contains nothing. It lacks the order of the right, written, black word. Writing introduces borderlines, a distance which is both temporal and spatial, within the act of signification. This distance seems necessary to escape its potential anarchy, its overwhelming power. This power is its tendency to become autonomous, its own reality which does not know an outside, much less transcendental values and faith, and – very important – no subject either. 'óur night ' whélms, whélms, ánd will end us.' In its more obvious religious implications, the painful entanglement of white and black, right and wrong, stands for the continual struggle of hostile forces within human nature. Yet even this fate of the human self is described by the poem as a text, a tale: 'Óur tale, O óur oracle!'

4. SIGNIFICATION AS DISTANCING

Writing creates distance. It introduces a temporal distance between its creation and its reception. It also creates a spatial distance between author and work as much as between work and reader by the simple fact that it requires a material representation, an artefact. Reading, on the other hand, abolishes this distance, but only through an act of simulation which is itself controlled by the forms of distance between artefact and percipient.[10] But is there also an internal distancing process at work within the mechanisms of signification, an intratextual distance?

Hopkins's poems give a double evidence for this. Despite the demands of 'inscape' and 'instress' to respond to the direct impact of phenomena, they depict the need of distance for their speakers and they exercise distance in their imagery. The creation of imaginary maps has already been identified as an appropriating feature in 'Pied Beauty'. A closer look at the process of building imaginary settings in the poems reveals that contrary to their impulse of gathering images, they also follow a movement away from the origin of the creation, the speaker. The very act of placing the images hides the creator of the imaginary units. The texts guide the reader's attention to the 'there', never to the 'here'. Even when the self of the poems is mentioned directly, the texts usually confront the reader with metonymies, substitutions (such as 'My heart in hiding' in 'The Windhover'). By mutilating the persona, the guise of the speaker, these substitutions create a self outside itself. It remains to be seen whether this internal contradiction reveals a central problem in the constitution of the self in Hopkins's poems, his notion of 'selving'. The first stanza of 'The Starlight Night' is exemplary of this distancing technique.

> Look at the stars! look, look up at the skies!
> O look at all the fire-folk sitting in the air!
> The bright boroughs, the circle-citadels there!
> Down in dim woods the diamond delves! the elves'-eyes!
> The grey lawns cold where gold, where quickgold lies!
> Wind-beat whitebeam! airy abeles set on a flare!
> Flake-doves sent floating forth at a farmyard scare! –
> Ah well! it is all a purchase, all is a prize.
>
> (66)

The place adverb 'there' plays a crucial role in the process of distancing, also the time adverb 'then' and the demonstrative pronouns and definite articles which are so frequent in Hopkins's poems. I have emphasised these elements in an extreme example, the first stanza of the already once quoted 'Morning, Midday, and Evening Sacrifice':

> *The* dappled die-away
> Cheek and *the* wimpled lip,
> *The* gold-wisp, *the* airy-grey
> Eye, all in fellowship –
> *This*, all *this* beauty blooming,
> *This*, all *this* freshness fuming,
> Give God while worth consuming.
>
> (84)

Demonstrative pronouns ('This') and definite articles, deictic (i.e. pointing) devices of the texts, are related to the concept of 'inscape', too. They are indicators of the autonomy of the natural objects, their 'thisness' (the Scotist term even contains the demonstrative pronoun). Most of the more descriptive poems consequently exhibit fewer of these devices. There, adjectives and compound nouns fulfil the same function as definite articles and demonstrative pronouns. A doubling becomes unnecessary.

Yet this autonomy as the result of signification has a double edge, too. It always indirectly invokes its starting-point as well. 'There', 'then', 'this', 'that', 'the' always define the outside of something, here the speaker. The dangerous quality of sensuous perception as much as the inherent pitfalls of aesthetic creation (and the very act of organising dislocated impressions into imaginary units is such a creation) are countered by this outward movement, this distancing effect.

Occasionally, this produces rather awkward results, when the seemingly unnecessary bombardment of distancing elements affects otherwise harmless poems. 'The Bugler's First Communion' is an example of such a digression (which is, incidentally, also a form of distancing) achieved by demonstrative pronouns and definite articles. These are its first four stanzas:

> A bugler boy from barrack (it is over the hill
> There) – boy bugler, born, he tells me, of Irish
> Mother to an English sire (he
> Shares their best gifts surely, fall how things will),
>
> This very very day came down to us after a boon he on
> My late being there begged of me, overflowing
> Boon in my bestowing,
> Came, I say, this day to it – to a First Communion.
>
> Here he knelt then ín regimental red.
> Forth Christ from cupboard fetched, how fain I of feet
> To this youngster take his treat!
> Low-latched in leaf-light housel his too huge godhead.

There! and your sweetest sendings, ah divine,
By it, heavens, befall him! as a heart Christ's darling, dauntless;
    Tongue true, vaunt- and tauntless;
Breathing bloom of a chastity in mansex fine.

(82)

Especially the prominent 'There' attracts attention. It appears twice in exposed position: in stanza 1, line 2 and stanza 4, first line – here even with an exclamation mark. Yet the two 'Theres' have entirely opposed significances. The first one indicates indeed distance, a very 'real' because spatial one ('over the hill'). The second 'There!', however, indicates no distance, but presence: Christ's presence in the Eucharist. An almost unbearable tension is expressed in this exchange of absence for presence – and eventually absence again, when the bugler is sent away towards his imaginary death. Away from the speaker: 'Let mé though see no more of him.'

The relation of signification and the self will be the focus of the next paragraph, and the analogies of modernist poetry and psychoanalysis will be discussed in a separate chapter. But – without reaching out too far already – one easily notices the speaker's hovering between forced distance, pressed intimacy, and uneasy release in the above poem. First introduced in an unimportant subclause ('he tells me'), the self gains dimension by the approach of the desired object. After an impersonal 'us' which indicates the priest's representative status, the speaker is transformed into the ambiguous 'My late being' and 'my bestowing' through the bugler's begging, i.e. the establishment of contact. But only the power of signification permits the speaker to present himself as 'I' in 'I say'.

The presence of the desired object is the fulfilment of desire, yet it also endangers personal identity.[11] When the bugler is finally 'Here' in stanza 3, the self can establish itself in an action even: 'how fain I of feet'. Nonetheless, the frantic activity expressed in 'fain' also hints at a potential danger inherent in the situation. Only a daring step can save the delicate equilibrium: the projection of the union of the self and the object of its desire on to the sacrament of the Eucharist. By the invocation of Christ, the ultimate example of fulfilled existence, the poem finds the ideal sign, one that embodies presence and absence simultaneously. *De Imitatio Christi*, the title of Thomas a Kempis's famous tractate, gains a rather new dimension here.

In Hopkins's most successful poems there is indeed a counterpoise of appropriation, the internalisation of impressions, and distancing, the externalisation of imagination. His most famous poem, 'The Windhover', starts with a verb that captures this ambiguity perfectly:

'I caught', here standing for 'took (imaginary) possession of' and 'perceived in the distance'.

> I caught this morning morning's minion, king-
>   dom of daylight's dauphin, dapple-dawn-drawn Falcon, in
>   his riding
>   Of the rolling level underneath him steady air, and striding
> High there, how he rung upon the rein of a wimpling wing
> In his ecstasy! then off, off forth on swing,
>   As a skate's heel sweeps smooth on a bow-bend: the hurl and
>   gliding
>   Rebuffed the big wind. My heart in hiding
> Stirred for a bird, – the achieve of, the mastery of the thing!
>
> (69)

'The Windhover' is an exercise in the control of imagery in both senses: the impact of images on the self, here represented by a speaker, and the speaker's distancing control of his vision, a vision that remains nonetheless – or exactly because of his achievement of distance – his own. On the surface, the poem describes the impression of the flight of a windhover on a speaker whose reactions become more and more ecstatic. The movements of the bird are convincingly modelled by a number of metaphors and similes (i.e. signification takes possession of the phenomenon, a fact also supported by the ambiguous compound 'dapple-dawn-*drawn*' – my emphasis).

Yet none of the expressions used in the description has objective scientific exactness. They derive from manifold paradigms apart from falconry or ornithology. There are feudal aristocratic terms, such as 'minion', 'dauphin', 'valour', 'pride', 'chevalier', 'gold-vermilion', as well as heraldic images, such as 'plume' or, somewhat hidden, 'wimpling'. Equestrian terms like 'riding', 'striding' and 'reign' contrast strangely with the image of the 'skate's heel', a pictorial deviation that predates later modernist techniques of associating incongruous images. Matter-of-fact expressions such as 'a bird' and 'the thing' and prosaic images like the plough and the embers of the last stanza of the poem are accompanied by colourful attributes such as 'shine' and 'gash'.

> Brute beauty and valour and act, oh, air, pride, plume, here
>   Buckle! AND the fire that breaks from thee then, a billion
> Times told lovelier, more dangerous, O my chevalier!
>
>   No wonder of it: shéer plód makes plough down sillion
> Shine, and blue-bleak embers, ah my dear,
>   Fall, gall themselves, and gash gold-vermilion.
>
> (69)

Again, the poem's technique is 'spreading out'. Not only is its imaginary object placed in a distance, a 'there', the sky. The text also makes sure that this object, the windhover, does not take over. It creates a subtle transition from the bird to Christ by the already mentioned diverse paradigms, by the windhover itself, one of Christ's traditional representations, and through the biblical allusion 'king-/dom of daylight's dauphin' (Luke 1: 78–9). Nevertheless, the poem does not ingeniously create yet another symbol of Christ. The windhover models Christ while remaining a bird. The distance remains between the *pictura* (the visual image) and the *subscriptio* (the abstract meaning), the two elements of the image. The unreconciled presence of two meanings, Christ and bird, makes the windhover an allegory. On the imaginary level, the bird does not leave the sky.

The curve of its flight hints at Christ's sacrificial death and the miracle of the resurrection. But it also indicates the simultaneous creation and destruction of meaning in the poem. At the point of greatest imaginary presence, preceded by a line containing no less than six unconnected nouns followed by Hopkins's usual expression of ultimate presence, 'here' ('Brute beauty and valour and act, oh, air, pride, plume, here'), the meaning of the poem collapses in the more than ambiguous 'Buckle!' Walter J. Ong regards 'Buckle!' as the description of the moment of 'instress' (Ong 1986: 17–18). If that is correct, then 'instress' presents itself as a phenomenon on the utmost borderline of language. Although the following lines seem to achieve a restoration of semantic coherence, it is evident that the imaginary unity does not fully recover. Embers, to use the image of the poem's final lines, may indeed gash once more. But then they die.

The imaginary self-destruction of the poem, this most radical act of achieving an internal distance, is indeed necessary to create a 'reality' within the poem that exists outside its structures, namely in their breakdown (Sprinker 1980: 3–19). The ultimate act of distancing within its act of signification permits the poem to come very close to Hopkins's ideal of 'inscape'. Only in destroying itself can the language of Hopkins's poems succeed. It must refrain from creating a meaning that would always remain inadequate, because artificial and secondary when compared to the reality with which it competes.

5. THE EMPTY SIGN: SIGNIFICATION AND 'SELVING'

Apparently, a system of signification that consists of the binary poles of appropriation and distancing – or internalisation and externalisation – offers very little space for the representation of the organising force that governs the action between these poles. The self of the poems is suspended over the abyss between two contradictory forms of signification. It is in the position of a paradox, because it must theoretically reconcile the two irreconcilable forces, if it is not – like the eye of a hurricane – an absence. The sign of the self in Hopkins's poetry must either be self-destructive or an empty one.

Both of these possibilities are, of course, paradoxical in themselves. Language can never unwrite itself (even when the French philosopher Jacques Derrida uses crossed-out words, he does not present an absence, but a presence, indeed a double one: that of the original word and that of its crossed-out status). Neither is there a sign that is completely blank. The very nature of the sign demands that it must be perceptible and – at least potentially – meaningful.

Nonetheless, a closer look at the representations of the self in Hopkins's poems reveals that most of them depict the self in exactly the paradoxical tensions described above. Albeit on the surface the dramatic poetic description of an actual shipwreck, *The Wreck of the Deutschland*, the poem generally considered the most difficult of Hopkins's works, 'the dragon in the gate',[12] deals explicitly with this issue. Not unimportantly, it is also the first of Hopkins's mature poems, written after a long poetic silence. Significantly, it starts with the line 'Thou mastering me' which sets the tone for the struggle of the self that it describes. Furthermore, three of the ten stanzas of its first part begin with the problematic pronoun 'I'. The two central stanzas of this part are an elaborate discussion of the constitution of this self:

4

I am soft sift
In an hourglass – at the wall
Fast, but mined with a motion, a drift,
And it crowds and it combs to the fall;
I steady as a water in a well, to a poise, to a pane,
But roped with, always, all the way down from the tall
Fells or flanks of the voel, a vein
Of the gospel proffer, a pressure, a principle, Christ's gift.

5

I kiss my hand
To the stars, lovely-asunder
Starlight, wafting him out of it; and
Glow, glory in thunder;
Kiss my hand to the dappled-with-damson west:
Since, tho' he is under the world's splendour and wonder,
His mystery must be instressed, stressed;
For I greet him the days I meet him, and bless when I under-
stand.

(52–3)

Stanza 4 stresses the two seemingly contradictory basic experiences of the self: stasis and motion. The conflicting states are analogous to appropriation and distancing. The positioning of the self is the primary form of taking possession of it. The stress on the simultaneous movement is the distancing aspect, for the movement is always from its starting point towards a new state.

The two dominant images of the stanza represent this paradoxical motion within stasis or stasis within motion. The sand in the hourglass, seemingly static, is nonetheless in a constant drift. The water in a well appears motionless, but is subject to pressure, a complex system of currents underneath its smooth surface. In both images the self is represented by material associated with formlessness: sand (here even a symbol of time, the most amorphous of all human concepts) and water. In both examples identity can only be achieved through the introduction of limitations, of form: the wall of the hourglass and that of the well (which is quite tellingly represented in anthropomorphisms, in images related to the human body).

The observation made in the analysis of 'Spelt from Sibyl's Leaves' – the formless anarchy of mere potentials requires limits imposed by signification to arrive at the stability of form and meaning – applies just as much, perhaps even more intensely, to the representation of the self. It requires an outside to constitute itself. Here, this outside is formed once more by signs. The signification of the self is therefore a double externalisation. Indeed, the closer Hopkins's poems approach their central issues, the more tightly they become entangled in the inevitable web of form. The externalising description of the self in part one of *The Wreck of the Deutschland* already takes place in the framework of a poem whose two parts represent exactly the internal and the external approach to the issue. And – not without reason – the externalising vision of stanza 4 (and stanza 5, too, as will be shown below) is positioned in that part of the poem which exercises the internal approach, i.e. in which the 'I' discusses itself. Yet another mirror is thus created.

Foucault describes the struggle of signification in terms analogous to Hopkins's techniques:

> Perhaps there exists an essential relation between death, the endless quest for the self, and the self-presentation of language. Perhaps the endless assembly of mirrors that opposes the black wall of death represents fundamentally every production of language, ever since language is no longer content to disappear without a trace. Even before writing was invented, language attempted to pursue itself *ad infinitum*, but not only because it did not want to die it decided one day to take shape in visual and unerasable signs. It is rather like this: something beyond writing had to happen in a space in which it could expand and manifest itself, something whose original and at the same time symbolic shape was drawn for us by Homer; something that is for us one of the few major ontological events of the utterance: its mirror-reflection beyond death and thus the constitution of a visual space in which the word finds unlimited opportunities for self-representation and can reflect itself endlessly behind or beyond itself. The possibility of the linguistic artefact has its origin in this duplication.
>
> (Foucault 1963b: 45; my translation)

The notion of reality – and the self – as a mere system of mirrors would, of course, be unacceptable for Hopkins. Although the mirror is a prominent symbol in the Victorian imagination (see *The Lady of Shalott*), it took Friedrich Nietzsche to herald this radical idea. Hopkins, as has been shown, strives towards a factual objective reality, a reality that gains its specificity by the interaction (the 'instress') of particular individual elements (the 'inscapes'). His poetry, however, the main tool for his endeavour, constantly undermines this aim. It remains, in Theodor W. Adorno's words, caught in the dialectic of mimesis (i.e. imitation) and construction (Adorno 1984: 65). This entanglement in its internal contradictions – and the attempts to escape from it – transport his poems into the realm of the aesthetics of modernism.

The problematic self that is – literally and metaphorically – in the centre of Hopkins's poems does not attempt its manifestations by externalisation only, by the 'thinking of the outside' in Foucault's terminology. It also directs its attention to the inside, towards the sensations through which the self reassures itself of its existence. These sensations are indeed physical in many of the poems. The 'inscape' of the self can be seen, felt, tasted and heard like that of every other object – and even more intensely. Hopkins, apparently very much a man of tastes and smells, describes this notion in his *Comments on the Spiritual Exercises of St Ignatius Loyola*:

> And this is above all true of that inmost self of mine which has been said to be and to be felt to be, to taste, more distinctive than the taste of clove or alum, the smell of walnutleaf or hart'shorn, more distinctive, more selved, than all things else and needing in proportion a more exquisite determining, selfmaking, power.
>
> (Hopkins 1953: 148)

Once more, a complex 'inscape', this time that of Hopkins's own person, is described through the contradictory procedures of appropriation (the list of comparisons charting the attributes of the self) and distancing (expressed by the repeated 'more' which indicates the opposite of identity, namely difference).

Thus, the expressions of psychological terror and suffering in the so-called 'Terrible Sonnets' should not only be read as metaphors. 'I am gall, I am heartburn . . . . / Bitter would have me taste: my taste was me', 'Selfyeast of spirit a dull dough sours' in 'I wake and feel the fell of dark, not day' (101) must also be understood literally as the description of the self by the self.

Painfully intense as these sensations might be, it is nonetheless evident that by naming them another externalisation takes place, this time within introspection. Even there, the self only ever succeeds in placing itself outside itself in its attempt to define its position. Hopkins's poems eventually devise two ways of breaking out of this vicious circle. One of the solutions is transcendental and religious, the second one aesthetic and poetic.

In stanza 5 of the first part of *The Wreck of the Deutschland*, the transcendental escape is beautifully illustrated. The stanza contains a two-way motion starting from the self and its ambiguous self-experience ('I kiss my hand') which is then directed first to the stars (i.e. towards infinity), then to the west, the direction of sunset. The sun is here, of course, the symbol of Christ and his sacrificial death. Only through the recognition of Christ and his sacrifice can the self arrive at a definition of itself: 'For I greet him the days I meet him, and bless when I under-/stand' (53) (note the triple 'I' of the line).

Christ is the simultaneous presence of the Divine and the human, i.e. the absolute 'inscape'. Only this climax of presence is capable of filling the bottomless absence in the place of the self in the poems. In this way the 'tall nun', the tragic heroine of the second part of *The Wreck of the Deutschland*, is capable of achieving spiritual fulfilment while being physically destroyed. Stanza 28 of the second part of the poem describes the union of Christ and the nun – or rather Christ's take-over of the nun's self:

> But how shall I . . . make me room there:
> Reach me a. . .Fancy, come faster –
> Strike you the sight of it? look at it loom there,
> Thing that she . . . There then! the Master,
> *Ipse*, the only one, Christ, King, Head:
> He was to cure the extremity where he had cast her;
> Do, deal, lord it with living and dead;
> Let him ride, her pride, in his triumph, despatch and have done
> with his doom there.
>
> (60)

The effect of this union is indeed the disappearance of the self altogether ('despatch and have done with'). Something in the ideal fusion does not quite seem to work. The poem refuses to end with this stanza either. It continues not only with a rather unnecessary praise of the nun's endurance, but also with a description of its own textual nature. It even discusses the relation of the production of language (which Hopkins, obviously in order to liken it to the important 'selving', names 'wording') and the described miraculous marriage. 'Read the unshapeable shock night / And knew the who and the why' (61) qualifies the nun's experience, but it is evidently also a description of the reading of the poem.[13]

This crucial flaw – the poem aims at creating a viable image of the self, yet makes this self disappear and only a poem materialise – shows that again the poem meets its most serious enemy in its own textuality. Reality and even Divine presence are not to be found outside it; they are only ever produced by it. The rather apologetic allusion to the beginning of the gospel according to John in the next lines, 'Wording it how but by him that present and past, / Heaven and earth are word of, worded by? –' (61), only leads to a question mark and another absence, the dash. The exclamation of the following line sums up the fundamentally contradictory nature of writing: 'The Simon Peter of a soul!' (61). Peter is indeed the person entrusted with the continuation of Christ's mission, but he is also the one to deny Christ three times. Signification is the only way to express concepts of the self, reality, and the Divine, but it will always be unfaithful to its task.

The 'Terrible Sonnets', written in the last years of Hopkins's life when he went through a particularly depressing exile in Dublin, deal with this feeling of disappointment very frankly. 'Comforter, where, where is your comforting? / Mary, mother of us, where is your relief?' asks 'No worst, there is none' (100), while 'I wake and feel the fell of dark, not day' illustrates the problem of Christ as the perfect transcendental sign which is as close to the self in Hopkins's view as a sign can get, yet still infinitely far away: 'And my lament / Is cries countless, cries like dead letters sent / To dearest him that lives alas! away' (101). The image of the dead letters is telling: the addresser does not lack the will to make an effort, yet language no longer fulfils its task of linking reality, the self, and the transcendental sphere. Thus, the self remains in its painful isolation – and indeed incomplete and empty, since it cannot establish the desired contact.

The only alternative for the self is to forsake manifestation, to exist in a space outside thoughts and language (an idea that Jacques Lacan formulated in the 1960s (Lacan 1977a: 146–78) expressed by Hopkins ninety years earlier). In the poem 'My own heart let me have more pity on', the speaker tells himself: 'Soul, self; come, poor Jackself, I do advise / You, jaded, let be; call off thoughts awhile / Elsewhere' (103). Yet the very fact that this advice is expressed through language in the shape of a poem indicates how difficult – if not impossible – this abandonment proves to be.

The second option for the self and the poems is the acceptance of their contradictory nature. What is formulated fairly early in 'As kingfishers catch fire, dragonflies draw flame',

> Each mortal thing does one thing and the same:
> Deals out that being indoors each one dwells;
> Selves – goes itself; *myself* it speaks and spells,
> Crying *What I do is me: for that I came.*
>
> (90)

is radicalised in the surprisingly optimistic 'That Nature is a Heraclitean Fire and of the comfort of the Resurrection':

> I am all at once what Christ is, ' since he was what I am, and
> This Jack, joke, poor potsherd, ' patch, matchwood, immortal diamond,
> Is immortal diamond.
>
> (106)

The tautological finale with its seemingly nonsensical repetition 'immortal / diamond, / Is immortal diamond', is much more than a dead end. It refers the poem to itself, but it also multiplies the symbolic quality of its final image by pointing outside itself while stressing that it is forever caught in its own material. The metaphoric attribute 'immortal diamond' that is among Christ's qualities is turned into a fact. Language becomes reality, or pretends to do so. It is exactly the hardness of the diamond – which makes it almost impossible to divide and thus to open up towards a reality outside it – which also causes its sparkle and thus its effect on this external reality. In this way the tragically closed poem as well as the distressing attempt to define a self, a subjectivity, within its limits, can become a valuable contribution to the Divine scheme of things – in the same way as the unceasing and undirected Heraclitean flux of elements[14] arrives at a strange, because poetic, symbiosis with the Christian promise of resurrection in the title of the poem.

6. MODERNIST HOPKINS

Poems which acknowledge their failure as a paradoxical success point towards a new aesthetics, the self-referential and self-destructive aesthetics of modernism. The preceding analysis has shown that Hopkins's poems cling to their central concept of 'inscape' as substantial and not merely as form. Yet the internal contradictions of the texts demonstrate that they only ever achieve an expression of 'inscape' through their very form, either within it or in its breakdown. The missing link between signifier and signified is clearly noticed – by the reader and the poems themselves in which the awareness of this central deficit creates despair. The lacking motivation of their material is ultimately the central problem of Hopkins's works.

Evolving out of a traditional mimetic approach, one that wants to believe in and depict a consistent reality (and through it an underlying Divine scheme of things), Hopkins's poems have to grant a power to themselves that transgresses the merely mimetic by far and uneasily strives towards a creation of their own. This is what Adorno calls the aspect of construction. Adequate expression is the paramount aim of the texts, yet all they ever arrive at is the demonstration of the instability of the relation between signifier and signified. As the analysis of 'Pied Beauty' has demonstrated, there remains an irreconcilable discrepancy between the conceptual map of the poems, their construction, and their imagery, their attachment to the mimetic. Those two poles are an exact reflection of Saussure's matching of conceptual and phonetic (in our case logographic [written] or ideographic [pictorial]) differences.

The dominant structures of Hopkins's poems present themselves as almost manic attempts to fight this lack of motivation. By erecting ingenious networks of alliterations, assonances, rhymes and rhythms, and especially by the inflation of nouns and descriptive adjectives and adverbs, most prominently their compounds, the texts strive for at least an internal motivation.[15] Even in this attempt, Hopkins's poems conform to Saussure's discovery that the sign may be motivated to a certain extent, yet only ever internally, within a network of signs.

Hopkins's poems try to counter the arbitrariness of the signifier by inflation. If one decided to adopt Jacques Lacan's radicalisation of Saussure's concept of arbitrariness, his 'notion of an incessant sliding of the signified under the signifier' (Lacan 1977a: 154; Jefferson and Robey 1982: 114–15), one could argue that the function of Hopkins's rows of related nouns and adjectives is to achieve at least momentary contact between representation and concept. For Lacan, the signified, i.e. that which the signifier tries to articulate, becomes so evasive as to be ungraspable. For Hopkins, this must not be. If his poems lost their point of reference, expressed in the 'inscapes' of things, they would lose their right to exist.

As has been demonstrated above, the pains with which Hopkins's poems describe and circumscribe relatively simple terms (such as 'Evening' in 'Spelt from Sibyl's Leaves') are their way of countering this threatening loss. In doing so, they provide a fine example of Roman Jakobson's important definition of the poetic: the projection of the paradigmatic axis on to the syntagmatic axis. 'The poetic function projects the principle of equivalence from the axis of selection into the axis of combination' (Jakobson 1987: 71). Hopkins's poems exercise exactly this projection of a field of meaning, a paradigm, on to the syntactical unit of sentence and lines.

Yet the underlying reasons for this procedure are not at all similar to what the Russian Formalists, the group of theorists that Jakobson is linked with, describe as the aim of poetry and all literary language: defamiliarisation. By making language strange, the Formalists claim, literature alerts the reader to its full potential, to its multitude of possible meanings. Hopkins's poems do not want to make language strange, they want to make it familiar, indeed so familiar as to help it break out of the limitations of its material. They strive to develop a stable relation between concept and manifestation; they desire a sign that is motivated, a perfect expression of God's scheme of creation. But they cannot find this sign in language, or rather they can only find it in three paradoxical forms: the empty sign (the absence, as in the description of the self), the breakdown of signification (the self-destruction of language), or the transcendental sign that cannot be questioned, because it cannot be rationally perceived (i.e. Christ, the vision of the Eucharist).

The three consequences of the breakdown of the belief in a stable sign will continue to appear in modernist poetry as absence, self-destruction and myth. Hopkins's poems are Victorian in their lament of poetry's lost grasp on reality. But they also manage to illustrate the origin of this loss in the very material of poetry, language, as well as the consequences of this discovery at a very early date. For the Victorian poets, loss becomes the content of their works. For Hopkins, loss shapes the form of his poems. All the endeavours of Hopkins's writings to establish contact with the concepts they try so hard to represent only ever end up in texts that are thrown back into their own structures. The compulsive internalisation that will be shown to be one of the characteristics of modernism displays its origin in the treatment of signification in his works. Its gloomy consequences for the self and its relation to reality are already vividly outlined there.

NOTES

1. The shifts of the concept of the sign are most clearly described in Foucault 1970: 40ff.
2. The status of Saussure's works is rather precarious, because of his habit of destroying the notes of his lectures. His seminal course is actually composed of notes taken by his students Bally and Sechehaye. Further references in the text are to the English edition: Saussure 1983.
3. Saussure is convinced of the primary status of speech. Writing is for him a secondary development.
4. I have provided my own examples to avoid Saussure's French ones.
5. Hopkins mentions these influences explicitly in a letter to his friend Dixon in October 1878 (Hopkins 1980: 71–4). A detailed discussion of sprung rhythm is Harold Whitehall's essay in Kenyon Critics 1975: 28–54.
6. All quotations are from Hopkins 1970. This is the most easily accessible scholarly collection of his works. The more recent complete edition Hopkins 1990 is recommended for the study of textual variants, etc.
7. Iser calls these gaps of meaning *Leerstellen* (Iser 1966: 371).

8. Gardner, who also claims a direct relation between Scotus and 'inscape', stresses the importance of Hopkins's choice of this philosopher of individuality and personality (Hopkins 1953: xxiii). See also Bump 1982: 38–41.
9. The Manicheans were a religious sect of the third to fifth century AD who believed that Satan was as powerful as God.
10. Peter Bürger regards this insight as the starting point of critical analysis: 'Scientific analysis of literature begins the moment one recognizes that the immediacy with which we perceive a poem as a poem is illusory (*Schein*)' (Bürger 1984: 4).
11. This is what so many descriptions of erotic bliss try to convey. The self forgets itself and thus ceases to exist – at least temporarily.
12. The expression was coined by Robert Bridges, Hopkins's friend and posthumous editor. See Bergonzi 1977: 157.
13. Hopkins read about the accident in *The Times* and *The Illustrated London News*. Still, his poem is indebted to the illustrations in the latter paper rather than to the newspapers' journalistic style. See, for instance, the sedate headlines of similar reports in the racier of the two papers, *The Illustrated London News*, reprinted in de Vries and van Amstel 1973: 148 ('The Wreck of the Irex') and 156 ('The Loss of H.M.S. Victoria').
14. Heraclitus is a Greek philosopher of the sixth century BC who claims that fire is the first element, since all things are in a constant mutation which leads them away from fire and back into it.
15. See Michael Riffaterre's view of the poetic neologism as discussed in Riffaterre 1983: 74: 'Far from arbitrary and anything but a foreign body in the sentence, the literary neologism is the most strongly motivated signifier that can be found in a text. . . . Coined expressly and created to meet specific needs, the neologism is the precise word *par excellence*.'

CHAPTER TWO

The Symbolic Approach and its Limits: W.B. Yeats (1865–1939)

1. THE FUNCTIONS OF THE SYMBOL

When Saussure claims that, in spite of their basic arbitrariness, signs may be motivated to a certain extent, he thinks explicitly of the symbol (Saussure 1983: 68). Within the textual network of signs this structure achieves a special status which permits it to overcome arbitrariness through a peculiar relation between signifier and signified. Saussure's statement highlights his theoretical position that knows nothing outside language, a perspective that – as the analysis of Hopkins's poems has shown – is a temptation for modern poetry from its beginning.

Charles S. Peirce, the second founding-father of modern semiotics, developed a more 'objective' theory of the sign based on his triadic model which includes an extratextual *referent*, an objective entity outside the text. This referent, its representation and its form (which Peirce regards as the relation between percipient and sign) add up to the sign. For Peirce, the symbol is consequently the least motivated of signs, since it lacks this objective referent. The *icon*, as a sign resembling the object it represents, and the *index*, a sign in a real relation with an object (such as smoke indicating fire), are the only motivated forms of signs for him. The symbol enters a relation to an object only by an act of will, i.e. interpretation or convention, and thus remains arbitrary (Krampen 1981: 23).

Saussure's claim that there exists a natural bond between thought and voice, and his denunciation of writing as external and corrupting, led to Derrida's attack on his semiotics in *Of grammatology* in which it is interpreted as a symptom of Saussure's *logocentrism*, his indebtedness and submission to traditional reason (Norris 1987: 87–94). For the present discussion it will suffice to note that the motivation of the symbol is always the result of an intention or a convention. It is never inherent in the symbol itself, but provided by an underlying system, either the personal symbolic system of the author or the symbolic system of convention. Usually, the two are closely related; i.e. the personal symbol is related to the conventional symbolic code by either conforming to, transforming or opposing the norm, while the norms of symbolic conventions are influenced and shaped by individual contributions.

Like every other sign, the symbol can be described as having two parts: signifier and signified. The distinctive feature of the symbol is its unconventional use of a complex visual signifier, the *pictura* (Latin: 'painting') in connection with an equally complex signified, usually that of an abstraction, the *subscriptio* (Latin: 'signature') (Link 1974: 168). The Greek root of the word symbol (*sumbolon* = 'watchword', deriving from *sumbállein* = 'to throw together') hints at its multiple functions. As a condensation, it acts as a shorthand for complex statements. Roland Barthes, in his concise comparison of the variants of signs, dryly states that 'in the symbol the representation is analogical and inadequate (Christianity "outruns" the cross)' (Barthes 1967b: 38). This inherent deficit of the symbol will become important in the following discussion.

The symbol's transgression of the language norm attracts attention to its form. This aesthetic appeal turns the symbol into a a potent rhetorical device. A conventional example is the symbol of the rose representing love. The complex *pictura* contains visual beauty, pleasant smell, fragility, but also the presence of hidden thorns. It is fused with the abstract *subscriptio* love: love is a unique and beautiful experience, highly sensual, but also short-lived and potentially painful.

Symbols that contain their 'explanation' as a part of their construction are called *emblems* (Latin *emblema* = 'inlaid work'; Greek *émblema* = 'insertion'; the *blem* derives from the same root 'to throw' as the *bol* in 'symbol'). These were particularly common in the Renaissance and the Baroque. When an arrangement of symbols achieves a personified and anthropomorphic character that correlates to its particular social and cultural function, it is called *allegory* (Greek for 'speaking otherwise'). A well-known example is the representation of justice as a blindfold woman holding scales.

2. SYMBOLS AND SYMBOLISM IN YEATS'S EARLY POEMS

Despite his claim that 'poems, like poets, are born and not made', even Northrop Frye has to admit that 'every poet has his private mythology, his own spectroscopic band or peculiar formation of symbols' (Lodge 1972: 425). Frye's professed attempt to distil unifying 'archetypes' out of the very varied history of literature, universal anthropological patterns which shape literary texts independent of their creators or historic background, is important, because it echoes exactly the tensions characteristic of much of W.B. Yeats's works. The symbol is placed in an intermediary position between the personal and the impersonal, the individual and the collective, or, when not seen as attached to the human sphere – as in religion and magic – the mythical. Yeats himself, not usually very good at analysing the features of his own works, perceived this mediating function of the symbol clearly when he defended the symbol against the allegory in his essay on Blake[1] published in *The Savoy* in July 1896:

> A symbol is indeed the only possible expression of some invisible essence, a transparent lamp about a spiritual flame; while allegory is one of many possible representations of an embodied thing, or familiar principle, and belongs to fancy and not to imagination: the one is a revelation, the other an amusement.
>
> (Melchiori 1960: 15)

The symbol is determined by an impersonal force, but it can only become part of the individual imagination by an act of revelation that is the poetic creation. Yeats's poetic work can be seen as suspended between these positions – and their interaction is a problem from the very start of his poetic career.

The first poem in Yeats's earliest collection *Crossways* of 1889, 'The Song of the Happy Shepherd', begins with an allusion to the inevitable interplay with tradition that every symbolic creation enters: 'The woods of Arcady are dead' (Yeats 1983: 7). This is the first of many death-claims which will be encountered in this study. The statement refers to an established fact, Arcady does not exist any more (if it ever existed at all), and to an artistic tendency, that of escapism. The easy poetic escape into the imaginary past is rejected. Or s seems. For the rejection of a traditional symbolic system does no to a ban on other symbolic constructs.

Of old the world on dreaming fed;
Grey Truth is now her painted toy;
Yet still she turns her restless head:
But O, sick children of the world,
Of all the many changing things
In dreary dancing past us whirled,
To the cracked tune that Chronos sings,
Words alone are certain good.

(7)

The very thing that has replaced Arcadian escapism, Grey Truth, a reference to the empiricism Yeats despised, is clothed in symbolic shape. It is presented as a painted toy that the world uses for her entertainment.

This world feeds on dreams, and dreamlike and uncertain are all things according to the poem – save one: words. The dreaming world itself may be nothing but a word. The poem is silent on the speaker or writer of this word, though it continues to fill its own realm with symbol after symbol. Chronos's cracked tune representing time has already made its appearance. It is followed by the warring kings of old standing for idle glory, and the stargazers with their barren wisdom. Most important, though, are the symbols representing that which the poem praises so highly, words. The sudden flaming word that is presented as the possible origin of the world is, of course, a biblical reference and alludes to the beginning of the gospel according to John.

The representation of creation as the word has strong links with the closed internalising nature of modernist techniques observed in Hopkins's poems. The texts can only imagine their outside to be like their own texture – with the result that they become their own cosmos. This phenomenon will be traced in all structural features of modernist poetry. It will be discussed in relation to psychoanalysis, economy and philosophy in the second half of this study. Here it it finds its reliable ally in the schizophrenic nature of the symbol which is both external – by its connection with tradition – and internal – as an individual artistic creation.

The central symbol of Yeats's poem is that of the 'twisted, echo-harbouring shell' (8) of its second stanza. It mirrors the lips of the addressee of the poem who by telling it 'his story' receives an echo of his words, his tale rewarded – until it fades away. (A variant reading of the poem gives 'Rewording' as the effect of the shell, thus stressing the symbolic activity even more strongly.)[2] The final lines of stanzas 2 and 3 explain the possible gain of the procedure: '[. . .] for this is also sooth' (8). The symbolic duplication of experience does not give it any sense, much less truth, not even material permanence. Yet within its structures, symbolic creation fulfils the function of a dream. It gives release from the daily fight against contingency, the idle struggle for fame (the kings of old), learning (the stammering schoolboy) and truth (the stargazers), by providing a universal frame for individual anxiety.

The central symbol of the shell also illustrates the uneasy position of the creator of the symbolic utterance. The humming sea and the echo-harbouring shell receive and repeat the message, his story. This story remains nondescript. The poem suggests nonetheless that it tells of the loss of all certainties save one: the certainty of words. Yet by telling his story, the protagonist of the poem only adds it to the meaningless noises of the sea and shell. His message loses any possible meaning, no matter how much the poem insists that the shell rewards (or rewords) it. The symbolic utterance produces a nebulous signified, yet one that is potentially more powerful than ordinary words. The hints at a mirror-function of the shell, its description as lips (rather than an ear receiving the message) which double and touch those of the story-teller (with obvious erotic connotations), and the adjective 'echo-harbouring' reveal its message as a mere reflection. Helen Regueiro describes the ambivalent relationship of man and nature in Yeats's poems as follows:

> Yeats's poetry, like Wordsworth's, thus stems from a profound sense of the loss of the unity of being. But where Wordsworth defines loss in terms of the self's relationship to nature, Yeats couches it, at least initially, in mythological terms.
>
> (Regueiro 1976: 96)

> The world Yeats constructs is thus at the very outset doomed by the self-consciousness with which it is created. It is a world constructed 'in nature's spite' and ultimately inimical to the very idea of poetic creation.
>
> (97)

This paradoxical status of the symbols in the above poem as starting-point and goal of poetic activity (if one regards the telling of one's life story as such) reappears in a more abstract symbolic construction of the poem, that of its speaker. As the title of the poem indicates, it is a song of the happy shepherd. The definite article is important, for it makes this shepherd the representative of a particular symbolic context. He is part of Arcady. But this Arcady is dead, and the speaker even repeatedly refers to its demise, finally and most drastically in the last stanza in which he talks about the grave of a dead faun, the impersonation of unreflected and undirected sensual energy, life in short.

When first published, the poem was entitled 'An Epilogue. To "The Land of Statues" and "The Seeker". Spoken by a satyr carrying a sea-shell'. Later, it became 'Song of the last Arcadian (He carries a sea-shell)'.[3] The transformation highlights some problems of the symbols in the poem. Its speaker is part of a dead or dying culture, yet he is described as happy. He shows a possible deliverance from the perils of existence in the transformation of his life into poetry through the shell. This transformation can only be that into symbols; the echoes of the shell in their relation to the noise of the sea correspond to 'invisible essence', the 'invisible flame' described in Yeats's essay on Blake.

From a semiotic perspective, the meaningless echo within the shell is the noise of language in its entirety, *langue*. Its relation to the thundering of the sea is not simply a mimetic echo, for it is not the sea one hears in shells. Out of this meaningless muddle of sounds, the speaker suggests one takes one's pick. The choice is governed by the particular situation of the addressee, but also the experiences, norms and conventions that have shaped him and his use of language. The echo received is personal experience clothed in signifiers, *parole*, but special signifiers: complex ideas illustrated by concrete images. The interaction produces symbols.

Only by this act of symbolisation can human experience gain meaning. Yeats formulates an insight in this early poem that he will re-encounter in philosophical shape in Nietzsche: all human history, be it individual or universal, is fiction and can only come to life and meaning in fiction. Thus, the 'last Arcadian' can be called happy despite the poem's veiled notion that his days are numbered. He has manifested himself and given meaning to his existence in the very utterance that is the poem.

Yet to leave it at that would overlook the darker aspects of the poem's symbolic message. Even this recently established identity is shown as doomed: it fades with the words that have helped to establish it in the first place. Furthermore, the constitution of identity through symbols is not entirely controlled by the protagonist. The shell has an active part in it, too. In the poem that follows and complements 'The Song of the Happy Shepherd' in Yeats's *Crossways*, 'The Sad Shepherd' (8–9), the shell refuses to echo the shepherd's story and turns it into an 'inarticulate moan'. As a consequence the shepherd's existence is forgotten. He vanishes from the symbolic stage of the poem so radically that he even ceases to be its grammatical subject. He is replaced by the shell which is too immersed in its 'wildering whirls' to take notice of him or his song. This is a first hint at the gyres of Yeats's later poems, his own version of the modernist vortex, the symbolic form that leads to permanence within the flux of reality and history and brings with it impersonality. Thus the refusal of personal identity for the shepherd. It is the direct result of the symbolic system taking over the poem.

The two above poems outline Yeats's model of symbolism. It requires inexplicable forces that determine the shape of the symbol, forces that choose their mouthpieces among men (a first hint at the élitism of Yeats's works, his notion of the artist as initiate). Yet it is up to the chosen prophet of these powers to provide the material of their echoing utterance from his own life. The protagonist of this symbolising activity, the poet, supplies his own story as the raw material for the symbolic transformation, not necessarily events from his own life only, but also thoughts and fantasies. Both artistic artefact and the identity of the artist are created by this interaction.

Following Lacan, Julia Kristeva calls this transformation the development from the imaginary or semiotic to the symbolic stage in the psychological development of the individual. It requires the clothing of impressions and sensations, also the perception of oneself, one's body (in Lacan's famous 'mirror stage') first in images. These are then transformed into symbolic shape when, with the aid of language, the self duplicates itself and posits itself as a controllable Other in an imaginary universe (Kristeva 1984: 19–106). This duplication inevitably entails a loss, for words can only ever be substitutes that represent unsuccessfully and incompletely what they stand for. This loss, however, is also a gain, because words give permanence to fleeting but 'whole' visions. It is a stage that must be undergone in the formation of the subject and leads to its stabilisation in an encoded identity which, however, remains alienated, lacking and external. Loss and the consequent feeling of incompleteness are, according to Lacan, the origins of desire. Loss and desire are also the motivations for individual actions which strive to overcome the fragmentation, but never achieve this aim.[4]

In Yeats's early poems, fragmentation as the consequence of symbolic representation is described in various forms. An objective symbolism employs objects and settings which either demonstrate lack and desire or its potential mastery, the latter usually in visions of successful love or the integration of the individual in particular historic, geographic and mythical settings. Subjective symbolism represents the protagonist of the texts in various guises, masks or personae (a technique very prominent in Browning's poetry and later perfected by Ezra Pound).

3. OBJECTIVE SYMBOLISM

Throughout Yeats's long poetic career his range of predominant symbols remains relatively limited. For a poet so consciously immersed in symbolism, this symbolic economy means a deliberate restriction. There are two possible explanations for this, starting from the different poles of Yeats's concept of the symbol. In his conviction that symbols are given to the artist by an external force Yeats relied heavily on dreams and dreamlike impressions to supply him with his material. Later he added the consciously invoked visions of his spiritualistic experiments and those of his wife to his store. He carefully recorded dreams and visions (as can be seen in his *Autobiographies*) and used them repeatedly in his works. The island symbol, for example, appears in his early verse play *The Island of Statues* of 1884. It reappears in the hero's quest through 'spice-isles' in the dramatic poem *The Seeker* (printed along with the former text), in the three allegorical islands of *The Wanderings of Oisin*, in 'To an Isle in the Water' (in which the island clearly stands for a woman) and eventually in 'The Lake Isle of Innisfree'.[5]

Economy of symbols therefore means faithfulness to the source of poetic inspiration. On the other hand, Yeats's sparsity of symbols is directly related to his painstaking attempt to develop his own unified symbolic system. This explains the multitude of poems sharing the same protagonist ('He', 'The Lover', 'The Poet', 'Owen Aherne', 'Michael Robartes', 'Crazy Jane', etc.) and the groupings of poems under the heading of the same symbol. The rose is the most important of these in Yeats's early poems.

The rose stands for a variety of things. First, it represents love, even a particular love, Maud Gonne, whom Yeats met for the first time in 1889 and who became the object of a tragic unreciprocated passion. Yet the rose also represents spiritual principles. It is the central symbol of the Order of the Golden Dawn which Yeats as well as Maud Gonne joined (Yeats in 1890). Its Rosicrucian symbolism employs the image of a rose with four leaves on a cross as the representation of a mystic marriage, both sexual (the rose standing for the vaginal, the cross for the phallic) and spiritual. The rose is also a symbol of Ireland, used, for instance, by poets like Aubrey de Vere and James Clarence Mangan whom Yeats mentions as his symbolic precursors in *The Countess Kathleen and Various Legends and Lyrics* of 1892 in which the poem 'To the Rose upon the Rood of Time' first appeared.[6] Paradoxically, it is at the same time a symbol of England, and thus mirrors Yeats's hybrid cultural background.

What makes the rose such an attractive symbol is its multiple meaning. Partaking in various symbolic systems, it brings a great complexity into relatively condensed poems. Its attraction is therefore also one of poetic economy. At the same time its polysemy offers a convenient screen for daring utterances. Passionate declarations of love can be passed off as philosophical or mystical speculations or patriotic fervour (the latter particularly successful with Maud Gonne). But also dubious and rather exotic Rosicrucian teachings can be disguised as love poetry (which always has a right to be irrational) or veiled political utterances. The procedure works in turn equally well for exclamations of Irish patriotism.

Although an ideal symbol, the rose is used in the same manner as the symbols hitherto analysed and also produces the same dangers. It indeed proves so powerful that it must be restrained. In the first and central rose poem in the collection *The Rose* of 1893, the already mentioned 'To the Rose upon the Rood of Time', its ambiguous attraction is fully illustrated. The speaker – in the guise of a Celtic bard – invokes the rose of his days (his love perhaps, or his faith, or both) while he sings of Irish legends. Through this rose he hopes to find eternal beauty, to cease being 'blinded by man's fate' (i.e. human contingency), and to see things with new eyes. But when the rose approaches (and the triple 'Come near' of the second stanza creates this impression), the speaker suddenly wants to keep his distance: 'Ah, leave me still / A little space for the rose-breath to fill!' (31).

What he fears is the loss of – interestingly enough – his hearing. Apparently, if the rose joined him he would only ever be able to hear eternal truths ('the strange things said / By God to the bright hearts of those long dead') and no longer the noises of real life. More important still, he would lose his ability to sing in a language comprehensible to men, he would 'chaunt a tongue men do not know' (31). Again, the perfect symbol would be the one to make the poetic utterance cease.[7]

The difficult tension which forces the poet to refine the symbols he cannot do without yet at the same makes it clear that a takeover of the poem by a perfect symbol would mean the collapse of poetic identity, thus of the poem itself, will be shown as a dominant problem in Yeats's later poems. There, two forms of dissolution will offer themselves as escapes from this structural impasse. The very illustration of this dead end in Yeats's poems, their awareness that the control of their textual mechanisms brings them close to their downfall, should be noted as a feature which places them within the structural canon of modernism.

4. SUBJECTIVE SYMBOLISM

The observation made in the analysis of Yeats's objective symbolism also applies to his symbols of the self, his subjective symbolism. The range of representations is limited and well organised. The symbols employed exhibit various degrees of imaginary distance: there are mythological figures as far removed and anonymous as the Arcadian shepherd or geographically distant as the Indian characters of the earliest poems. These, however, are soon replaced by equally mythical, but more precise figures, such as characters from Irish mythology; King Goll, Fergus, Cuchulain and Oisin. Their nature is determined by the tales spun around them. The symbolic system they inhabit shapes the nature of these symbols.

All of these protagonists are tragic figures characterised by loss and madness as well as quest and fight. Yet their intertextual determination does not disqualify them as parts of Yeats's idiosyncratic system. All of his symbolic characters share a close resemblance; one could even argue that Yeats's work is attached to mere variants of a single self.[8] This self is scrutinised and illustrated in its various aspects by carefully chosen personae.

The multiple aspects of a single character can also be detected in the polarised personae of some poems. Michael Robartes and Owen Aherne are, for example, representations of proud intellect and unrestrained emotions. The traditional Platonic division into mind and body is driven even further and to Victorian proportions in the characters illustrating spiritual and physical love, the lady and the chambermaid.[9]

Symbolically, the division into pure and distant love object and soiled sexual partner is indeed only overcome in Crazy Jane. This prominent character in Yeats's later poems comes up with a Blakean statement in her quarrel with the bishop, the representative of abstract spiritual values: 'Love has pitched his mansion in / The place of excrement' (259–60).

This love in all its aspects (as shown in the rose symbol) is central in most of Yeats's poems. This is self-evident in his early and middle period. Yet even his later and last poems circle around the issue, although the treatment is now a different one, and the poems try to envisage love in connection with universal laws and forces located outside the individual.

Yeats's personae can represent the lover as a tree (in 'The Two Trees') or, more often, as an animal, such as the hound with the phallic red ear in 'He Mourns for the Change'. More prominently, he can be depicted as a bird, one of the white birds of the poem with the same title, or a swan, the symbol Yeats employs so frequently.[10] In 'The White Swans at Coole' the symbolic equilibrium is so delicate that Yeats himself saw only the description of an actual observation in the poem. Yet it is obvious that the image of 'nine-and-fifty swans' paddling peacefully 'lover by lover' contains the apparent symbolic reason for the speaker's sore heart. There is one solitary swan left over with whom the speaker of the poem implicitly identifies his own situation.

Overt symbolic representations of the lover are, of course, the lover and the poet of the early poems, as well as the 'He' of so many poems in *The Wind Among the Reeds* of 1899. All three personae are autoreferential conventions and direct the attention to the fact that they are the producers of texts. Although only the most basic grammatical representation of identity, even 'He' is a symbol. It is the least specific persona, because it lacks description. At the same time this lack gives it potentially unlimited significance. In Lacan's psychoanalytic theories it is the purest and most radical symbolisation of the ego.[11]

Surprisingly, the poet and even the lover are more detached from love. Both discuss the way in which they perceive it rather than their love itself. The poet is indeed more concerned with his artifice than with the beloved person. In 'A Poet to His Beloved', the poet's activity forms the frame of the text: 'I bring you with reverent hands / The books of my numberless dreams' (63). The adored object remains little more than the 'White woman', i.e. pure spiritual love, despite her contradictory description as worn by passion 'As the tide wears the dove-grey sands' (63). In this respect, she is also the white page, still uninscribed by the poet. Physical love and poetic creatic are equalled. This equation will reappear in Yeats's later poems, most prominently in 'Leda and the Swan'. Yet the poetic creation is apparently more important than the characteristics of the love-object. This is another hint at the self-determination of symbolism which, once let loose, soon eclipses objects as well as the subject. The insight that symbolic poetic creation, as much as love, is always coupled with possible destruction can already be detected in 'Coole Park and Ballylee' of 1931 where the 'stormy white' of a swan is even declared an 'emblem', and one that 'can be murdered with a spot of ink' (244).

The lover, though already more direct in his address (i.e. he does not talk about what he says, but talks to his beloved) is still concerned with the mechanisms of his affections rather than with the object of his love. In 'The Lover asks Forgiveness because of his Many Moods' the hurt loved one is merely the puppet of the speaker. Her actions, intended as a remedy for the lover's moods, are prescribed by exactly those moods. Not even the grammatical subject of the poem is clear in places. Although, in the part in quotation marks, it must be the insulted woman, the speaking lover never ceases to be in symbolic control of the scene.

Love that is self-aware loses sight of its object and becomes self-possessed, i.e. narcissistic. This seems to be the implied message of the poem. It also applies to the symbolism of Yeats's early poems. A symbolism that is completely in control and functions unproblematically does this only within a hermetic textual closure. The texts created in this way are incapable of envisaging and reacting to phenomena outside themselves, because their assembly of ill-defined signifieds produces a universalist 'fog' of meaning, one big indeterminacy that clouds their entire perspective. Even in seemingly traditional love poems Yeats implicitly formulates this modernist crux. He dramatises the problematic role of the symbol in poetic imagination even more drastically in his later poems.

The opposite of a controlled symbolism is the unrestrained flow of symbols. This is what happens when the symbols take control of the poems rather than being employed within a strictly defined symbolic network by a controlling identity. Some of the most powerful poems in Yeats's *oeuvre* are the result of this toppling of poetic hierarchies. 'He mourns for the Change that has come upon Him and his Beloved, and longs for the End of the World' (61) is one example. It is a poem filled to the brim with symbols, some deriving from Irish myths, some Christian, others allegorical. The clash of the complexities of these symbols prevents the poem from establishing a clear message. What remains is the impression of sheer visionary force directed towards the apocalyptic dissolution of its finale – in which the mythical Boar of Irish legends brings about the end of the world. This end of the world is clearly analogous to the end of poetic identity. The collapse of symbolism, here paradoxically initiated by a symbolic overcharge, catapults the poem out of its symbolic system back into the vagueness of the imaginary.

This dissolution does not automatically lead to meaninglessness, though. The breakdown of symbols can lead to different structures, such as the metonymy which scatters dislocated images across a poem, or the metaphor providing isolated and often obscure fusions of images. These tropes create different forms of semantic coherence. In the above poem, for instance, the collapse of symbolic coherence is connected with the very issue of the poem and thus completely functional. It produces mutilated symbols and allegories, such as 'hatred and hope and desire and fear' or 'Time and Birth and Change' which are merely 'hurrying by' without a chance of creating a stable message. The symbolic breakdown is even the creator of a kind of joy, a joy of disintegration (in the 'Boar without bristles' 'grunting and turning to his rest' of the poem's finale) that can be seen as a precursor of the Nietzschean tragic gaiety in a poem like 'Lapis Lazuli'. It can also be associated with Roland Barthes's *jouissance*, the pleasure of the text (Barthes 1975).

'The Valley of the Black Pig' (65) is another example of a double surrender to the forces of dissolution. This valley is the setting of an apocalyptic prophecy in Irish mythology; therefore the expectation of destruction expressed by those 'weary of the world's empires' in the poem (Jeffares 1984: 59–61). Yet the text itself already presents this surrender symbolically in its uncontrolled gathering of dreams which become so powerful that they dissolve the border between waking and dreaming.

The speakers of Yeats's poems yearn for their own destruction. They beg for release from the symbolic settings which shape and control their existence and long to immerse themselves in a broader, because unrestrained, imaginary wisdom (the imaginary stage of psychoanalytic theories). In 'Fergus and the Druid', it is Fergus, King of Ulster, who demands release. He is both chained to his position of power and to his mortality, both of which restrict him as a subject and therefore become the symbols of another chain, the one called 'the chain of signification' by Lacan – on which desire only ever moves along, but is never overcome. Fergus is granted his wish and sees his life (or lives rather, for his vision is that of a succession of rebirths) float by in various images. Yet this imaginary knowledge leads to a destruction of his symbolic identity: 'But now I have grown nothing, knowing all' (33). Man cannot exist without his symbolic identity, even though it brings with it eternal restriction and lack. 'Ah! Druid, Druid, how great webs of sorrow / Lay hidden in the small slate-coloured thing!' (33), the druid's bag of dreams, cries Fergus.[12]

The second and more deeply hidden message of the poem is that only the initiates are in control of the border between the symbolic and imagination. For Yeats, these initiates are the magician and the poet. Yet their control is never complete and entails not only perils for their identity, but also an awareness that is hard to bear. Yeats's middle and later poems illustrate some of the difficulties evolving out of the interaction of imagination and poetic control through symbolism. The difficulties are again produced by the source of the poet's vision which Yeats locates in a transcendental reality outside the human sphere. This external motivation clashes with the creativity of the individual, with human decisions and autonomy, both of which are expressed in history.

5. SYMBOLS AND HISTORY

The intermediate position of the symbol between invisible unchangeable essence and an individual poet subjected to the contingencies of existence creates a tension within the symbol from its very conception. It can only function as part of a symbolic system that is by its very nature slow to change, in its ideal form immutable even. Yet as the personal poetic utterance of a particular poet it is also subjective, closely attached to its temporal context and therefore prone to transformation. The conflict can seemingly be reconciled if the symbolic system becomes a closed one that includes even its creator. When an individual position with its cultural and historic context is abandoned, a drifting into ahistoricism becomes a permanent danger. Already some of Yeats's early poems, such as 'The Man who dreamed of Faeryland', express the suspicion that the escapism of a hermetic symbolism is eventually unsatisfactory. There seems to remain something outside the poems that a hermetic symbolism is unable to grasp. The early poems suspect that it is life itself, the ever-changing life of the individual as well as the people, both of which are shaped by history.

One of Yeats's first poetic attempts to come to terms with history, 'Easter, 1916', consequently exhibits a rather derogatory attitude towards its own material and the source of symbols, language. '[P]olite meaningless words' (180) it calls its speaker's reaction to the protagonists of this particular Irish tragedy, the Easter Rising. A 'mocking tale or a gibe' (180) is all that he can think of in such dramatic times. He is not part of the struggle, but removed in the bourgeois safety of his club. Yet not even there does he remain untainted by the events. He feels that he belongs to the same culture as the people involved in the struggle. This is exactly the point where symbols enter the poem again. Without them, it seems, the speaker cannot explain his position in more than the grey facts of an empirical description, nor can he react to the events with more than 'meaningless words'. Neither would fit the complete change and transformation that are his impressions. The symbol he chooses for them is the birth of a terrible beauty.

The oxymoron describes the ambivalent aspects of the Rising. It was utterly stupid, yet heroic. The deaths caused by it were cruel and shocking, but they had the splendour of mythical heroic sacrifice. Even the hopes and fears connected with the Rising were ambiguous. Aspirations for direct political change were completely shattered. Nonetheless, the dead and those executed after the Rising instantly became martyrs whose memory kept the revolutionary spirits alive.

A completely universal symbol, however, cannot be tolerated by the tensional concept of Yeats's symbolism. Even his symbols of historic events display connections to the personal sphere. In the second stanza of 'Easter, 1916' the change that is the poem's central theme is attributed to Constance Gore-Booth who, according to Yeats, was transformed from a beautiful girl to a shrill political fanatic by her political activism. Yeats's description reveals that he still regards women in true Victorian fashion as wives and mothers, even though their contemporary roles hardly agree with these conservative views. 'That woman' becomes an aspect of the all-encompassing symbol of the 'terrible beauty', even though the change cannot erase her personal history.

From a different angle, the stanza therefore describes a more essential loss than that of a girl Yeats once admired. It laments the intrusion of universal history into the personal sphere. Change caused by historic events (or, more generally, time) interferes with the well-organised symbolic system of one's personal life. Yeats's decision to write about these external events is therefore not altogether altruistic.

Even if this change intrudes from outside, it is nonetheless also at least partly generated inside the personal realm. The protagonists of the historic drama of 'Easter, 1916' were driven by 'excess of love'. Political visions have the same origins as poetic ones. What applies to poetic works consequently also applies to political actions: it is their creators' responsibility to shape their vision. An escape into the apologetic evocation of transcendental powers, fate, Heaven, etc., is more than dubious: 'O when may it suffice? / That is Heaven's part, our part / To murmur name upon name' (of the victims; 181). If excess of love hardens hearts, then excess of imagination probably paralyses the mind. At least it prevents action. 'I write it out in a verse –' (182) is such an action, the poem claims. It is both pathetic compared with the rebellion and has greater authority, for despite its reduced historic significance it achieves an insight into universal history provided by the superhistorical view of the symbol. Nietzsche's view of history as a subjective vision (an idea familiar to Yeats) is important in this context (Nietzsche 1980, vol. 1: 243–334). This idea burdens poetry with a responsibility that cannot be met with visions of fairyland.

History can only be grasped in symbolic form if the poems take account of their position in the tension of impersonal and personal forces. 'Nineteen Hundred and Nineteen' is another attempt to depict factual history, here the violence of the Black and Tans, in symbolic constructs. The poem's topic is loss, but this time the examples of cultural decay are not Irish, but artefacts from ancient Greece. The particular Irish events are projected on the matrix of Western culture as a whole. They are integrated in a historical scheme that surpasses their time and space and turns them into general symptoms of cultural decline. The lost Greek artefacts are also diminished in their value when they are placed in the context of the 'pretty toys' (207) the speaker had when he was young.

Historic loss is the inevitable price to be paid for cultural maturity, just as much as symbolic loss is the price of personal identity. The prospects of this growing-up, however, are rather bleak. The poem is pessimistic. It denies historic progress, and – when naming the reason for its absence – employs generalisations: 'rogues and rascals' (207) are to blame. These anonymous forces represent the poem's deterministic and mythical outlook. 'Nineteen Hundred and Nineteen' illustrates the destruction of its historic ideal with images from a vague past: cannon, Parliament, king, trumpeters and guardsmen. It eventually has recourse to biblical prophecies (Isaiah 2: 4 in the image of the transformed ploughshare (Jeffares 1984: 230) and finally the apocalyptic vision of the dragon from Revelation 12: 1–12). The image of the dragon merges with folkloristic demon riders and finally the realistic image of the riders of the Black and Tans. The subtlety of the transition makes it almost an equation. By piling signs from different backgrounds on top of each other, the poem creates a myth. Again, the text is not content with factual historic events. They have to be put into a universal frame.

Intellectual escapism, thinking within closed symbolic schemes, is condemned at the end of the third stanza of the poem for its mistaken assumption that it is exempt from the turmoil of history and human brutality. Yet the central concept of history in the poem once more places symbols in the focus of historical understanding. The knowledge of history demands the reading of 'the signs' (207), a grasp of its symbols. Again, this intellectual capacity is linked with sexual potency. Only the chosen fulfil both requirements. The vision granted to them is pessimistically Romantic: everything is vain – except the true work of art. This work of art is the perfect symbol, one that keeps the balance between individualistic symbolism, the closed fairyland of the egotistical poet, and the realm of visions in which all meaning dissolves in an imaginary flux. The chosen artist is a modern Daedalus, elevated, lonely and constantly endangered. His eventual destination is extinction, for all his powers derive from passion: 'Man is in love and loves what vanishes, / What more is there to say?' (208).

The poem has more to say, though. The inevitable human failure is seen in a larger context provided by Yeats's own model of repetitive decline and ascent in *A Vision*, the Platonic Year (Yeats 1937: 243–63). Incomprehensible barbaric forces determine historic rise and fall – and thus also the fate of the artist and his works. The only option for the individual is to participate in this seemingly chaotic and yet coherent tumult: 'All men are dancers and their tread / Goes to the barbarous clangour of a gong' (208). Individual existence, the symbolic creation of coherence and therefore also poetic creation, are only attempts to participate in a larger concept, that of myth. This is the second direction of a radical symbolism that Yeats's poems indicate.

The third part of 'Nineteen Hundred and Nineteen' consequently symbolises poetic creation (hitherto noticeably absent from the list of artistic activities mentioned in it) as the flight of a swan, one of Yeats's favourite symbols.[13] The swan image undergoes a transition from comparison to myth marked by the repeated use of the word 'Satisfied' (208). When immersed in the universal system of myth, the deficient symbol is no longer experienced as lacking and can become an ideal mirror, here of the soul. The swan's preparation for its flight is the stage preceding artistic creation. The dark powers of the approaching night, the formless muddle of the imagination, are subject to his control. He rides on or plays with them.

An understanding of the relation of artistic creation, personal fate, and impersonal forces does not automatically lead to an escape from their tensions. The second and third stanzas of part three of 'Nineteen Hundred and Nineteen' recall two dangers of symbolism already observed several times. The complete immersion in a symbolic system leads to the loss of the self, to isolation and blindness, or to dissolution and destruction. Neither is acceptable and brings relief from the troubles of existence and the subjection to death.

Still, neither participating in the brutality of the world (as suggested in part four of the poem) nor mere ironic distance (as illustrated in part five) suffices as an adequate reaction to this difficult position. The uncontrollable tensions and unforseeable developments of existence must be accepted, suggests 'Nineteen Hundred and Nineteen'. Destruction as well as cultural creation have to be seen as expressions of universal schemes. In this connection, the 'terrible beauty' of 'Easter, 1916' reappears, this time in the image of the strangely beautiful horses and riders. They represent actual violent events as well as aesthetic spectacle, anarchic chaos and universal order (since their running in circles corresponds to the eternal cycle of the Platonic Year). They also mark the shift from realistic historic description via symbols to the folkloristic and mythical finale of the poem. The question whether evil originates from the destruction of beauty, or beauty is the result of destruction, cannot be answered by a text thus entangled in its own mechanisms.

On a more personal level, the inextricable connection of creation and destruction in one's own emotional and sexual impulses shifts into the focus at the end of the poem. 'Herodias' daughters' (210), spirits who unwillingly harm men falling for their beauty, and Lady Kyteler with her demon lover Robert Artisson as the representative of those suffering and destroying because of their insatiable need to be loved, illustrate the roots of violence and destruction in individual passion.[14] Yet this passion is also the source of creativity. It is founded on the same lack and desire that also leads to its very opposite. Yeats's poems try to reconcile these contradictory impulses by illustrating a symbolic alternative: the dissolution of deficient symbolism in an imaginary flux or its integration in a universal myth. Neither of these options can convince before it tackles the very root of this problematic symbolism: the poetic imagination.

6. THE LIMIT OF THE SYMBOL: IMAGINATION

If history threatens the symbol from its outside by highlighting the static nature of its construction, the internal limits of the symbol are exposed by the failure of one or more of its constituents. This happens in the collapse of overdetermination, when too many or too complex symbols produce an overcharge of meaning, as in 'The Valley of the Black Pig'. Rarer in Yeats's works is the fading away of symbolic interrelations which leaves isolated metonymies. A poem depicting the problem of writing symbolic poems after the loss of symbolic connections is the one tellingly named 'Symbols' in *The Winding Stair and Other Poems* of 1933 (239–40). A third form of dissolution is the complete integration into myth: once the symbols become part of a truth, they lose their status as deficient signs, because they are no longer measured against an external referent. An example of this incorporation in myth has just been encountered in the last lines of 'Nineteen Hundred and Nineteen'.

In this final section of the discussion of the symbol, the problem of its source will be analysed. Imagination describes the relation between poetic identity and the origin of its images. In Yeats's own imagery it is visible in the connection of, for instance, shepherd and shell in the discussed early poems. There, the source of symbols is transcendental, a different mystical reality. Its spokesman, the artist, is chosen to provide the material for the symbol from his own life. The symbol's eventual shape is determined by this interaction.

Yet throughout Yeats's works contradictions appear about the control of symbols. Is it in the hands of the artist or his external transcendental source, the 'invisible essence' or 'spiritual flame', as he calls it in his essay on Blake? Texts such as the 'Shepherd' poems see the transcendental origin of symbols as the controlling force. Other poems, especially those which feature the protagonist as magician or explicitly as artist, grant the poet control of his symbols. An early example is the poem 'To a Shade', a more elaborate and much later one 'The Tower'.

Important enough to provide the name for the collection *The Tower* of 1928 which initiates the later phase of Yeats's career, the poem is a complex discussion of old age and death, issues that became more and more important to Yeats – then already sixty-three years old. Old age threatens the artist's control of symbols, since for Yeats poetic power is closely linked with physical and especially sexual potency. Both are doomed to fade in old age. Death is an even more radical threat, because it unveils the ultimate limits of the symbol. It is possible to symbolise death, but every representation of this final absence automatically gives away its inadequacy. The same applies to the afterlife which can only ever be illustrated in images taken from actual life. The symbolisation of a counter-reality proves impossible.

Old age, however, is fairly easy to conquer symbolically. The beginning of 'The Tower' externalises the issue by presenting it in the image of a 'sort of battered kettle at the heel' (194). The speaker of the poem is shown as an abused dog to whose tail this object is attached by an unmentioned force. He tries hard to argue that old age is only a physical misfortune that his body suffers. His imagination, he is keen to stress, is more alive than ever. As a proof he indulges in an idyllic vision of his childhood days.[15]

The poem's second part then reveals the vision as what it is: poetic artifice. The speaker is presented as a magician on top of a tower, calling for visions. The tower, whose importance is stressed by the title of the poem, recalls the élitist position of the chosen artist, his capacity for generalising judgments, but also his isolation. It is also a phallic symbol, equating again poetic and sexual potency (Jeffares 1970: 30). Furthermore, it implicitly hints at the danger of the artist's symbolic vision: the view from the tower is a survey of its surroundings, but hardly a glance at its own construction. The successful symbolic system remains blind towards its own devices.

The desired visions indeed appear, and it is not difficult to explain why: the speaker has never left the realm of the imagination. His visions are memories. All those fantasies stress the importance of perception over reality. Since imagination inevitably transforms impressions, perception is never objective. And it must not be, because only imagination is capable of uniting dislocated events into the symbolic unity of fictions. This is the importance of the anecdotes of this section of the poem. They tell of the absolute power of a feudal landowner, but also of the beauty of a peasant girl. More important, they mention the power of song to drive men mad, and thus link the theme of power to that of artistic creation. The powerful poet is blind Raftery, but he is quickly substituted by Red Hanrahan whom the sixth stanza of the second section of 'The Tower' declares the creation of the poem's speaker. The circle has closed again. Everything is now inside poetic imagination and part of the symbolic system it creates.

An absolute command of this imagination, however, leads to a loss of objective views. The blind poets Homer and Raftery are impersonations of this principle. Absolute imagination, the triumph of the poet, is a tragedy. Its result is madness (even though the poet himself seems miraculously exempt from the tragedy he creates). An ideal fusion of subjectivity and objectivity remains a paradoxical endeavour, as is shown in the symbol of the '[o]ne inextricable beam' (196) of moon and sunlight. Yet not an objective unity is desired, but again an imaginary one, as the verb 'seem' indicates. But even this emphasis on perception rather than objective reality (Bell 1980: 35) does not resolve the tension produced by the overwhelming imagination of the poem. The control of the poem's speaker still rests on an identity that is itself symbolic: the magician.

The end of the seventh stanza of part two of 'The Tower' shows what happens when imagination takes over completely. Hanrahan (here in the position of the magician which is also that of the poet) transforms a pack of cards into a hare and hounds. The card game mirrors the text with the cards as its symbols. When these symbols take over, the structure of the text is disturbed. The result is mad discourse, the violation of rules, and the end of the game. The little anecdote illustrates this danger, but threatens to become dangerous itself by growing out of proportion. It has to be stopped. This can only be done by forgetting, i.e. countering the symbolic permanence.

The poem's third part then tries to achieve a balance between the desire of its speaker to manifest his identity through his recollections and the dangerous power of his imagination. It juxtaposes stock phrases and images from Yeats's earlier poems with great pathos in what is declared to be the speaker's will. Yet all he manages is to prepare his peace with '[p]oet's imaginings / And memories of love' (199) again. The symbolic process offers no escape. Its orientation is towards myth, the 'superhuman / Mirror-resembling dream' (199). After trying to break out of its symbolic structures, the poem arrives full-circle at its roots in the imagination again.

Consequently, the final part of 'The Tower' can only offer a pseudo-alternative. The jackdaw building its nest with stolen material represents the poet and his use of eclectic material (in what Claude Lévi-Strauss calls *bricolage*). This is the materialist option. Yet never content with grey truth, Yeats also offers a transcendental escape which is a paradoxical turn against the rest of the poem: 'Now shall I make my soul'. An Irish expression for coming to terms with death, it also indicates that the mechanisms of imagination shall be grasped with imagination. This is wishful thinking, and the poem is aware of it. It does not even try to present a symbol of this miraculously achieved state of permanence capable of countering the vividly depicted old age and approaching death. The attempt, however, is important. It is much more than just a symptom of excessive imagination, as Harold Bloom seems to believe (Bloom 1970: 350). It outlines a crucial modernist concept, that of a complete integration of reality into the imagination which achieves a simulated permanence in the symbolic poetic structures.

'Sailing to Byzantium', the first poem in *The Tower*, also contains an attempt to symbolise transcendental permanence – in the shape of the artificial golden bird. It is doomed to disappoint because of the structure of the symbol which always relies on actual phenomena as the source of its *pictura*. Its construction also requires an identity that cannot catch itself in its own net. Therefore the golden bird of 'Sailing to Byzantium' remains a toy and proves painfully inadequate both as a representation of the perfect work of art and as an attempt to conquer temporality. The inadequacy of the symbol in the face of the metaphysical, of issues that transcend physical reality, also makes 'The Tower' leave its reader with the naked 'soul' of its speaker. This soul cannot be clothed in symbols, and therefore remains unconvincing in a poetic structure relying on symbolic certainties.

Symbols cannot grasp phenomena outside human experience; thus death, for instance, can only be shown in its physical manifestation, not in its nature as an absence. Transcendental concepts like the soul can only be depicted in materialist reductions, in reifications (even if these are clever ones, such as the deliberately imprecise 'Shade more than man, more image than a shade', 'death-in-life and life-in-death', and 'Miracle, bird or golden handiwork, / More miracle than bird or handiwork' (248) in 'Byzantium', Yeats's renewed attempt to envisage an afterlife).

The symbol is indispensable for the creation of reality, history, and personal identity. At the same time it brings with it closure and paralysis. This becomes perhaps most evident in the stone sculpture of the Chinamen in 'Lapis Lazuli'. It is meant to represent life of all things (Levine 1970: 21–2). It is painfully obvious, though, that it remains an ornament, a grinning little reminder that life (and death) are much more complex than symbols are capable of depicting. Yet this does not mean that one can freely abandon symbols. When symbolic coherence is blasted, the result is the collapse of semantic structures, mad and chaotic discourse in which the remnants of the symbols function as metaphors and metonymies, as will be shown below.

In his last poems Yeats laments the loss of security (especially that of poetic inspiration) which is always the consequence of the abandonment of coherent symbolic systems.[16] 'The Circus Animals' Desertion' illustrates this loss. The connection between the source of visions and the poet has vanished: 'my ladder's gone' (347). Left are the disconnected symbols of a poetic career. Yet slyly Yeats tries to preserve one last intact symbol, the heart. But even this is now a 'foul rag and bone shop' (348).

The second option for an inadequate symbolism is illustrated in another late poem, 'Long-legged Fly'. It, too, consists of fragmented images which were once part of Yeats's symbolic system. Yet the fly of the poem's title, although not really a full-fledged symbol itself, at least knows how to react in the face of all this chaos. It stubbornly keeps its position on the stream whose pace and currents it can ignore. Its mind is fixed on silence.

The path is cleared for the ahistorical modernist myth, capable of integrating the fragments of a shattered Western culture. As will be shown in the chapter on Ezra Pound, myth feeds on dissolved symbolic systems and gives them a new meaning within its own concept – which knows nothing of the dangers that threaten the symbol. Similar to a completely closed symbolic system, yet much more universal and untroubled by internal problems in its in-built blindness towards itself, myth fills the silence after the crumbling of symbolic certainties with its own mighty voice.

NOTES

1. That Blake rather than Arthur Symons is the source of Yeats's symbolism has now become critical consensus. See, for example, Driscoll 1975. The influence of French Symbolism is also questioned in Hahn 1971: 15–17.
2. Yeats 1950: 8. Yeats's handwriting is notoriously difficult to decipher.
3. The poem was first published in the *Dublin University Review* in October 1885, then under the second title in *The Wanderings of Oisin* in 1889. See Jeffares 1984: 3.
4. Lacan 1977a: 1–7 ('The mirror stage'). On misrepresent see 'The direction of the treatment and the principle 226–80 (263). On the importance of the word in activity see 'The function and field of speech psychoanalysis', 30–113.
5. For a psychoanalytic evaluation of the islands in Webster 1974: 4–37. She regards them as 'an altern

and Yeats's first attempt to work his fears [of women and sex] and guilt feelings [about oedipal urges] into a traditional framework' (8).

6. On the rose as a symbol see Jeffares 1984: 20–4 (21). The Rosicrucian symbol was also used as a cover illustration for the first edition of *The Rose* (1893). A reproduction is on the front page of Driscoll 1975.
7. On the rose as a symbol of inspiration and its dangers see Hessenberger 1986: 43–5. Also Bloom 1970: 110–12.
8. Thus the title of Richard Ellmann's biography, *Yeats: The Man and the Masks* (1961).
9. Yeats's disgust at genitals and sexual activity is discussed in Webster 1974: 15–16.
10. On bird symbolism in Yeats see Saul 1966: 245–56 (246).
11. Still, the radical constitution of the subject by naming itself remains a misrepresentation. In Lacan's words: 'It is not a question of knowing whether I speak of myself in a way that conforms to what I am, but rather of knowing whether I am the same as that of which I speak' (Lacan 1977a: 165).
12. On the loss of the coherence of speakers in Yeats's poems see also Bloom 1970: 110–12.
13. The poet mentioned explicitly in line 1 is therefore rather Yeats himself in ironic representation than Shelley, as suggested in Jeffares 1984: 233.
14. For the legendary sources of these images see Jeffares 1984: 234–6.
15. This vision contains elements with erotic overtones: the rod, the worm (used as a symbol for the penis in 'The Chambermaid's Second Song'), and the ambiguous 'spend', a Victorian euphemism for ejaculation.
16. Bloom puts it this way: 'The poet is in despair for the lack of a theme, but he has gone beyond the possibility of finding a fresh one' (Bloom 1970: 457).

CHAPTER THREE

From Metaphor to Metonymy: T.S. Eliot (1888–1965)

1. THE BIRTH OF MODERNISM

T.S. Eliot is the first poet in the present study whose works leave no doubt which tradition they belong to. His poems are icons of modernism. They exhibit the structures associated with the 'fragmented reality' apparently so poignant in the years between the two world wars. Two of these structures, metaphor and metonymy, and their relation within the development of the aesthetics of modernism, will be discussed in this chapter.

Eliot's poems also mark the beginning of what is conventionally called 'classical modernism'. The term is in fact an oxymoron, since modernism can be defined as a reaction to its historic models, thus also as anti-classicism. Eliot's poetry, too, breaks with the preceding standards of English poetry and constitutes an essential rupture. In its radicalism, this denial of its status as yet another development in the history of literature is a new phenomenon. Modernism indeed tries to present itself as generated out of itself, as a *machine célibataire*.[1]

This tendency of declaring itself fatherless, and, more especially, motherless, points at modernism's roots in the Enlightenment, the first movement in Western intellectual history to give itself its own rules and premises. The latter has implications on modernism as an exclusively male project, an issue which will be discussed in the chapter on psychoanalysis and modernist poetry. Modernism therefore presents itself as a paradoxical production out of itself. Its 'immaculate conception' thus also echoes the capitalist production of surplus, an analogy which will become crucial in the chapter on the economy of the modernist poem. In a world in which everything becomes a commodity, even one's history is no longer a matter of fate, but of acquisition. The denial of tradition influences modernist poetry on various planes. Yet it remains a deception. Modernism is indeed infatuated with its own past. One of its characteristics is the use of traditional texts in montage and collage techniques, as quotations.

In this respect, it is crucial that modernism with its continual stress on the threatened role of subjectivity (a problem already observed in the problematic position of the self in Hopkins and Yeats) actually shows this subjectivity in almost unlimited control. It is even presented as capable of drawing a line where it would like to see the limits of its own manifestation. This tendency of strengthening the role of the subject while showing it as endangered will reappear throughout the present study and will eventually help to delineate one of the limits of modernism.

Modernism's view of itself as a *machine célibataire*, a celibate machine existing out of and for itself, has crucial implications for its self-reflective potential. Here, its loss of a history, a tradition, eventually every form of reality outside the texts which could act as a point of orientation, is progressively turned into a denial of an outside altogether. One of the basic failures of modernism, that to establish contact with an external reality, is transformed into one of its primary achievements. Its virtue is that of blindness. Modernism is constantly in danger of losing control because of its limited self-criticism which is produced, paradoxically, by an overemphasis on self-reflection. It is the effect of its fixation on its material, language, its own constructive aspect. This explains in part the drift of many modernists towards fascism. This fatal weakness is only the most drastic result of a universalism that arises when all external means of comparison have vanished. Jean-François Lyotard consequently claims that modernism is the prototypical example of a master narrative, an all-encompassing explanation presenting itself as truth, which inevitably becomes totalitarian and eventually terroristic (Lyotard 1984: 31–7).

This seems a rather radical claim when one considers T.S. Eliot's *oeuvre*. Obviously, here is a poet concerned with very personal failures which correlate with a hostile and fragmented reality, a writer of 'reflections from a damaged life' – to use the subtitle of Adorno's *Minima Moralia*. It remains to be seen if the crucial elements of his works point towards general patterns of modernism.

2. THE STRUCTURE OF THE METAPHOR

The interest in the metaphor is as old as the human concern with language. In the relation of language and reality the crucial role of the metaphor lies in its intermediate status between figure of speech and cognitive image, a form of perception.

From a purely linguistic point of view, the metaphor is a displacement, an exchange of signifiers. Yet – unlike the symbol – this displacement is not a substitution, but a synthesis. The metaphor merges the associations of two signifiers, their paradigmatic fields. For instance, the sentence 'He is a lion' takes the associations of majesty and strength that the signifier 'lion' contains and places them on a particular person. The merger is motivated by a semantic similarity (the Greek word *metaphorá* means 'transfer') (Link 1974: 149).

This union, however, also influences the perception of the objects which provide the signifiers of the merger. Both the lion and the person described by the metaphoric statement achieve a new status through their metaphoric coupling. Eva Feder Kittay remarks in her comprehensive study of the metaphor that this cognitive aspect was already noticed by Aristotle. She summarises his ideas in his *Topics* as follows:

> as argumentation, metaphorical expression is always obscure because metaphor results in the same object being placed in two different genera, neither of which includes the other. If a genus is regarded as a perspective upon an object, metaphor results in the placing of an object in two perspectives simultaneously. From this juxtaposition results a reconceptualization, sometimes permanent, more frequently transient, in which properties are made salient which may not frequently have been regarded as salient and in which concepts are reorganized both to accommodate and to help shape experience.
>
> (Kittay 1987: 4)

Metaphors therefore do not depict an existing similarity of objects, but persuade their percipient of this similarity. 'Eliot was not comparing anything to anything when he promised to show us fear in a handful of dust', states David A. Cooper (Cooper 1986: 184). And Kittay claims that 'the opening to "The Love Song of J. Alfred Prufrock", as much as any metaphor, creates a similarity rather than records an antecedent one' (Kittay 1987: 18).

Kittay suggests the following structural outline of the metaphor, using as her example the 'Bees of England' from Shelley's poem 'Song to the Men of England' (29):

TERM:

/bi:z/
the concept of bees

referent: some actual bees in the world

METAPHOR:

the TERM 'bees'	/bi:z/
	idea of bees and their social hierarchy
the idea of workers (and their social and economical hierarchy)	

Figure 1

In the analysis of modernism, this creation of new similarities is central. All discussions of modernism as a mere mimetic depiction of a fragmented reality tend to ignore this creative aspect. In the analysis of the ambiguous role of personality in modernist poetry, the use of metaphors can provide crucial answers. It remains to be seen whether there is a particularly modernist way of employing metaphors. The title of the present chapter hints at the suspicion that the role of metaphor is threatened in modernist poetry, that its status is liminal and eventually shifting towards a different figure of speech, the metonymy, whose structure will be outlined after the discussion of the metaphors of Eliot's early poetry up to *The Waste Land*.

3. METAPHORS IN ELIOT'S EARLY POETRY

One of the striking features of Eliot's poems in *Prufrock and Other Observations* of 1917 is the dominance of what Jürgen Link calls the 'daring metaphor'. According to Link's structuralist model, daring metaphors fuse images of such remote origins as to make the area in which they overlap almost empty of mutual associations. When it is completely empty, he calls the structure an 'absolute metaphor' (Link 1974: 150). The famous opening lines of 'The Love Song of J. Alfred Prufrock' contain the most renowned example of this technique in Eliot's works:

> Let us go then, you and I,
> When the evening is spread out against the sky
> Like a patient etherized upon a table;
>
> (Eliot 1974: 13)

The lines contain one straightforward metaphor, the term 'spread' applied to 'evening', and a simile that compares this evening to an anaesthetised patient. Yet, as Kittay rightly remarks, 'In simile, the "like" is itself a metaphor. Thus metaphor is not merely one "among endless devices"; it is the pragmatic device for pointing out analogies and making comparisons which cross the bounds of our usual categories and concepts' (Kittay 1987: 19).

A crucial distinction between simile and metaphor is the fact that the simile makes the reader aware that someone or something is drawing the analogy, whereas the metaphor hides its producer. In this respect the similes in Eliot's early poems are connected with the poems' preference for evasive, but still coherent narrators.

The lines from 'Prufrock' quoted above therefore contain a double metaphor whose rhetorical effect is very convincing. The reasons for this are easy to see: the daring metaphors mirror the modern mind's perception of reality as an arrangement of non-compatible sensations and impressions. The poem delivers the modern head 'brought in upon a platter' (to use the allusion to the biblical story of John the Baptist in the poem). Yet this should not deceive us about the status of the images: they are not so much mimetic, i.e. representing reality, as cognitive – in the same way that 'He is a lion' does not describe an actual physical similarity, but the way in which someone perceives the person. They illustrate mental states, but these mental states are also in turn created by their depiction in Eliot's poems.

This creation of mental landscapes, which are often expanded into themes and are taken by many critics to represent directly the turmoil of either the First World War or the inter-war years, will appear again and again not only in Eliot, but also in Pound's works. It is important to keep this interrelation between perception and artistic creation – or rather the blurred borderlines between the two – in mind for an evaluation of the modernist attitude towards tradition.

In Eliot's 'Prufrock' these clusters of metaphors can be interpreted as symptoms of a universal development. They illustrate the growing autonomy of the world of objects which in turn leads to a questioning of the autonomy of the subject. This subject can only ever constitute itself through the objects which form its reality. In this manner, the evening becomes anthropomorphised at the beginning of 'Prufrock', only to be instantly declared passive, drugged and helpless, the very image of human subjectivity threatened by the growing dominance of the objects surrounding it. These objects, such as the 'certain half-deserted streets' which become '*muttering* retreats' and 'Streets that *follow* like a tedious argument' (13; my emphases), gain a life of their own. They are suddenly filled with malicious intentions. Their 'insidious intent' (13) forces the speaker of 'Prufrock' to an overwhelming question which is apparently central to the poem, since it appears at various strategic points of the text.

Balachandra Rajan claims that this question is related to a general theme in Eliot's works, his 'life–death ambiguity', as he calls it. True living presupposes the acquisition of knowledge through experience. Yet this knowledge is shocking (Rajan 1976: 8–9). Rajan does not explain the reason for the shocking nature of knowledge. But it is easy to guess that the shock is the insight that the subject's efforts to constitute itself through actions and objects only ever prove its attachment to the world of objects. It continually fails to attain true autonomy. The most elaborate attempt to become a fulfilled subject, i.e. to live, only leads to the ultimate dissolution in death. Death and forms of losing consciousness and therefore control in sleep, anaesthesia and sexual activity prove that subjective autonomy remains a fiction.

In his later works, Eliot seems to accept this lack of autonomy reluctantly. The deficient subject becomes the basis of a religious framework which pretends to overcome the lack. In his early poems, however, there is no such remedy. The deficiency seems to derive as much from external factors as from internal failures of the protagonists of these miniature dramas. 'Do I dare?' is the continual question of the speaker in 'Prufrock', but his hesitation is related to very physical manifestations of bodily decline – such as thinning hair. Again, perception unites psychological disposition and physical reality. In this respect it becomes clear that it is not important whether the speaker in 'Prufrock' is indeed ageing or merely a hypochondriac. The images he employs to describe his position are indeed metaphors, even if their status often remains disguised:

> Time to turn back and descend the stair,
> With a bald spot in the middle of my hair –
> (They will say: 'How his hair is growing thin!')
> My morning coat, my collar mounting firmly to my chin,
> My necktie rich and modest, but asserted by a simple pin –
> (They will say: 'But how his arms and legs are thin!')
>
> (14)

The above lines could be read as a realistic self-description of the speaker. They are indeed a fairly complex tissue of metonymies, too. A closer inspection, however, shows that most of the elements of the description exhibit exactly the danger of the increasing autonomy of objects: the hair is *growing* thin (a very subtle pun), the collar is *mounting* (my emphases). Nowhere is a trace of active interference of the subject with these objects to be found. The objects are in control. Even worse, the constitution of the subject is only possible through these objects and the comments of other subjects who act as onlookers. These do not judge its particular values, only again its external appearance through physical aspects (the arms, the hair).[2]

This interference of the material with the life of the subject finds its most drastic expression in the line 'I have measured out my life with coffee spoons' (14), although here, for once, the subject appears to be in control. This control remains fictional, however, since what is taken control of cannot be controlled. The line is concerned with time. This time, according to the philosophy of Henri Bergson, whose lectures Eliot attended in Paris, is only conceivable as space for a mind raised in the Western metaphysical tradition. This space again has all the qualities of the dominant object.

The recurring images of time in its various shapes, the biblical 'fulfilled time' of Ecclesiastes, the 'unfulfilled time' of mechanical repetition, as well as the potentially fulfilled time of individual existence depicted in the images of walks, visits, and stairs, all coexist in 'Prufrock'. Yet their coexistence is not harmonious, it creates tension. Since there is no hierarchy of time schemes, all of them strive to become dominant. Indeed, it is not easy to decide which concept of time each action represents. Is the walk suggested at the very beginning of the poem (but never really undertaken) an example of fulfilled time? Certainly not. But could it hint at potential fulfilment – just like the overwhelming question – or is it merely a recurring ritual utterly devoid of meaning? The poem gives no answer to this question, and this is its most tragic aspect.

For the metaphors in a poem like 'Prufrock', the instability of the time schemes creates problems on a structural level. Metaphors seem to exist outside time, since they are a fusion of paradigms which coexist simultaneously without distance on the syntagmatic level, the axis of narration. Yet if objects that are the sources of metaphors necessarily exist within time, and this time even becomes an object itself, the notion of a timeless realm becomes highly dubious. Time itself enters the ranks of material things, but by doing so it at least partly robs the texts of their potential to depict perceptions in metaphors. It introduces an internal spatial distance within metaphors that drives them closer to metonymies. Images refuse to become fused into unified metaphors and remain isolated and fragmented metonymies. This is the structural reason for the continual tendency of modernist poetry to replace symbols and metaphors by metonymies.

The above self-description of the speaker in 'Prufrock' is a proof that the fusion no longer works. Some later lines in the same poem also demonstrate the dilemma:

> Shall I say, I have gone at dusk through narrow streets
> And watched the smoke that rises from the pipes
> Of lonely men in shirt-sleeves, leaning out of windows? . . .
>
> (15)

The images strive to become an impersonal metaphor of loneliness, hopelessness, perhaps even decay and exploitation. Yet they remain a metonymy. This metonymy even stresses that it is the manifestation of a particular subject – in spite of its description of subjectivity as endangered or indeed absent in the rhetorical question 'Shall I say'. It is the fiction of a speaker who is even capable of referring to himself and his expressive potential.

4. THE STRUCTURE AND EFFECTS OF THE METONYMY

Metonymy is the displacement of signifiers on the syntagmatic axis of texts, the axis of narration on which signs are connected according to the rules of grammar and word order. Metonymy either describes the relation of fragmented parts of an image or a figure of speech that appear in various parts of a text or a fragmented image representing something more complex than itself (as in the *pars pro toto*, the 'part for the whole'). The Greek term *metonymia* translates as 'change of names'. The effect of the metonymy can be twofold. A consistent metonymic structure creates the impression of a tightly knit argumentative unit, a kind of organic coherence of the text, whereas incoherent, far-fetched, or too drastically reduced metonymies produce ambiguity, obscurity, or even illegibility.

In all cases, the reader is forced to supplement the missing syntagmatic links. In the case of the coherent metonymy, this supplementation results in a near-perfect simulation of coherence. In all other cases, there are either semantic overlappings creating ambiguity, gaps in the semantic network producing obscurity, or even doubts concerning the adequacy of the applied code of interpretation leading to the illegibility of a text (Riffaterre 1983: 9–12).

In Eliot's *oeuvre*, there is a tendency for metonymies to become more and more radical, until – in a poem like *The Waste Land* – they become the most important elements of the text, and the whole poem turns into an extended metonymy. In Eliot's earlier poems metonymies are employed to give a pattern, even a temporal structure to the texts. 'Rhapsody on a Windy Night' is the finest example.

In 'Prufrock', the structuring metonymy is that of the street scenes which appear repeatedly representing various times of the day. Again, time is related to space in the manner of Bergson's theories. In 'Portrait of a Lady', the seasons of the year form this pattern, each one with an attribute that is itself a recurring image in Eliot's works. The winter of its beginning is linked to the familiar smoke and fog; the spring of its second part to lilacs (which, like many flowers in his poems, hint at eroticism). Summer – also in part two – is connected with the sound of a broken violin (music representing memory and potential fulfilment, yet here it is 'out-of-tune'); and eventually the autumn of its third part with the image of the walk.

In 'Preludes' the times of the day are again depicted in various street scenes or voyeuristic glimpses into houses. In this poem, the clearest representation of time as object – which is then in turn anthropomorphised – can be detected: 'The winter evening settles down' (the first line of part I) and 'The morning comes to consciousness' (23) (the corresponding line of part II). These are mirrored by the corresponding third and fourth part of the poem which thus achieves a perfectly symmetrical shape. Here it is a woman and a man who are described in exactly the same positions as the preceding evening and morning. Eliot's poems turn the perception of modern reality into psychological landscapes, but they also function in a diametrically opposed way and transform individual psychology into objective states.

Eliot's own theory of the 'objective correlative', the linking of intellectual notions with images from life or memory, is therefore more radical than its author believed. He defines the term in the following way:

> The only way of expressing emotion in the form of art is by finding an 'objective correlative'; in other words a set of objects, a chain of events which shall be the formula of that particular emotion; such that when the external facts, which must terminate in sensory experience, are given, the emotion is immediately evoked.
>
> (Eliot 1975: 48)

What his concept neglects is that neither objects nor events but only their representations in signifiers appear in works of art. The choice and meanings of signifiers are already governed by conventions which are not only personal, but also collective. Still, these signifiers do not automatically relate to any given reality (not even a psychological one). They form a reality of their own – which in turn influences their shape and choice. The signifiers are metaphors and metonymies, and therefore both visual and cognitive. When read in this light, Eliot's 'objective correlative' remains a splendid example of the growing awareness of the importance of objects and language in the formation of subjective identity.

If the metonymy acts as a structuring and organising device in Eliot's early poetry by relating time and space, it fulfils a rather different function when it comes to the representation of individuals. Here, the metonymy prevents characters from achieving coherence. In fact, it very often reduces them to a state in which one can hardly call them personalities at all, where they are the victims of a reality that does not know and much less permits fulfilment. What interferes with any possible development towards 'whole' personalities is not only objects, but also – equally turned into objects, reified, that is –

other people. '*L'enfer, c'est les autres*' (hell is other people), Jean Paul Sartre's famous statement, also applies to Eliot's works.

One of the reasons for this has already been observed in 'Prufrock': the constitution of identity is only possible through the observations and value-judgements of others. Yet these others are just as fragmented as the individual who relies on them – and they in turn rely on the perception of others, including the incomplete individual at the beginning of the chain. This correlates with Lacan's concept of desire as continual displacement on the chain of signifiers. There is no fulfilment to be found in 'the Other', yet this Other remains the necessary point of orientation for the constitution of the individual self.

On a structural level, this tragic incompleteness of characters is depicted by the metonymy in Eliot's poems. The speaker of 'Prufrock' is represented by his thinning hair and his pathetic arms and legs in the passage quoted above. Women (the favourite 'Other' in Eliot) are presented as their hair, their arms (sometimes full of flowers – a further displacement) or their smell. A poem drastically depicting the struggle of two identities in their mutually exclusive constitution is the rarely discussed 'Hysteria', Eliot's only collected prose poem.

In 'Hysteria', a male speaker describes his feelings when faced with the laughter of a woman who has accompanied him to a restaurant or tea-room. This woman is presented as an extended metonymy: 'her laughter', 'her teeth', 'her throat', 'her breasts'. In the first two sentences, which can be read in Freudian terms as a prototypical description of castration anxiety, the speaker imagines himself swallowed by the woman and undertaking a masochistic journey through 'the dark caverns of her throat, bruised by the ripple of unseen muscles' (34).

The rhythm of these sentences, the first consisting of two long parts, the second of four short ones, corresponds to the structure of violent laughter as well as to that of sexual intercourse. In this respect, it is interesting that the special talents of the woman's teeth are stressed, thus creating the image of the *vagina dentata*, the vagina with teeth, a powerful allegory of male fears. In the process, the speaker's 'I' is transformed from being 'aware', 'becoming involved', 'being part', being 'drawn in' and 'inhaled' to being 'lost' and 'bruised' (34).

This is a perfect description of the radical failure of the constitution of the self. The failure is even more devastating as it occurs in connection with the one activity that should represent the perfect way of affirmation for the self, its relationship with others, here even with that special Other, the partner in a sexual relationship. The failure happens because this partner is perceived as fragmented; not as a subject, but as a succession of objects that do not form a whole, but an abyss.[3] The speaker is not presented as a subject either, but also becomes increasingly objectified in the course of events.

When the poem returns from the psychological landscape of its first two sentences to a realistic description of the setting, there are still reverberations of the process just undergone. The waiter who tries to usher the two embarrassing guests into the garden, the second male character of the poem and the only one described in his physical appearance, is elderly and has trembling hands. The poem's images of masculinity are as negative as its descriptions of the feminine.

The final sentence of the text shows the speaker again in ironic control. Nonetheless, it states that the occurrence has altered his perception of reality. It is shattered and lies in fragments:

> 'I decided that if the shaking of her breasts could be stopped,
> some of the fragments of the afternoon might be collected, and I
> concentrated my attention with careful subtlety to this end' (34).

The final subclause reflects back on the poem's constitution: it is nothing but the subtle attempt to gather the fragmented impressions of an event (and it is not important whether this event is fictional, since it is a psychological one) into a coherent shape.

According to Freud, hysteria results from libidinal impulses prevented from reaching their goals (Freud 1973–86 vol. 8: 31–164). Compared to archaic ideas about the organic reasons of hysteria (the term derives from the Greek *hustera*, 'womb'), Eliot's poem is indeed the description of an unusual variant. The obvious hysteria of the poem applies to the laughing woman, but its male speaker also displays the symptoms of lost control. His wild visions contrast strangely with his obvious paralysis. His desire is at the same time sexual and directed towards his partner as it is pointed towards the establishment of his own identity. Both fail, primarily because their means of manifestation, language, intervenes. The metonymy can be an adequate or indeed the only way of coming to terms with a fragmented reality. Yet it has serious effects on the establishment of identity. In 'Gerontion', a self constituted by meaningless memories of interchangeable events, people, and objects deplores its own vacuity and hopelessness. Himself a mere metonymy, 'a dry brain in a dry season' (41), the speaker fails to find solace in others. They fragment and swallow him ('To be eaten to be divided, to be drunk', 39), an effect also highlighted by their exotic names: Hakagawa (hack),

Madame de Tornquist (torn/twist), and Fräulein von Kulp (gulp). Distraction and confusion characterise a world in which reality has become a cunning and deceptive story and the self a memory of non-events. The inevitable conflict of reality and self in their metonymic representations is brought to its breaking point in what is generally regarded as Eliot's most radical poem, *The Waste Land.*

5. ABSENCE AS STRUCTURE: *THE WASTE LAND*

As an elaborate and repetitive device, metonymy fulfils two functions in modernist poems. It depicts a fragmentation of perception – which it in part creates as well. It also constructs a new coherence, one that is unlike the linear structure of conventional narratives, but rather resembles a network or – to use a post-structuralist model – a rhizome. One of the central problems of modernist poetry is indeed its attempt to overcome the traditional narrative, the epic tradition that brings with it coherent characters and personalities (easily visible in the epic heroes) as well as a linear view of history. Both of these points of orientation were threatened by the ever-increasing speed of modern life in a late industrial society as well as by the most radically unsettling experience in history so far: the First World War.

Still, the abandonment of the epic tradition proved much more difficult than the early attempts of the modernists suggested. Imagism, for example, thought to overcome the traditions of its poetic predecessors by simply refusing to develop coherent arguments. A single image was declared sufficient, and narrative to be avoided at all costs. Yet the price that Imagism had to pay for its radical reduction of poetic technique was its inability to make statements. As its name implies, images were all it produced, and these in turn displayed tendencies to become merely ornamental.

Mere ornaments were not acceptable for the modernists who were all too keen on promoting their views of history and culture, in some cases religion as well. New techniques of writing epic poems had to be developed which would avoid the pitfalls of traditionalism, since the defeat of tradition was programmatically declared the offspring of the modernist movement. In this struggle, the metonymy proved the most reliable ally.

In Eliot's *The Waste Land*, metonymies are the bases of the three dominant textual layers of the poem: its landscapes, its characters and its quotations. The landscapes of the poem are the desert (already implied in the name of the poem), the garden (the antithesis of the desert), the city, the river, and the sea, all of which appear in various connections. It proves difficult to decide which scenery is connected with which part of the poem, for all sections display various settings – with the notable exception of 'Death by Water', the shortest part, which features one scenery and one protagonist only.

The other four sections contain recurring images of sceneries in various combinations. Rather like props in a theatre production, they are used repeatedly and become significant through their ever-changing combinations. In part I of the poem, 'The Burial of the Dead', the desert scene of the very beginning is followed by a reminiscence set in a restaurant in Bavaria. This is replaced by another desert scene which is followed by the prototypical garden scene of Eliot's early poems, the one featuring the woman with flowers in her arms, the 'Hyacinth girl'. The last two paragraphs of this part take place in a nondescript setting for Madame Sosostris and a city scenery that already contains hints of the important image of the river (London Bridge is mentioned and the verb 'flowed' is used repeatedly). The very end of its last part, however, returns to the images of the garden and the desert which it links in the potent image of the planted and flowering corpse.

The effect of this metonymic creation of sceneries is twofold and seemingly contradictory. The poem refuses to create a coherent realistic setting. There is no landscape that could possibly fit its description. At the same time the text manages to build its own reality, one that is by various hints identified as a mental one: 'Unreal city', the 'mixing' of 'memory and desire'.

Furthermore, the elements of this psychological landscape also have clear symbolic value. As indicated by the amusing sequence featuring Madame Sosostris, there is an underlying significance to all settings. Her cards show for the first time the Phoenician sailor who reappears in 'Death by Water'. The 'Lady of the Rocks' called 'Belladonna' (literally 'beautiful woman', but also a poisonous plant) is related to the ambiguous descriptions of women as desirable but also potentially threatening. The crowds of people walking round in a ring correspond to the anonymous masses flowing though London as well as to all characters in the poem engaged in repetitive activities without clear goals. The most drastic ones are certainly the typist and the carbuncular young man engaged in their dreary love-making.

In this way the landscape metonymies of the poem are interrelated to form a symbolic landscape peculiar to the poem itself. They also create the mental landscape of the text which can be related to the modern mind as well as the mental state of its creator, Eliot. Furthermore, the metonymies of the poem's settings also establish connections with the characters who inhabit them, and these connections in turn create new structures of meaning with potential symbolic value. The fragmentation caused by the excessive use of metonymy leads to a complex semantic network.

The same can be observed in the analysis of the characters of the poem. Many of them appear only once and are then seemingly forgotten. Examples are the speaker at the beginning of 'The Burial of the Dead', called 'Marie' by her cousin; Madame Sosostris; Stetson; the hysterical woman in 'A Game of Chess'; the pub characters of its end (Bill, Lou, May); Mr Eugenides, the Smyrna merchant; Elizabeth and Leicester. There are others who reappear, either clearly identified or thinly disguised, such as the Phoenician sailor, the Fisher King, Tiresias and Christ. Still, despite Eliot's claim in the 'Notes on the Waste Land', there is no central character of the poem. Like the settings, the characters are metonymic figures whose interrelation establishes their semantic potential.

Tiresias – whom Eliot himself proposes in his notes to be the central character – is not only blind but also androgynous. The Fisher King, so popular with critics who see the poem as an elaboration of the Grail legend, is not present in parts two and four of the text.

The unidentified voice who is the dominant narrator of the poem does not seem to belong to any identifiable character, but keeps hovering between all characters. Its in-between status makes it the expression of the network of metonymic interrelations rather than any particular part of this network. This corroborates Michael Beehler's claim that one of Eliot's achievements is the expression of the relational status of points of view:

> For Eliot, 'facts are not, in the realist sense, given; they are produced by . . . a "system"' or by an ineluctable non-neutral, situational point of view. The conditions of that point of view are [. . .] unexpressed and yet implied, and are acknowledged by Eliot to be 'irreducible'. What Michaels emphasizes about Eliot's pragmatism is the understanding of facts, of the universally and immanently real or basic, as 'determined by local "conditions" whose "transcendence" involves not their theoretical absorption into a higher whole but what might instead be called a lateral movement from one set of local conditions to another', with each locality being

> 'in no way more self-conscious, no more able to be reflective about its subjectivity' than any other.[4]

A similar observation can be made concerning the third dominant metonymic structure of the poem, that of intertextual references, its literary allusions. They also appear repeatedly, form patterns, but no identifiable statements, much less a fixed 'meaning'. Their foremost function is the development of a common cultural basis between poem and reader, a shared cultural background. They are cultural clichés in Michael Riffaterre's terminology (Riffaterre 1984: 15–16). In the case of *The Waste Land*, the reader-controlling function of allusions is closely connected with the poem's theme of cultural fragmentation and decay.

Maud Ellmann calls the poem's attitude towards its cultural heritage 'blasphemy', which she defines as 'affirmation masked as denial' (Ellmann 1987: 95). This indeed makes sense when one recalls that the poem exerts an ambiguous influence on its material, language, the medium that transfers cultural heritage into the text. Its reliance on the metonymy fragments the sources it uses. At the same time the poem creates new relations between the fragments, its own semantic network – or rather it urges its reader to perform this act of creation. This explains why *The Waste Land* has become a prime example of a text hardly visible under the heap of interpretations it has engendered. Again, the poem creates the loss it laments (here: the loss of Western civilisation).[5] At the same time it counters this loss by the creation of its own reality. Harriet Davidson describes this ambivalent effect as follows:

> First, the poem makes the reader experience the absence of expected connections. This reader-response observation capitalizes on the existential confusion which readers may feel and does not necessarily lead beyond the state of subject confronting object. Secondly, and more profoundly, the poem discloses absence ontologically as a state of the world, not as the state of a consciousness trying to know a world.
>
> (Davidson 1985: 3)

This groundless reality of *The Waste Land* derives much of its power from the ingenious linking mechanisms between its layers of metonymies. All of its central structures, the intertextual one of references and allusions, the lyric one of landscapes and other settings, and the dramatic one of vivid characters not only form independent patterns of their own. They also melt into one another, so that the created network becomes very dense. The second part of the poem, 'A Game of Chess', provides a striking example. It starts with the lyric description of a boudoir into which suddenly the intertextual allusion to the myth of Philomel enters.[6] This in turn is replaced by a dramatic sequence (although it consists most likely of a woman's monologue countered by the thoughts of her male partner). This dramatic outburst is followed abruptly by a very different allusion, this time to a music hall song, the 'Shakespeherian Rag', which then blends into a scene, once more dramatic, in a pub. The very end of this pub scene then subtly becomes another literary quotation, the last words of mad Ophelia in *Hamlet*.

The merging of various forms of discourse in the poem is related to its inability to draw a borderline between an interior of the text and a 'reality' outside it. It functions like the mind of a neurotic, incapable of differentiating between fiction and reality; thus the egalitarian status of quotations, lyric reflections and realistic dramatic scenes. On the textual level, this corresponds to the extraordinary density of the tissue of metonymies. Their overlappings create areas with a high density of meaning as well as serious gaps, the *Leerstellen* in Wolfgang Iser's theory of reader-response.[7] These gaps derive from the combination of distant fragments and signifiers as well as from their displacement all over the wide space of the text. As its title implies, *The Waste Land* has indeed epic ambitions, although these are pursued in an unorthodox structural way. Johnson assesses it in the following way: 'The path to be followed by the reader is not the discursive one of plot development, but that of a vertical ascent-descent through the text's stratification till resonance between identical signifier poles is set up' (Johnson 1985: 407).

An example of semantic networks created through metonymies is the episode featuring Elizabeth and Leicester gliding down the Thames in a barge in 'The Fire Sermon'. First, the episode is a reference. It derives directly from a sixteenth-century manuscript.[8] Yet its presentation takes the form of a lyric poem. The scenery evoked in the passage is the river, but it refers to the city as well. The scene is familiar: the unsuccessful attempt to establish a functioning relationship between the sexes. It is set on the river (embodying time) in a barge (the fixed form, perhaps of the restrictions of society). Additionally, the sequence is interspersed with the refrain 'Weialala leia / Wallala leialala' (73), an allusion to Wagner's *Ring des Nibelungen* where it is the song of the Rhine daughters.

The short sequence contains a metaphoric construction employing the three familiar forms of discourse, lyric, intertextual and dramatic (although here the interchange is silent, it is not less powerful). This construction is then metonymically linked with other parts of the poem. The frustrating sexual relationship, for instance, corresponds to the one in 'A Game of Chess', the love-making of the typist and the young man, and the rape also to be found in 'The Fire Sermon'. In this respect, it is not unimportant to note the ambiguous 'brisk swell' and 'Rippled' (73), reminiscent of the masochistic fantasies in 'Hysteria'. The theme of the polluted river is connected with the flow of people in the 'brown fog of a winter dawn' (65) in 'The Burial of the Dead' and, more obviously, with the description of the river at the beginning of 'The Fire Sermon' itself. This river bears, significantly (since the negation evokes presence), '*no* empty bottles, sandwich papers, / Silk handkerchiefs, cardboard boxes, cigarette ends / Or other testimony of summer nights' (meaning, most probably, condoms) (70; my emphasis). The Wagnerian interlude in turn relates the episode to the beginning of the poem where a quotation from *Tristan und Isolde* introduces the theme of unfulfilled desire.

Yet there are also the inevitable gaps in the metonymic network visible in the same sequence. The theme of social constraints interfering with a relationship, which is evoked by the story of Elizabeth and Leicester, does not appear anywhere else. Neither is there a logical link between the originally jubilant song of the Rhine daughters and the frustrating scene depicted in this part of 'The Fire Sermon'.

The Waste Land combines the metaphoric approach (the first and constantly dominant metaphor is indeed its very title)[9] with the metonymic and creates its discursive strategy out of their interactions and the tensions between them. The poem has many different meanings in the sense that it is an invitation to interpretation. But it is more than merely an open, polysemic text. As Harriet Davidson points out, 'the poem seems to expose the conditions for the possibility of all interpretations of this text and any text' (Davidson 1985: 5). It questions the very nature of interpretation and thus the relationship between text and reader and their status as interdependent object and subject.

The poem creates an almost musical sense of movement (which will reappear in even more elaborate form in *Four Quartets*), yet it refuses to name, outline, or even support the belief in a goal of this movement. If it is a quest myth, it is

> indeed that of interpretive being. The fertile land is created from the waste by the quest, but, as is evident from Jessie Weston's book, the quester in the myth generally does not know how to reach the object of the quest, certainly does not know how to reach the goal,

> and is usually unaware of what he has done to bring fertility to the land. Often asking questions is enough to fight the barrenness – no answers are necessary, because none are available.
>
> (Davidson 1985: 113)

Its dislocation of the firm expectations which are part of any reading-process, its questioning of the subject–object relation which underlies reading, exposes the constitution of the reading-experience. It thus creates what Davidson calls a 'hermeneutic universe' analogous to Heidegger's 'linguistic universe' (7), a world governed and created by interpretation rather than firm transcendental bases.

In doing this, *The Waste Land* also foregrounds and questions the conditions of its own production. This makes it a milestone of modernism, indeed a crossroads from which the way leads either to the acceptance of this lack of groundedness as the starting point of a new aesthetic or to attempts to fight the deficiency with the means that have remained in the control of the artists. These compensation strategies are the reliance on the material and the retreat into the closure of a linguistic and hermeneutic world. The threat of Eliot's poem remains, no matter which tradition artists and critics have chosen to follow, because it unveils the basic paradox within the determining forces of modern reality:

> if the self is determined by language and language is determined by culture and culture is surely a human creation, then there is a lack of groundedness here – a continual deferral of the origin of meaning.
>
> (Davidson 1985: 33)

> The human world is created in the desire to escape the absence defining our existence. The symbols, myth, art, and all of society attempt, in the endless elaboration of a relational linguistic world, to cover the absence. Lacan identifies this human activity as the 'metonymy of desire', which reveals our lack of wholeness and sufficiency even while it tries to hide this lack. Human life is a constant conjunction of death and desire to escape death.
>
> (103)[10]

The transition from metaphor to metonymy in Eliot's works is a symptom of this attempt and the paradoxes created by it.

6. FROM NETWORK TO PATTERN: *FOUR QUARTETS*

If 'Gerontion' marks Eliot's move from ironically relativistic characters to dislocated voices or 'areas of consciousness', as Anthony L. Johnson prefers to call them (Johnson 1985: 403), and thus an important transition from metaphor to metonymy in his poems which eventually culminates in *The Waste Land*, then 'The Hollow Men' and *Ash-Wednesday* can be regarded as stages in the development from metonymic fragmentation to a new symbolic unity. The problematic nature of this renewed wholeness will be analysed in this concluding section. Both 'The Hollow Men' and *Ash-Wednesday* exhibit two related features which become dominant in the symbolically most coherent of Eliot's poems, *Four Quartets*: repetition and self-reflection.

'The Hollow Men' surprises by the relative coherence of its narratorial voices. Although the visions of these voices are very similar to the fragmented reality of *The Waste Land*, the speakers are not only capable of naming themselves, they can also describe their position and their relation to the reality surrounding them. Although their outlook is deeply pessimistic (and even apocalyptic, as the end of the poem demonstrates), they display an intact subject–object relation, something that is completely absent from *The Waste Land*. The reason for this restoration of subjectivity is twofold. On the one hand, subjectivity in the poem establishes itself *ex negativo*. It defines itself through its own destruction. On the other hand, it creates itself in the ritual, by repetition.

Repetition and anaphora, the doubling of verse beginnings, abound from the poem's first lines. Its monotonous rhythm supports its ritualist aspect.

> We are the hollow men
> We are the stuffed men
>
> (89)

> [. . .]
> This is the dead land
> This is the cactus land
>
> (90)

> [. . .]
> The eyes are not here
> There are no eyes here
> In this valley of dying stars
> In this hollow valley
>
> (91)

Repetition is introduced in a variety of ways. There is, for instance, the parody of the well-known children's rhyme 'The Mulberry Bush' at the beginning of part V, which substitutes 'prickly pear' for the original plant. The playful ditty with its innocent connotations of old fertility rituals has been replaced by a very personal evocation of sexual frustration (Smith 1974: 106–7).

It is followed by one of the most intense passages in Eliot's poems, one that contains a minimum of words repeated over and over again. The central noun 'shadow' ends all stanzas. It questions the reality of the discussed concepts (idea, reality, motion, act, conception, creation, emotion, response, desire, spasm, potency, existence, essence, eventually descent) and unveils them as nothing but words, signifiers. This corresponds to the repeated 'Between' at the beginning of lines which is exchanged for the mere paratactic 'And' and eventually for 'Falls'. This is a concise description of the deconstructive attitude of Eliot's poems. Meaning is only established 'between' signifiers, through their connection ('And'), either on the paradigmatic or the syntagmatic level. Yet increasingly this connection fails, the results are gaps, absences into which the meaning of the texts together with their textual identities 'falls'.

The construction of this ritual of negation with excerpts from the liturgy throws an ambiguous light on the development of Christian belief in Eliot's works. In the absolute lack depicted by these lines, the repeated 'Thine is the Kingdom' has obscure referents. Traditionally the end of the Lord's Prayer, it represents the Christian belief in God and the hope for redemption in an afterlife. Connected with the absolutely negative images of the poem, however, the address can also be interpreted as an attack on Christian faith – if the 'Kingdom' is regarded as just one of death's kingdoms in the poem. This is supported by the fragmentation of the formula in the poem's penultimate stanza. In both cases, the recourse to the absolute (whether it is God or death) is necessary to complement the enormous absence of meaning created in the text.[11]

In *Ash-Wednesday*, repetition is even more dominant, and again this is connected with a clearer focusing on a narrator. Its first part contains no less than eleven lines beginning with 'Because'. There are six cases of anaphoric doublings of first words in subsequent lines and even two examples of triple anaphoras. Part VI of the poem contains a similar cluster of anaphoras.

Its other parts highlight the second reason for the symbolist appearance of this poem. It contains metonymies that are not only repeated over and over again, but which can also be linked with symbolic concepts and thus inhabit an intermediate realm between metonymy and symbol. The Lady of part II becomes associated with Dante's Beatrice, and the speaker relates his own state to the sacrifice of Prometheus (Smith 1974: 136–9). These are by no means all intertextual references or invitations to discover such cross-references similar to the allusions of *The Waste Land*. Yet what makes these metonymic patterns different from those of an open text like *The Waste Land* is exactly their underlying symbolism. They are all related to the now overtly Christian values of submission, sacrifice, humility and redemption.

The transition from metonymic fragmentation and openness to a new symbolic unity is achieved through the vertical arrangement of metonymic structures. Their paradigms thus establish relations which – when the metonymies are carefully selected to fit this aim – form a unified message, eliminate overhanging and unconnected semantic elements and leave no more gaps of meaning. This and the pleasant melodious character produced by repetition explain why a poem like *Ash-Wednesday* seems more pleasant to many readers than *The Waste Land*. A poem with a re-established symbolic coherence created out of discursive fragments relocates the position of the reader and frees him from the exhausting task of positioning himself constantly. It no longer questions his role in the reading-process, his subjectivity and autonomy. In Roland Barthes's terms, the poem becomes a classical *readerly* work again – and is no longer a *writerly* one that exposes the problems of its own constitution (Barthes 1974: 3–4).

In *Four Quartets* this shift from metonymic fragmentation to symbolic coherence is accomplished in an even more ingenious way. The text not only discusses the procedure, but tries to justify it at the same time. It starts with a philosophical discussion of time which sets the tone for the dominant theme of the poem, that of universal and individual history, their connection, and the consequences for the life of individual, nation and, eventually, mankind. Yet the problem of synchronising universal and individual history, the two time schemes familiar from Eliot's earlier poems where they often appear in images of the ocean and the river, is also related to the problem of integrating dispersed metonymic structures into a coherent symbolic unity.

Dislocated metonymic structures create semantically open texts whose meaning cannot simply be pinned down. The metonymies achieve this polysemy by forming rhizomes and networks with areas of higher semantic density but also gaps of meaning. Consequently they oscillate in the reading process (see *The Waste Land*). Yet they can be brought to a standstill when they are carefully superimposed to form a stable pattern of internal relations. The pattern resembles the symbolic systems analysed in Yeats's poetry. Still, the main difference between traditional symbolism and the symbolism in Eliot's later poems is that the latter is only internally motivated and remains a mere structural reproduction of transcendental beliefs, whereas the former derives its authority from a belief in an actual link with transcendental concepts outside the text.

In an essay on time in *Four Quartets* Ole Bay-Petersen describes the procedure:

> In *Four Quartets* the theme of time is associated throughout with the concept of a pattern which – like the still point – unites the temporal with the eternal. We have already glanced at the aesthetic pattern in which 'words or music reach / The stillness . . .' ('Burnt Norton'). This pattern is analogous with the external pattern. As Eliot writes in 'Burnt Norton': 'The detail of the pattern is movement . . . .' This implies that the pattern itself is still, and events that unfold in human time form tiny details in a pattern which attains significance and completeness only *sub specie aeternitatis*.
>
> (Bay-Petersen 1985: 148)

The time scheme created through mere internal motivation in *Four Quartets* is in fact the traditional pre-modern one. Foucault calls it the belief in 'linear succession' and illustrates it in the following way:

> . . . beneath the shifts and changes of political events, they [the historians] were trying to reveal the stable, almost indestructible system of checks and balances, the irreversible processes, the constant readjustments, the underlying tendencies that gather force, and are then suddenly reversed after centuries of continuity, the movements of accumulation and slow saturation, the great silent, motionless bases that traditional history has covered with a thick layer of events.
>
> (Foucault 1972: 3)

The musical analogy evoked by the title of the poem corresponds to the belief that both past and future are contained in the present moment. Individual history is only a point on the axis of universal history. It is located in a particular space. Thus the titles of the four quartets: places of particular importance for Eliot; and the concentration on the interaction between place and personality in 'East Coker'. The impression that the quartets are linked and interact is supported by semantic congruences between the vertical layers of their metonymies. A stability and permanence is created which is reassuring, but at the same time isolated and even frigid. 'Love is itself unmoving' says a line in 'Burnt Norton' (195) that describes this effect of the poem's construction of certainties.

The quasi-archaeological examination of the layers which form the history of mankind, a nation, and the individual eventually leads to a circular fatalistic view. 'East Coker' demonstrates the necessity of decline and renewal for the continuity of life in its images of food and excrement, procreation and death. An impersonal viewpoint is created which strives towards a Nietzschean superhistoricism, a detachment from history.

With 'The Dry Salvages' an even more cosmic tone enters the poem. In its evaluation of the progress of the human race, a pessimistic outlook is developed. Civilisation is depicted in the taming of streams, the symbol of individual history, here as an allusion to youth via the reference to Mark Twain's Mississippi. Its origin, however, and its eventual goal are illustrated by the image of the sea, the great formlessness which also represents universal time. The river as the individual text of life originates from and is eventually absorbed into the universal unity of dissolution, *parole* becomes *langue* again. Yet by outlining this most universal concept of language, history and reality, the text counteracts its very argument. It does not demonstrate a dissolution, but a constitution, that of its own symbolic system.

The fact that this symbolic system lacks motivation by any external authority and its complete closure become evident in the final quartet, 'Little Gidding'. It is a deliberately retrospective summary of Eliot's poetic career, an evaluation of the influences that have shaped his poetic voice. The identity of 'Little Gidding' creates its own ghostly mirror-image in its dialogue with its compound other self.

This process is constantly linked with a Christian view of humility – which in turn derives from the insight that the seemingly permanent can easily turn out to be very transient indeed (an impression certainly influenced by the impact of the Second World War). Nonetheless, it ultimately remains the expression of the same hubris that produces Yeats's line 'Now shall I make my soul'. The attempt to rescue a stable identity out of the fragmented reality of experience is one of the central aims of modernism. It leads to a closed system of poetic thought. It can appear in many shapes, such as the stress on the youthfulness of the imagination despite physical decline in Yeats, or, in Eliot's case, the disillusioned humility of an ageing self that renounces something it never had or appreciated: desire and love. Yet it always generates similar structures.

All modernist endeavours which refuse to accept the irrevocable fragmentation of existence, the loss of firm points of reference, inevitably end up in structures that, although only internally motivated, become universalist and totalitarian. Thus the replacement of 'here' by 'England' in 'Little Gidding', of free verse by the traditional metre of *Piers Plowman* in 'The Dry Salvages' and the echo of its beginning in 'Little Gidding'. Fragmented 'areas of consciousness' are exchanged for a coherent speaker. His humility when faced with the fragmentation of reality only thinly disguises the arrogance of his presence when all ground for subjectivity is lacking.

The transition from 'open' metaphoric and metonymic text to a 'closed' symbolic one can be detected *in nuce* in the beautiful opening lines of 'Little Gidding'. Already its very first term, 'Midwinter spring', confronts the reader with a daring metaphor which is both immediately convincing and immensely complex. Its metaphoric status is openly discussed in line 3: 'Suspended in time, between pole and tropic'. It sets the tone for the paradoxical and yet complementary imagery of the section: the contrast between extreme cold and intense brightness and heat. It also already implies the notion of timelessness so crucial to the whole of *Four Quartets* which M.L. Rosenthal rightly calls 'the immanence of eternity' (Rosenthal 1978: 197). Timelessness can be achieved by the metaphor alone. Eternity, however, requires transcendental prerequisites which elevate the temporary poems into a larger framework. Thus the expansion of mere apparition into epiphany: not merely 'sun flames on ice', but 'pentecostal fire'.

Individual anxiety, 'windless cold that is the heart's heat', is extended into the impersonal (and already vaguely Christian) image of 'soul's sap quivers'. Indeed both empirical reality and the individual are ushered out through the back door: 'There is no earth smell / Or smell of living thing'. The poem clears the space for a vision with clear biblical overtones: the miraculous blossoming of a hedgerow in winter (reminiscent of apocryphal stories of Mary and the flight to Egypt). Rosenthal describes the effect of the line accurately when he claims: 'The passage is more deceptive than the illusion it describes – an act of incantatory magic' (47). It creates the impression of a transcendental reality outside the text by linking its metaphors and metonymies to established, namely religious, symbols, thus supplying them with a symbolic aura. The effects are impersonality and anti-realism – and this exempts the passage from rational scrutiny and closes it to interpretation. Rosenthal's correct yet almost entirely positive view of the poem supplies attributes whose quality appears more questionable in the context of the structural assessment of the present study: 'Eliot's genius, in large part, lies in his ability to combine the language of the most evocative immediacy with hints of deep mysteries rooted in the subtlety of his own mind. He writes in clear riddles' (45–6).

The importance of the oxymoron (what is a 'clear riddle'?) will become evident in the evaluation of modernist poetry in the context of the entire 'modernist project' in the conclusion of this study. Other, less striking characterisations of this crucial part of *Four Quartets*, such as 'illusion', 'visionary joy', and 'efforts . . . to restore presecularist modes of thought' (46–9) – when seen in connection with Thomas Mann's critical questions concerning 'seeming' in modern art – show that the aesthetics of *Four Quartets* are in reverse gear. Eliot's long poem returns from modernist dissociation and fragmentation to a renewed mystical integrity. This makes the drastic request for salvation possible which concludes this section of 'Little Gidding': 'Where is the summer, the unimaginable / Zero summer?', and supplies the authority for the soothing symbolic finale of the entire poem:

> And all shall be well and
> All manner of thing shall be well
>
> (233)

NOTES

1. 'Celibate machine' is a central term in Deleuze and Guattari's *Anti-Oedipus: Capitalism and Schizophrenia* (Deleuze, Guattari 1984: especially 16–22). It stands for the seeming production of the subject by or its confusion with the 'desiring machine' which represents libidinal urges (17).
2. There is a recurring association of hair and arms (and also hair on arms) with eroticism in Eliot's poems (as in 'La Figlia Che Piange'). The use of arms and hair in such a derogatory description in 'Prufrock' can therefore be read as a hint at the speaker's (imagined) loss of erotic attraction.
3. Ruth Nevo's remarks on *The Waste Land* also apply to 'Hysteria': '. . . disunification, or desedimentation, or dissemination (to use Derrida's terminology) is the *raison d'être* of the poem; . . . in it the strategies of self-consumption, *mise en abyme*, and influence anxiety can be inspected at large' (Nevo 1982: 453–61 (454–5)).
4. Beehler 1987: 16. Beehler is referring to an article by Walter Benn Michaels, 'Philosophy in Kinkaja: Eliot's Pragmatism' in Samuel Weber and Henry Sussman (eds), *Glyph 8* (Baltimore, 1981) in this quotation.

5. Anthony L. Johnson takes the famous line 'These fragments I have shored against my ruins' to be a sign of this attitude: 'The line . . . is itself paradoxical. Nothing fragmented normally props up anything, least of all 'ruins'. The truth of the matter, surely, is that this is a case of reversed representation – representation by an opposite, in Freudian terminology. A true innuendo could be unscrambled if we reconstructed: 'I have used these fragments to break up my world picture' (Johnson 1985: 399–416 (413–14)).
6. Philomel was raped by her brother-in-law Tereus who cut out her tongue to prevent her from accusing him. Philomel communicated the crime to her sister Procne by weaving it into a cloth.
7. In claiming that the metonymy is capable of forming coherent semantic networks I contradict Anthony L. Johnson's otherwise excellent article '"Broken Images"' (Johnson 1985). He tries to demonstrate a polarity between paradigmatic integrity and syntagmatic fragmentation in the poem. This explains perhaps why he never uses the term metonymy in his essay, since it already implies that elements dispersed on the syntagmatic axis can also form coherent structures. Yet he also eventually arrives at the insight that the only true continuities of the text are to be found in its gaps. See in particular 403–4.
8. See Eliot's note to line 279 of *The Waste Land*: 'V. Froude, *Elizabeth*, Vol. I, ch. iv, letter of De Quadra to Philip of Spain', 83–4.
9. Calvin Bedient explains its function as follows:

   > Already, as an allusion to the devastated land of Arthurian Grail romance, it distances us from the putatively actual, secular, if hardly less mythic city of Eliot's poem, with its London Bridge, Saint Mary Woolnoth's, honking horns, drying combinations, gramophones, cigarette ends, Shakespeherian Rag (an import from the *Ziegfeld Follies*), etc., etc. This presumptive metaphoricity continues within the body of the poem itself, holds sway there – so that, for instance, the phrase 'A heap of broken images' anticipates by many lines a 'naturalistic' itemization of the contents of the secular realm. Throughout, the metaphors act like preventive medicine, giving us a measure of immunity in advance to everything abject (which in this poem is everything we ordinarily think of as real).
   >
   > (Bedient 1986: 1)

10. The reference attributed to Lacan actually derives from an article on Lacan by Jean Laplanche and Serge Leclaire, 'L'Inconscient', in *Les Temps Modernes*, 17 (July 1961): 81–129.
11. See the discussion of the philosophical equivalent of the problem in Marquard 1989: 64–86 (69).

CHAPTER FOUR

Modernism and Myth: Ezra Pound (1885–1972)

1. MYTH AS FRAME AND SUPPLEMENT

In their *Dialectic of Enlightenment*, Adorno and Horkheimer claim that magician and trickster are the two positions left to man after his discovery that language is no longer tied to what it tries to represent, to its referent. Its position of relative autonomy in relation to everyday practice is also the source of its arbitrariness and seeming inadequacy. The magician consequently tries to reconcile language and objective reality, the trickster accepts the rupture between word and reality and exploits the resulting possibilities to their utmost (Adorno and Horkheimer 1979: 60–2; 69–72).

Michel Foucault develops a different, though not contradictory model of the history of the relation between language and reality. In *The Order of Things* he distinguishes three stages in the development of the sign. Phase one (from the Stoic philosophers of ancient Greece to the Renaissance) is characterised by a threefold structure of the sign which unites signifier, signified, and the *conjuncture*, their relation. The Renaissance fuses these three elements by stressing the aspect of relation. It becomes associated with similarity and thus assumes aspects of both signifier and signified. This muddled but still tertiary structure is then superseded in the Enlightenment (i.e. the late seventeenth and early eighteenth century) by a binary model deriving from the dissociation of sign and reality (Foucault 1970: 42–3). This is the compound of signifier and signified encountered in Saussure. Foucault mentions, among others, Hobbes, Berkeley and Hume as thinkers of this rift.

Jacques Derrida is one of many theorists who claim that the sign has undergone a further structural change in what can be interpreted as the shift from modernity to modernism, i.e. in the process of the questioning of rationality by this very rationality. The signified has disappeared and left only the signifier (Derrida 1978: 280–1).

The consequences of the above shifts are thorough. From being a mere mark attached to things like a stigma, i.e. from being only material, language creates two new layers around itself by the introduction of the concept of similarity. One of those layers is the commentary created 'on top' of language by rearranging the given signs. The other is the text that is now postulated 'underneath' the signs as their origin and creator (Foucault 1970: 40–1).

Foucault goes on to explain that although the mysterious, quasi-prelapsarian 'nature' of language has continued to shine through its use, it cannot possibly be reconstructed. Although he tentatively grants literature at least the capacity to remind us of this 'nature', he is careful to point out that neither a hermeneutic nor a materialist (i.e. semiotic) approach to language and literature can avoid falling into either the category of the commentary or what he later labels the critique of texts. Every form of interpretation is caught in the classicist position (43).

In the light of these theorems, the endeavours of modernist poets can be put in either of Adorno and Horkheimer's categories. The ritualist repetitions of Eliot's poems become evidence for a magical approach. They try to generate their own magical logic designed to re-establish the connection between the text and the increasingly fluid and evasive – and thus threatening – reality outside it. The finale of *The Waste Land* is the most overt example. It functions as a magic spell with all the qualities of the latter. 'Shantih Shantih Shantih' is foreign, i.e. its meaning is only known to the initiate. The triple repetition is a standard device in magic and rituals. Perhaps the traditionally masculine character of the number three is not unimportant in a ritual devised to fight, among other things, fears of impotence. Eventually the poem tries to achieve 'Shantih', peace, with this ending.[1]

Still, as the further development of Eliot's poetry shows, a reliance on ritual and magic does not suffice when the issue at stake is the proper and permanent recovery of the connection between text and an extratextual reality. The mere evocation of foreign cultures only gives a surface-authority to the texts. This throws a rather different light on the cosmopolitanism of many modernist texts. It is not so much an achievement as a necessity. The unstable cultural background of modernist poems is only seemingly stabilised by the authority – and the glamorous surface and élitist seduction – of fragments of foreign cultures.

The piling-up of layers of meaning manages to form coherent and convincing texts, but no more than texts. The nature of the employed material remains too obviously textual and continually throws the texts back into their closed sphere. This is one of the vicious circles of modernist poetry: it is generated by the desperation over the monadic state of language and fuelled by the horror of its isolation, yet all its endeavours only ever confirm its hermetic closure.

The way out of this circle always leads through the imposition of symbolic systems on to and into the texts. History and Christianity combined provide this necessary framework for Eliot. In Yeats's case, it is his esoteric view of cultural history. For D.H. Lawrence, whose poetry is not discussed in the present study, the organic coherence of primitive human instincts serves the same purpose. It is, of course, arguable that all of these seemingly external points of reference are equally fictional, that their connection with poetry is structurally not at all different from the mere inclusion of fragments of foreign cultures.

A poet who is not only aware of this dead end, but devises a way out of it that radicalises or, as he would have preferred, purifies some of the structural traits detected in modernist texts, is Ezra Pound. He is therefore both magician and trickster according to the above model. This makes an evaluation of his poetic development, concentrating on his use and treatment of myth, indispensable for an exploration of modernist poetry.

The present study concentrates on myth as a form of narrative, an underlying and pervasive or explòited structure, a text that forms part of other texts. As a textual category myth fulfils a double function: it provides a framework inside which utterances attain legitimacy and authority, and it supplements these utterances in their logical construction. As a framework, myth is similar to the symbolic network, yet with the crucial difference that symbolism remains attached to a personality and a particular historic position. Myth is by definition both impersonal and ahistorical. This becomes evident even in attempts to connect symbols and myths (as, for instance, in the works of C.G. Jung who develops a theory of archetypal symbolism). The structural reasons for myth's denial of its origins are elaborated in Roland Barthes's *Mythologies*. His concept of myth shows it as a meta-language imposed on an original utterance (which he calls 'object-language'). This is his model (Barthes 1973: 124):

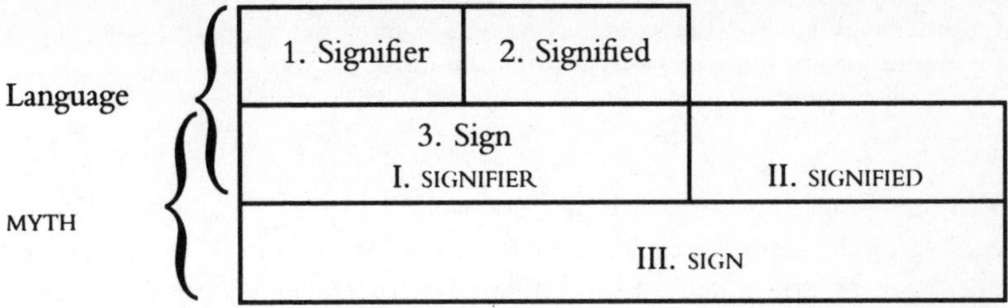

Figure 2

The similarity between Barthes' model and the concept of metaphor outlined by Kittay is striking. The position given to the sign in Kittay is held by a complete utterance in Barthes. Myth transposes a complete portion of discourse into another sphere which is not merely metaphoric, but also metalinguistic, beyond language.

The consequences for the 'processed' utterance are enormous. They affect its self-reflective potential as well as its relation to established norms, not only of linguistics, but also of politics and ethics. In his *Structural Anthropology* Claude Lévi-Strauss merely alludes to the close relation between myth and ideology:

> . . . what gives the myth an operational value is that the specific pattern described is timeless; it explains the present and the past as well as the future. This can be made clear through a comparison between myth and what appears to have largely replaced it in modern societies, namely, politics.
>
> (Lévi-Strauss 1963: 209)

Barthes is sharper when he calls myth a theft of language and a transformation of history into nature, thus an affirmation of the historic *status quo* (Barthes 1973: 135–6, 140).

The problems evolving out of myth's denial of its linguistic origins are even more complex. Paradoxically enough, they become visible when this denial is so absolute as to hide the presence of myth altogether – as in philosophy. Karl Jaspers describes the hostile relationship of philosophy and myth in the following way:

> Philosophy saw in myth an adversary insofar as it paralyses the transformation of narrative into a term by its overwhelming power. Myth became one of philosophy's objects which wants to be understood by it as an alien, but indispensable attire of truth. It eventually remains the borderline of philosophy, for when philosophy shipwrecks in its thinking, it still hears the language of myth. Myth therefore becomes a momentum of philosophy itself

> which, in its own thinking, although in vain, creates myths. It is the other way round. The content of myth is an origin of philosophy. If philosophy translates that into its thinking, it cannot replace mythical language.
>
> (Jaspers 1964: 7; my translation)

Derrida is more aggressive in his essay 'White Mythology': 'By an odd fate, the very metaphysicians who think to escape the world of appearances are constrained to live perpetually in allegory. A sorry lot of poets, they dim the colours of the ancient fables, and are themselves but gatherers of fables. They produce white mythology' (Derrida 1982: 213).

If the use of myth has such serious implications, why has it proved so influential on poetry in an age that can hardly be regarded as attracted to traditional norms and certainties? Why is myth the magnetic force towards which most modernist poetry seems to drift? The recourse to myth is a survival strategy. As Adorno points out, art disavows myth in order to come into being. Yet to avoid being swept aside by a now nearly all-powerful rationality, art has to point out the limits of this rationality. It achieves this by a renewed recourse to myth (Adorno 1984: 79–80). In an environment characterised by an ever-increasing speed of life and an evasive fluidity of reality, the language of poetry seemed in danger of becoming inadequate. Neither could the position of a narratorial voice be legitimised any longer. Poetry itself seemed on the verge of becoming an obsolete art form. This was clearly perceptible at the time when modernism had only just begun to emerge. Compare Edmund Wilson's assessment of the future of literature:

> As language becomes more international and more technical, it will become also less capable of supplying the symbols of literature; and then, just as the development of mechanical devices has compelled us to resort to sport in order to exercise our muscles, so literature will survive as a game – as a series of specialised experiments in the domain of 'symbolic expression and imaginative values attained through the free combination of the elements of language'.
>
> (Wilson 1931: 225)

The position to be adopted is neatly described by an analyst of modernism's final phase, Marshall McLuhan, when he illustrates the strategy of his first study of contemporary culture:

> As this method was followed, *A Descent into the Maelstrom* by Edgar Poe kept coming to mind. Poe's sailor saved himself by studying the action of the whirlpool and by cooperating with it. The present book likewise makes few attempts to attack the considerable

> currents and pressures set up around us today by the mechanical agencies of the press, radio, movies, and advertising. It does attempt to set the reader at the center of the revolving picture created by these affairs where he may observe the action that is in progress and in which everybody is involved. From the analysis of that action, it is hoped, many individual strategies may suggest themselves.
>
> (McLuhan 1967: v)

If one swaps 'reader' for 'poetic identity' one attains an accurate description of the position of modernist poetry. The most important strategies of coping with this position in Pound's poems will be discussed below.

2. PERSONAE AND MYTH IN POUND'S EARLY POEMS

On His Own Face in a Glass

O strange face there in the glass!
O ribald company, O saintly host,
O sorrow-swept my fool,
What answer? O ye myriad
That strive and play and pass,
Jest, challenge, counterlie!
I? I? I?
   And ye?

(Pound 1968: 35)[2]

Pound's early poetry abounds with first-person narrators who are – explicitly or implicitly – identified as anything but a modern poet, let alone Ezra Pound himself. Franz Link divides these poems into metamorphic ones (those with a non-human speaker – such as the various tree poems – in the tradition of Ovid) and those employing personae (i.e. masks), characters who supply a voice and, more important, their history (Link 1984: 13–31). Both concepts are by no means unproblematic. Their underlying theoretical uncertainties are indeed similar. What lies behind the mask, or, what is the starting point of the metamorphosis? Is it the author, i.e. a historic consciousness, or – as Wolfgang Iser puts it – an 'implied author' (a term that provokes exactly the same questions and acts as just another mirror in the cabinet)? The important aspects for the present study are: what is the function of metamorphosis and the use of personae?

Link draws the connection between persona and myth quite clearly in his discussion of the metamorphic tree-poems 'The Tree', 'La Fraisne', and 'A Girl'. In all these cases he sees a mythological subtext as the point of reference of the poems. In 'A Girl' this subtext is the myth of Apollo and Daphne, more precisely, Ovid's version of the same in his *Metamorphoses*. The reference is an intertextual one. In 'La Fraisne' the subtext is Celtic mythology. The explicit hint is the pseudo-Celtic place name 'Mar-nan-otha', the implicit one the symbolic significance of the ash-tree (the meaning of 'La Fraisne') in Celtic and Germanic myths. One might add the stylistic similarity to some of Yeats's poems dealing with Celtic mythology (14–23).

Paul Smith argues therefore that Pound's use of personae is closely connected with his 'reflexive' method. Smith characterises it as an awareness and discussion of the conditions of producing poetry, the 'recurrent positioning of the poet in relation to his material' (Smith 1983: 8). The use of personae as a self-reflective or even metapoetic device explains why the subtext that provides the personae in the early poems always causes problems. Even the simplest of the metamorphosis poems, 'The Tree', exhibits discrepancies in its intertextual nature. Its form refers to Yeats, its content to two Greek myths, that of Apollo and Daphne and that of Philemon and Baucis. The latter combination is itself contradictory, since the first couple is an example of unfulfilled, the second one of fulfilled love. Its language, to add to the difficulties, is a mixture of Yeats's and a pseudo-archaic English without relation to either Yeats or the mentioned myths. All of these styles clash with the colloquial final line of the poem and its 'rank folly'.

In 'A Girl', the discrepancies are even more radical, because they extend to the poetic persona and split it into two or three different ones. Its first stanza describes the experience of metamorphosis, the second one comments on the metamorphosis from outside, and its final line is eventually a self-reflective statement that classifies both the experience and its poetic description as 'folly'.

'La Fraisne' goes even further. It again introduces several themes and planes of reference by simultaneously employing the classic motif of tree-metamorphosis, but also invoking Yeats again, this time his railing against old age. Yet it also alludes to the troubadour topic of madness caused by unhappy love, whose importance is highlighted by the Provençal title of the poem. Furthermore the poem illustrates the clash of these themes in its language.

> For I was a gaunt, grave councillor
> Being in all things wise, and very old,
> But I have put aside this folly and the cold
> That old age weareth for a cloak.
>
> (4)

'La Fraisne' oscillates between traditional poetic form and metre (as in the first stanza above – which is very Yeatsian) and its continual dissolution. This eventually leads to complete fragmentation in stanza 8 which contains only one complete sentence among six incomplete ones.

> Once when I was among the young men . . .
> And they said I was quite strong, among the young
> men.
> Once there was a woman . . .
> . . . but I forget . . . she was . . .
> . . . I hope she will not come again.
>
> . . . I do not remember . . . . .
>
> (5)

This fragmentation is only partly overcome in the final lines of the poem. These are more like a hurried summary of what has been said before than a proper conclusion.

> I do not like to remember things any more.
>
> I like one little band of winds that blow
> In the ash trees here:
> For we are quite alone
> Here 'mid the ash trees.
>
> (5)

The language of the poem mirrors the situation of its speaker. Its representation is a situational rather than a mimetic one, i.e. it does not draw the image of a speaker, but provides a glimpse of one particular moment of this speaker's existence – and withdraws him with the end of his utterance. This is the main difference between Pound's personae and their tableau-like presentations in the works of Pound's model, Browning. Browning's speakers gain a life of their own, yet not immediate presence as do Pound's transient and contradictory, yet immediate voices.

The reasons for this discrepancy are easy to see, because they result from the poetic techniques of the two authors. While Browning chooses personae to express events and sentiments unsuitable for a Victorian contemporary, Pound employs them not to legitimise a particular utterance, but as a justification for *any* poetic utterance. His personae are more than devices, they are necessities. This explains their transient status, the apparent lack of control which makes them change shape within a single poem and fragments their messages.

The problematic status of the speaker in Pound's poems corresponds to his preference for personae from a troubadour background, professional outcasts whose fortunes depended on their protectors as much as their work was subject to the favours of its chosen object, usually the adored woman.[3] Two aspects of the troubadour existence offer particular parallels to the situation of modernist authors: the need to identify themselves in their works (troubadour poetry is one of the first examples of literature after antiquity placing emphasis on its authors) and the problem of defining oneself in terms of status and position. The biographic analogy plays an important part, too. All the poets gathered in the present study are in some way exiles: Hopkins through his faith (and in his later life in Ireland), Yeats by being Irish in a dominantly English cultural background (and paradoxically also the other way round, by belonging to the Protestant Anglo-Irish minority in Ireland), both Eliot and Pound by being Americans.

Pound stresses this in-between status by setting his best-known troubadour poem on 'the open road'. 'Cino' thus also manages to allude simultaneously to Browning (through its opening line) and Whitman (and his 'Song of the Open Road'), while the theme 'I have sung women in three cities, / But it is all the same' (6) refers to Symons (Ruthven 1969: 49–51). Through its intertextual references the poem outlines its own genealogy. But it does more than merely position itself in a poetic tradition. It also shows why it breaks with that very tradition. This break does not lie in the outspoken refusal to sing of women any more, but in the shift of emphasis from the struggle with a love-object to a struggle with its own poetic form. The interest of the poem is not its theme, but how to leave that theme behind. It drifts towards pure self-reflection, and that is its modernist aspect.

The speaker of the poem, similar to the one in 'La Fraisne', only constitutes himself by his loss of a theme, therefore losing also the justification of his utterance. Indeed, rather than his song about women, the only descriptions we get are those of him by women:

> They dream us-toward and
> Sighing, say, 'Would Cino,
> Passionate Cino, of the wrinkling eyes,

> Gay Cino, of quick laughter,
> Cino, of the dare, the jibe,
> Frail Cino, strongest of his tribe
> That tramp old ways beneath the sun-light,
> Would Cino of the Luth were here!'
>
> (6)

They are also characteristically contradictory:

> Once, twice, a year –
> Vaguely thus word they:
>   'Cino?' 'Oh, eh, Cino Polnesi
>   The singer is't you mean?'
>   'Ah yes, passed once our way,
>   A saucy fellow, but . . .
>   (Oh they are all one these vagabonds)
>
> (6)

The technique is similar to that of Eliot's 'Prufrock' whose speaker also depends on the judgement of others (and again some of these others are women). Yet while their comments are clearly interpreted as negative in Prufrock's case, the contradictions of 'Cino' leave the speaker of the latter in a void, a metaphorical 'open road' with only memories as an orientation ('. . . eh? . . . they mostly had grey eyes' (7)) and a rather dubious direction for the future ('I will sing of the sun' (7)).

This future orientation must be taken seriously, although it is instantly ridiculed in the doggerel verses to Phoebus Apollo ('Pollo Phoibee, old tin pan' (7)). The song to nature and its deities is, of course, as worn-out as the praise of women, and the irony of the poem is aware that breaking out of a tradition only ever leads into another one. Yet the three final lines of the poem, at first glance merely a repetition of its pervasive theme ('I have sung' versus 'I will sing' as the description of the position of poetic identity), hint at a possible new direction in Pound's poetry, that of his short-lived Imagist period. The need for a mythical base as starting-point of the poetic utterance is revealed as the addiction to tradition. Once they have discovered this, Pound's poems display a very ambivalent attitude towards myth, one that is destructive and reconstructive at the same time.

His assemblage of styles and traditions hints at the fact that coherent mythical settings are no longer available. In spite of the multitude of seemingly accessible points of reference, none of these represents a coherent text, a mythical frame for the poetic utterance inside which both a narrative and a coherent narrator are possible. Instead, the speaker of the poems juggles with fragments of narratives while constituting himself out of these snippets in the process. By no means all of them are actually his. What, for instance, does Phoebus Apollo mean to an Italian troubadour of the late thirteenth century? The Victorian assurance concerning the free availability of culture has become very frail indeed. The speaker of Pound's poems appears like an image produced by a kaleidoscope: a fragile pattern produced by the delicate equilibrium of colourful fragments whose ultimate connection is merely their gathering in one vessel, the poetic form. But even that displays widening cracks – as the fragmentation of Pound's early poems shows.

Nonetheless, the very existence of nameable speakers and especially the use of irony – which by creating critical distance at least simulates a detached point of view – demonstrates that, although questionable, poetic identity has not yet been shattered in Pound's early poetry. This leads to coherence in spite of their fragmentation, but it eventually condemns the poems to remaining within a tradition that they expose as dead. Pound's later rejection of some of his early works as 'stale creampuffs' is a hint in this direction.[4] More revealing is a remark on the poem 'Cino' in a letter to William Carlos Williams of 1908: '"Cino" – the thing is banal. He might be anyone. Besides he is catalogued in his epitaph' (Ruthven 1969: 49). Pound criticises his poem for containing a speaker who is both impersonal and a distinct person. The contradiction unveils an essential impasse of modernism: both complete anonymity and a traditional personality are unacceptable. The former leads to a text without a centre, the latter to traditionalism. The assemblage of fragments, mythical or otherwise, creates either an unconvincing mess or a seemingly coherent image which remains, however, as dead as a tin-pan Apollo. The simple use of dead myths does not create a living one – at least not as long as their gathering takes place within established forms. The personae cannot be manipulated as easily as the early poem 'Histrion' tries to make its reader believe:

> No man has dared to write this thing as yet
> And yet I know, how that the souls of all men great
> At times pass through us,
> And we are melted into them, and are not
> Save reflexions of their souls.
> Thus I am Dante for a space and am
> One François Villon, ballad-lord and thief
> Or am such holy ones I may not write
> Lest blasphemy be writ against my name;
> This for an instant and the flame is gone.

> 'Tis as in midmost us there glows a sphere
> Translucent, molten gold, that is the 'I'
> And into this some form projects itself:
> Christus, or John, or eke the Florentine;
> And as the clear space is not if a form's
> Imposed thereon,
> So cease we from all being for the time,
> And these, the Masters of the Soul, live on.[5]

The poem's later deletion from his personal canon by Pound is a sign of his disillusionment with the simplistic use of personae.

3. FRAGMENTS OF CULTURE

The problems of time and history, the generation and loss of culture, are central to Pound's poems. The fictionality of historic time, the need to define one's position through one's cultural background and the difficulty of doing so – since to be part of one's culture and history all their elements inevitably undergo a reification – surface in many of his early poems. The problem eventually culminates in *The Cantos* (Harmon 1977: 3). In *Guide to Kulchur* Pound summarises the dilemma: 'A man does not know his own ADDRESS (in time) until he knows where his time and milieu stand in relation to other times and conditions' (Pound 1938: 82–3). Yet, as he had pointed out earlier in *The Spirit of Romance*, history – and even one's individual history – could no longer be regarded as 'linear, sequential, segmental, homogeneous and continuous' but had to be perceived as 'non-linear, non-sequential, unitary, multiform and discontinuous' (Nänny 1973: 18):

> It is dawn at Jerusalem while midnight hovers above the Pillars of Hercules. All ages are contemporaneous. It is BC, let us say, in Morocco. The Middle Ages are in Russia. The future stirs already in the minds of the few. This is especially true of literature, where the real time is independent of the apparent, and where many dead men are our grandchildren's contemporaries, while many of our contemporaries have been already gathered into Abraham's bosom, or some more fitting receptacle.[6]

The problem is obvious: where in this flux can the individual find a position for a personal – poetic – utterance? Where is the material of this utterance, and what is its shape? The first question puts the finger on the significant void between the 'I have sung' and the 'I will sing' of earlier poems like 'Cino'. The second one leads directly to Pound's technique of fragmentation.

The idea of the self as a screen on to which, for some timeless instant, the reflections of great souls are projected (as elaborated in 'Histrion') serves as justification of the experiments with manifold personae. Not so much their personalities count in the emulation, but their experiences. In the words of Max Frisch's anti-hero in *Mein Name sei Gantenbein* (Gantenbein be my name), a novel on identity: 'I try stories on like clothes' (Frisch 1964: 30; my translation). Yet the attempt to project other people's experiences on to a contemporary speaker creates two problems: the experiences are mutilated to fit into the new form; and they remain distant, their historic remoteness can never be fully overcome. This is not a contradiction to the immediacy discovered in the analysis of Pound's personae. The access to a past experience does not automatically transform its content into a contemporary one. Thus its value must remain limited. Both mutilation and distance inevitably produce fragmentation. The poem 'The Picture' describes technique and effect:

> The eyes of this dead lady speak to me,
> For here was love, was not to be drowned
> out.
> And here desire, not to be kissed away.
> The eyes of this dead lady speak to me.
>
> (73)

The immediate effect of the artefact, a picture by Jacopo del Sellaio, as a footnote to the poem informs the reader, is countered by the apparent message of the poem. It talks about things past: 'For here was love [. . .] And here desire'. Even in the sly indirect reference to what is perhaps the present of the poem it is concerned with loss. Obviously there is – in contrast to the love depicted by Sellaio – a love that can be drowned out, a desire that can be and perhaps has already been kissed away. And yet the object of the poem is doubly remote since its production took place 400 years ago (the footnote gives 1442 to 1493 as the dates of Sellaio's life), while its theme is even older, namely mythical: the goddess Venus.

The poem that follows 'The Picture' in Pound's *Collected Shorter Poems*, 'Of Jacopo del Sellaio', is another elaboration of the subject and even more explicit about the internal and external problems of Pound's retrospective method. Internally, the suspicion raised in 'The Picture' – the present can never be as perfect as the past, since, paradoxically, it cannot outlast that which is already history –

is confirmed by the lines 'And here's the thing that lasts the whole thing out: / The eyes of this dead lady speak to me' (73). They devalue the preceding statement 'And now she's gone, who was his Cyprian, / And you are here, who are "The Isles" to me' (73). It is important that both Sellaio's Venus and the person addressed by the speaker are removed from the temporary context of the poem by their epithets 'Cyprian' and 'The Isles' which are synonymous references to islands where Venus was worshipped (Ruthven 1969: 186). The status of the mentioned women is that of mythological quotations.

The dilemma in which Pound found himself because of his attempt to create a present with fragments of the past is exposed by two of his contemporary critics. Yeats, a friend of Pound's, puts him in 'Phase 23' of the historic cycle of his *A Vision* and makes him a representative of the man of the moment. Wyndham Lewis, less amicably, states in *Time and Western Man* that 'His field is purely that of the *dead*' (Harmon 1977: 6).

There are frequent examples in Pound's early poems of a rather uncertain appreciation of the present, one that only works by turning the present moment into a thing of the past. In Adorno's terminology, this would be called a reification of experience, its transformation into an object which can be recalled and modified, but also evaluated against other moments and experiences obtainable as memories (if they belong to the subject of the texts) or as other texts (if they belong to others). This reification always leads to mutilation. Adorno's views on the 'deadly' quality of art will be discussed in the conclusion of the present study.

An early poem on the subject of the happy hour of love, 'Horae Beatae Inscriptio', describes this ambivalent attitude. The present is only cherished because of its potential value as memory. The 'Inscriptio' of its title hints at the explicitly textual nature of the transformation. 'Erat Hora' is another poem on the reification of experience. Its first lines read:

> [. . .] Nay, whatever comes
> One hour was sunlit and the most high gods
> May not make boast of any better thing
> Than to have watched that hour as it passed.
>
> (40)

Making an inventory of experience as a 'thing' and the stress on the past tense in 'passed' are evidence of the observed tendencies.

It is not only experience which offers itself *a priori* in a fragmented form (this is what the common superficial notion of the fragmentation of modern experience suggests). This fragmentation is also consciously produced in modernist poetry. It is the effect of the same attitude as that concerning cultural heritage in *The Waste Land*. Yet Pound's poems no longer lament the fragmentation taking place in them. As a later example will show, they even revel in it. What remains the same in Eliot and Pound's poetry are the underlying reasons that make fragmentation necessary. In both cases it is not a willingly adopted manner of an ego so strong that it can accept its own mutilation. Although the textual identity appears to be stronger in Pound, because it is at least without obvious internal contradictions, even in his works fragmentation is a rescue-mechanism.

If a poet like Hopkins has to distort language, invert syntax and pile signifier upon signifier in compounds and lists to grasp single sensuous and/or emotional experiences, Pound's task is even more demanding. Although he, too, deals with moments of individual experience, these are only ever employed to create a larger entity, a story or even history. The fragments he manipulates are not those of direct personal experience, they are pieces of other stories and histories. They are mythological fragments according to Odo Marquard's definition of myths as means of making truths accessible and bearable in life:

> . . . the mythical technique – the telling of stories – is something essentially different – namely, the art of bringing available truth within the reach of what we are equipped to handle in life. For the truth is, as a rule, not yet there when it is either (like the results of the exact sciences, as, for example, formulas) too abstract to connect with or (for example, the truth about life, which is death) unliveably awful. In such cases, stories – myths – not only can but must come forward in order to tell these truths into our life-world, or to tell them, in our life-world, at the kind of distance at which we can bear them.
>
> (Marquard 1989: 90)

In this respect, Pound's mythological *bricolages* are not so much means of conveying a particular message[7] as expressions of the basic dilemma already encountered in Yeats's works: what is the status of art and the artist in an ever-changing and destructive world? While for Yeats the dilemma emerges out of the experience of the artist's own physical decline and fears of mortality, Pound's poems show it as a challenge affecting not only the individual artist, but the entire profession. As William Harmon observes in his discussion of Pound's *Cathay* poems: 'Again and again in *Cathay* the relatively peaceful poetic surface is set against the turbulence of some kind of temporal transition' (Harmon 1977: 75).

Relief cannot be found in an 'increased attention to his [the artist's] immediate surroundings and his own powerful art', as Harmon claims (74) for the poet Rihaku (Li Po) in 'The River Song'. Even this speaker is aware of the inextricable connection of the delight in his art with its impermanence:

> But I draw pen on this barge
> Causing the five peaks to tremble,
> And I have joy in these words
> like the joy of blue islands.
> (If glory could last forever
> Then the waters of Han would flow northward.)
>
> (128–9)

The poem knows no real stability. It talks of vanished kings in the same way as it describes the present Emperor (who, characteristically, 'inspect[s] his flowers' (129), the frailest of organisms). It abounds with wind images and bird songs, symbols of impermanence. Eventually the poet compares his own utterance – a melody played on a flute – to the sound of the new nightingales in the gardens at Jo-rin. The image shows him as a replaceable ornament, in fashion today, outdated tomorrow. It recalls the description of the poet moping 'in the Emperor's garden, await-/ing an order-to-write!' (129) in the preceding line which in turn mirrors the image of five-score nightingales singing aimlessly in the same stanza.

The only artistic artefact of lasting value in the poem is not the boat so meticulously described in its first lines. That is drifting 'with the drifting water' (128). It is a song by Kutsu, the Ch'u Yuan of Pound's 'After Ch'u Yuan' (Ruthven 1969: 207), characteristically the same medium as the poem itself (which is also described as a song in its title). Yet even the position of this song is odd: it 'Hangs with the sun and moon' (128). The image evokes the classical idea of worthy persons and objects being elevated to the status of celestial objects (as, for instance, Castor and Pollux), and thus the attainment of mythical value by the perfect work of art (Yeats's 'artifice of eternity'). At the same time the verb 'Hangs' as well as the paradoxical position of the song 'with the sun and moon' (recalling Yeats's image of sun- and moonlight as one inextricable beam in 'The Tower') show the desired mythical position as impossible and again deadly.

If Pound's early poems make a statement about art, it is the very pessimistic one that perfection is no longer attainable, that it can only be recalled imperfectly in fragments and translations. Translation is a similar form of acquisition of stories and histories, again with an inevitable effect of mutilation. On the positive side, however, it connects distant texts (either removed in time or place, i.e. culture and language) and the present in which these texts gain a new, albeit transformed life. 'The Song of the Bowmen of Shu' as well as 'The River Merchant's Wife: A Letter', 'Lament of the Frontier Guard' and other poems in *Cathay* share the same background as laments uncertain of being heard. Their fictional survival provides a hope for poetry.

Yet searching the archives for material whose transposition into a contemporary poetic language provides both a subjective platform for the utterance and the assurance of possible survival (and thus an in-built justification of the action itself) does not automatically solve the problems which engendered the fragmentation and its discussion in the present study. Where is the poetic ground on which the fragments are assembled, and what happens when the foreign texts bring with them – through their personae – an alien discourse that threatens the identity it is supposed to create?

A poem like 'Papyrus' that radicalises both the fragmentation and the translation aspect represents one direction in which Pound explores the possibilities of reducing both the narrative side of his poems and the ornamental aspects of their language.

> Spring . . . .
> Too long . . . . . .
> Gongula . . . . . .
>
> (112)

One could argue that the poem consists more of absences, of dots, than words. It is indeed a transcription of an existing document, in spite of the considerable licence taken by Pound in his rendering of the text (Kenner 1972: 54–5). It is a Sapphic fragment, and Pound uses this connection to transform it into a love poem that is in essence Imagistic. It is also completely impersonal – or would be, if it were not connected to the stories surrounding Sappho and her lovers which are evoked by 'Gongula' (who is mentioned by Suidas, a Greek encyclopaedist of AD 1000, as one of Sappho's disciples (Ruthven 1969: 190–1)). Even in its most radical reduction, the use of fragmentation does not permit impersonality, since the fragment as a *pars pro toto* always evokes its context which then interferes with the attempt to create something new. Only Imagism whose reductionism is non-fragmentary holds these opportunities, but at a different cost. It will be discussed below.

The second impasse, that of the personae transported into the new discourse by translation, is discussed in poems like 'Villanelle: The Psychological Hour'. Harmon calls it 'the piercing of artificial persona' (78). Indeed the poem with its description of the growing uncertainty of a speaker eagerly awaiting fictional guests is a surrender to the insight that one's position is hardly strengthened by the construction (or reconstruction) of a seemingly similar point of view in an imaginary Other. What Foucault shows, in *The order of things*, to be at work in Velázquez's *Las Meninas*, a painting which places its percipient in a position already occupied by other viewers shown in a mirror in the picture, succeeds in a medium which, as a visual artefact, can be perceived even when it is a *trompe l'oeil*.[8] It does not work so easily in a text that only becomes one if both its reader and the message awaiting him are granted a position, so that an interchange becomes possible. The character of language as representational in its function, but not in its nature, gets in the way.

The attempt to introduce authenticity through a persona or various personae is brought to a deliberate collapse in 'Near Perigord'. In a splendid example of deconstruction *avant la lettre*, the poem first subverts the traditional arrangement of the strata of personae and then busts the form completely by leaving its initial questions and topics aside to concentrate on its own formal problems – which are thus exposed. The conventional construction would be: the speaker of the poem tries to see things through the eyes of another (earlier) person (the persona) who in turn tries to get access to an even earlier experience by yet another character. As in a system of optical lenses, the perspective narrows the closer one gets to the present (i.e. the 'natural' time of the poem). The 'original' experience that is the goal of these arrangements retreats into the background and is only present in fragmented form. Here it is the question how Bertran de Born, the Provençal poet, could allegedly be responsible for many political upheavals of his day and at the same time write love poems (Ruthven 1969: 177–84). The arrangement is that of Barthes's model of myth: the original experience is the object-language which is appropriated and transformed by a secondary system, here the poetic utterance.

However, 'Near Perigord' works rather differently. It disclaims the older poet's right to greater authenticity. In fact, the speaker of the poem, after invoking a persona named Cino to solve this historical problem, finds his helper insufficient. This is hardly surprising, since he does not get any answers from him. Not even bringing in another possible source of help, the 'biographer' of the troubadours, Uc de St Circ, helps.[9] Eventually, the speaker takes over completely, first implicitly by speculating about the case himself (and thus demonstrating that, as a historian, he probably knows more than the characters involved in the case), then explicitly in part II: 'End fact. Try fiction' (154). This is the poem's claim for autonomy.

At the same time it presents itself as a farewell to the false mythical authority produced by the personae. These are unveiled as what they are: puppets controlled by a traditional poetic identity. For suddenly Cino replies, though characteristically without answering the speaker's question. Instead he reflects on the very position of this speaker (another evidence of the essentially metapoetic character of Pound's personae): '"I am an artist, you have tried both métiers"' (156). Cino claims that the poem's speaker tries to be artist and historian, both factual and the creator of fictions. When it finally comes to the use of other people's points of view to support one's own (or to make it possible), Cino's warning is '"Do we know our friends?"' (156). The poem remains inconclusive on the dominant problem of personae: the dangers produced by the appropriation of the discourse of others. 'Or take En Bertrans?' (156) is the circular ending of its second part. Its final third part then indulges in the visualising of Bertran's experience, i.e. in accordance with the motto 'End fact. Try fiction' it freely appropriates his perspective. The end of the part (which is actually a discussion of Bertran's image of a particular lady) sums up the effect of the use of fragmented experiences of others. It is both the antithesis of the image drawn in the poem 'On His Own Face in a Glass' and its supplement. It creates 'A broken bundle of mirrors . . .!' (157).

4. IMAGISM AS ANTI-MYTHICAL MYTH-MAKING

Imagism is essentially a radical poetic reduction technique. It attempts a 'direct treatment of the thing' by eliminating merely ornamental aspects in poetry (i.e. unnecessary adjectives and meaningless rhythmic conventions), and – most importantly – by rejecting both explicit and identifiable speakers and narratives.[10] This restraint tries to overcome the metaphoric aspect of poetic language, i.e. it tries to reduce the paradigmatic axis of Jakobson's model. The terms employed in an Imagist poem are meant to be neither metaphors nor symbols. But the rejection of narrative also mutilates the syntagmatic side of the text.

While the desire for greater austerity is a recurring phenomenon throughout the history of literature, Imagism deserves a special status, because its restraint is directed against the poetic nature of language itself. Imagism is a self-destructive, an anti-poetic poetics. Not only does it attempt to eliminate epic elements from its texts, it tries to force language to be referential. It cannot accept what Saussure discovered to be the basic feature of language: its arbitrariness. Pound states this programmatically in *Gaudier-Brzeska: A Memoir* of 1914: '*Nomina sunt consequentia rerum*' (words are the consequences of things).[11]

The products of this austere poetics are mainly short poems, often no longer than one stanza. Most of them are either syntactically incomplete or semantically incoherent. The Imagist movement, if it can be called one at all, was short-lived, and its output varied greatly in shape and quality. Still one could argue that Pound's Imagist poems are the most radical ones in that they adhere most closely to the Imagist doctrines. A poem like 'L'Art, 1910' approaches the ideal:

> Green arsenic smeared on an egg-white cloth,
> Crushed strawberries! Come let us feast
> our eyes.
>
> (113)

It certainly contains no coherent narrative, neither is there a word that is merely ornamental and could be left out without altering the meaning of the text.

The poem plays on various oppositions: between colours (green, egg-white, and, implicitly, the red of strawberries), wholeness and destruction ('smeared' and 'crushed' versus the cloth which is not only white, but 'egg-white', thus evoking the frailty and perfection of an egg), the edible and the poisonous (egg and strawberries versus arsenic), eventually between two sensual activities, eating and seeing (in 'feast our eyes'). In doing so, the poem demonstrates convincingly the process of generating Images as Pound saw it. In the essay 'As for Imagism' of 1915 he describes his ideas concerning the nature of the Image:

> The image can be of two sorts. It can arise within the mind. It is then 'subjective'. External causes play upon the mind, perhaps; if so, they are drawn into the mind, fused, transmitted, and emerge in an Image unlike themselves. Secondly, the Image can be objective.

> Emotion seizing upon some external scene or action carries it intact into the mind; and the vortex purges it of all save the essential and dominant or dramatic qualities, and it emerges like the external original.[12]

The above quote already shows the crucial problem of the concept: its inability to draw a clear line between the subjective and the objective, external reality and internal sensation. The 'thing' in Imagist poetry is not at all an actual object, it is a state of perception. There is no real difference between a perceptual and a conceptual image (Link 1984: 53). Is it the objective reality of a stained cloth that produces the impression, the Image of 'L'Art, 1910'? Or is it the observer (who classifies the green as arsenic, the cloth as egg-white, the whole scene as a feast for the eyes) who creates this objective reality by naming it?

Wolfgang Iser takes this as a proof that the Imagist reduction is not a simple return to an origin. The Image is neither to be found in the object(s) referred to nor in the perception of the reader. It oscillates between the two poles and thus creates Pound's 'apparition' so successfully described in the master-poem of Imagism, 'In a Station of the Metro' (Iser 1966: 369):

> The apparition of these faces in the crowd;
> Petals on a wet, black bough.
>
> (109)

Pound openly accepts and endorses the notion of the in-between status of the Image, its evasive nature:

> An 'Image' is that which presents an intellectual and emotional complex in an instant of time . . . . It is the presentation of such a 'complex' instantaneously which gives that sense of sudden liberation; that sense of freedom from time limits and space limits; that sense of sudden growth, which we experience in the presence of the greatest works of art.
>
> (Pound 1954: 4)

This liberating aspect of the Image leads back to its relation to myth. What the Imagist reduction technique tries to achieve is precisely a freedom from historic constraints, a liberation from empiricist restrictions in the perception of reality. As Iser puts it, it rejects the division into primary and secondary qualities of things (as advocated by John Locke). Perspective becomes a component of reality, its ordering scheme. The Imagist Image suggests that reality emerges from a plurality of perspectives. Each singular definition is unveiled as illusory. Eventually the individual shape of an Image foregrounds a constitutive imagination which is in an unconstrained relation with objective reality. It thus leads to a reshaping of experience and creates a new model of perception (Iser 1966: 371–2).

In textual terms the freedom from conventional perception – which is also a freedom from established coherent and linear notions of history and personality – is a de-automatisation of the reading process. Yet both Pound's term 'purify' (which derives from Mallarmé) and Iser's critical claim that this de-automatisation is not a defamiliarisation[13] hint at a basic ambiguity of the technique that also pervades its relation to history and myth. The de-automatisation of a process does not abandon the process but highlights it. The reduction of language with the aim of stressing the complexity of a phenomenon and thus making it more accessible still has to deal with two given entities: the nature of language and the reality of objects. Pound's formula 'make it new' captures the impasse in its grammatical object 'it' – which stands for the oscillating phenomenon created by the interaction of language and perception, the apparition within a text. Yet the remaking of a traditional object only ever reproduces this object in a modified shape.

Iser points out one reason for this limitation of the Imagist technique. It remains analogous, i.e. the poetic construction strives towards some kind of mimetic correlative, for instance in its use of the term 'bough' for platform, 'petals' for faces in 'In a Station of the Metro'. The Image does not alter the role of the creative subject, despite its attempt at impersonality. Nor does it overcome its attachment to history. It merely replaces its historic limitations with a superhistoricism that is eventually mythical again. The position desired by the identity of Imagism is that of Nietzsche's *Übermensch*, the superman.

Access to this elevated perspective is sought through the perfect work of art. Here Pound is in accord with Yeats. But what is the perfection of the most elaborate artefact for Yeats (the golden bird of the 'Byzantium' poems) is, at least theoretically, the most spontaneous product for Pound. His stress on the instantaneousness of the creation of Images tries to recall a quasi-archetypal situation of artistic production. This shifts the perfection from the product to the artist and makes Pound's élitism both more poignant and more dangerous than Yeats's.

Barthes calls this tendency of modernist poetry its desire to become substance rather than remaining a mere attribute (Barthes 1967a: 48–9). Yet this desire is undercut by the very instability of language itself. Language does not permit an unambiguous representation because of the continual shifts of meaning within its structures. Even an attempt to overcome tradition and conventional history by a direct treatment of 'the thing' brings back the mythical in the shape of the authentic unmediated experience. It assumes the role of the original, the object-language that the poetic text transforms into a nuclear myth. A truly new poetic must consequently be concerned with the basics of language, not merely with the complexities of its use. Pound realises this when he abandons Imagism in favour of Vorticism – which stresses the metaphoric drive behind poetic creation in a way that will be re-encountered in Nietzsche below. Yet only a much more radical assault on language, his ideogrammatic method, manages to overcome the limitations imposed by the still present signified through which personality and history enter the texts.

5. THE TRAP OF TRADITION: *HUGH SELWYN MAUBERLEY*

> The 'age demanded' chiefly a mould in plaster,
> Made with no loss of time,
> A prose kinema, not, not assuredly, alabaster
> Or the 'sculpture' of rhyme.
>
> (188)

Hugh Selwyn Mauberley shows Pound's awareness that neither the persona technique with its epic overtones nor the radical anti-narrative strategies of Imagism succeeded in creating a poetry which was more than a plaster-cast of the time of its conception. Outdated as quickly as it was produced, its value became questionable from the start. Apparently, poetry had lost its status as a monument of the times, an approving or critical commentary on the present. If it was not to lose its justification completely, radical new forms were required which incorporated the vital characteristics of what Max Nänny calls the 'Marconi era' as opposed to the 'Gutenberg era' preceding the modernist age (Nänny 1973: 18).

Hugh Selwyn Mauberley is Pound's self-conscious coming to terms with the past, with dead poetic traditions – including those of his own early poems. The poem – or arrangement of poems – contrasts voices which are unveiled as equally threatened identities (or aspects of a single identity). These lose as much in the process as they depend on it for their constitution. The theme of the sequence is the impasses and the death of traditional poetry, represented by the fictional character Hugh Selwyn Mauberley. The first poem, however, is declared an ode for the sepulchre of E.P. The initials are, of course, Pound's. This is not so much a gesture which proves Pound's detachment from the problems described in the sequence. Rather it is a jocular, yet also serious admission that he is not at all exempt from them, that the personal identity of the poet, the identity of his texts, and the personae representing this identity (Mauberley or E.P., for instance) are inextricably connected.

Mauberley, the failed poet, is portrayed as an artist whose attachment to realism is the basis of his art as well as the reason for his failure: 'His true Penelope was Flaubert' (187). This applies, of course, just as much to the realism, albeit very historicised and aestheticised, of Pound's early poetics. A hint is the labelling of the sequence as a farewell to London in the footnote to the title page of the poem, which links the theme of abandonment with Pound's biography. As the discussion of Imagism has shown, its reliance on 'the thing' or its 'apparition' with its overtones of originality and authenticity is nothing but a complex form of realistic mimesis.

Mimesis, however, only coexists with construction in a problematic tension. The descriptions referring to the altered state of things in *Hugh Selwyn Mauberley* are therefore unambiguously negative. The 'grimace' of part one is the first indication that the poem is more than a farewell to old standards. It is a lament. Its third part appears as a list of reproaches of the new age which is accused of diluting and perverting the strengths of a rather hazy classical period. In a very Nietzschean fashion this 'before and after' list compares classical beauty to modern ornament; original art to its mechanical modern parody (embodied in the pianola); Dionysos to Christ; the phallic and ambrosial to homeopathic dilutions, and eventually sensuality and ecstasy to their cheap simulations in the popular media. The summary of these damnations is in the centre of the part:

> All things are flowing,
> Sage Heracleitus says;
> But a tawdry cheapness
> Shall outlast our days.
>
> (189)

Paul Smith regards this as a hint at what later becomes 'Pound's vehemently restorative politics' emerging from the conviction that 'contradiction is ultimately a threat, or treated as something accidental or transient which could be rectified or repaired' (Smith 1983: 30).

Even though a lost tradition is lamented, the poem is aware that it will not be resurrected. The reasons for this are outlined in the fourth and fifth parts of *Hugh Selwyn Mauberley*. The First World War with its decimation of the younger generation and shattering of established norms has also destroyed any possible aesthetic consensus. This radical break does not produce a new aesthetic. It merely leaves a void and creates nostalgia – which in turn traps any attempt at new forms in obsolete ones. The following two parts of the poem are mere reminiscences about the radicals of the last generation. This nostalgia is criticised in the protagonist of the second poem, M. Verog, who is described as 'out of step with the decade' (193). It is unveiled as pure myth-making.

The aggressive overtones of the reminiscences eventually dominate the subsequent parts of *Hugh Selwyn Mauberley* in which current literary attitudes are attacked. The first victim of the onslaught is characteristically a Jew. He is criticised for denying his cultural heritage. The second one is a literary opportunist, the third an esoteric stylist. The charges are directed against every form of neglecting one's history, one's belief, eventually the demands of life. This central concern of Pound's early poems is still dominant. It cannot be satisfied in 'soft' poetry with its psychologising and ornamentalising tendencies of which so many contemporaries of Pound – and he himself – were guilty. Eliot especially comes to mind in poem XII which is reminiscent of his 'Portrait of a Lady'. Such poetry must remain 'snapping at empty air', an image which appears repeatedly.

The circular movement of *Hugh Selwyn Mauberley* is evident. The complaint of the first half reappears in the second one, hardly disguised, since 'The Age Demanded' bears the subtitle 'Vide Poem II. Page 188' (201). The text is aware of its uncomfortable closure, its inability to break out of the formal constraints it criticises. Although it manages to discuss the problem in exemplary dialectic fashion, a solution is not in sight. Indeed, the very fact that the issue is dealt with in a poetic text devalues it (as the ironic use of inverted commas for 'The Age Demanded' in part two of the poem indicates). Pound's footnote to the entire poem, which offers the reader the option to skip the text, shows his realisation that even criticising one's own tradition turns into an empty mythologising of the past.

6. THE MATERIALITY OF *THE CANTOS*

Like many major modernist works, *The Cantos* came as a surprise in Pound's *oeuvre.* There is evidence that he started planning them as early as 1909,[14] and undoubtedly many of their features are radicalised characteristics of his earlier works. Yet their sheer length and organic growth alongside the life of their author, the highly complex if not chaotic character of *The Cantos*, their use of many forms of cultural discourse which by far exceeds Pound's usual strategy of exploiting the lives and works of other poets,[15] and last but not least the impossibility of finding a central message, accounts for the special position of this text, not only in Pound's works, but in the history of modernism.

In their relation to myth, *The Cantos* employ a double strategy. On the one hand, the poem abounds with mythical fragments. It starts with a reference to the mythical hero Odysseus who remains a central topic throughout the poem. It comes across many other myths in the course of its creation. Yet – unlike Pound's earlier poems – *The Cantos* do not transform the fragments they incorporate into their system. These are left remarkably unchanged, which often accounts for radical clashes in their montage. Even the translations of fragments from other languages remain faithful to their originals, very dissimilar to Pound's earlier 'translations' which hijack the foreign texts and force them into a new contemporary frame. The organising principle of *The Cantos* is that of contrast. It can already be detected in the radical break between canto I and the beginning of canto II. The former is concerned with Aphrodite and ends with the line 'Bearing the golden bough of Argicida. So that:'; the latter starts with 'Hang it all, Robert Browning' (Pound 1987: 5–6). Despite the colon, there is no continuity. The subject-matter of the succeeding lines is entirely different, and their style incongruous: lyricism versus drastic direct speech. Examples of radically contrasting discourse appear throughout *The Cantos*.

The Cantos try to maintain the 'solidity' of the discourses they employ by refusing to integrate them into a new harmonic unity. Their method is paratactic, i.e. adding up. This purges the text of a conventional identity. It also prevents the poem from creating new myths out of fragments, at least at first glance.

The most radical attempt to achieve solidity is the use of ideograms. They emphasise the main driving force behind Pound's poetics: the concern for proper expression. The Chinese character *cheng ming*, introduced in canto LI (252), represents this idea. It signifies 'correct name(s)' or, more literally, 'correct rank'. Pound's etymology of the term claims that the character derives from those of 'governor' and 'waning moon over the mouth' and therefore has ideographic connections with its signified. This is very dubious, not only because the history of the Chinese language is rather different from what Pound and his source Fenollosa believe.[16] The term 'correct name(s)/rank' refers to abstractions without ideographic equivalents.

The contradiction exposes a crucial problem of *The Cantos*: how can they deal with their central issues of language, culture, and history without 'diluting' them with inappropriate terms? The problem is defined by Pound economically as usury. It soon becomes apparent, however (especially in cantos XLV and LI) that the term has a much wider application: 'Usury kills the child in the womb'; 'Usury is against nature's increase' (both in canto LI; 250). Usury becomes a universal force of substitution, devaluation and betrayal. As such it also refers to the distinction between phallic strength and anal laxity that is an undercurrent in Pound's early poems and now becomes prominent, explicitly in the so-called 'Hell Cantos' XIV and XV.[17]

Yet the problem also reflects back on Pound's poetics where inflationary trickery, the exploitation of the autonomy and arbitrariness of language, are condemned as the first step towards the decline of literature, culture, and eventually – full circle back to the beginning of the chain – nature. For, despite all the radical metonymies of *The Cantos*, their sometimes brutal contrasting of discourses, their underlying model of thought is still organic. A.D. Moody describes Pound's 'cosmic' model in the following way:

> there is but the one intelligence: human intelligence, and the intelligence in nature, these are (or ought to be) one and the same. Real intelligence is seminal intelligence, the intelligence that is of the vital process. Hence Pound's 'paradiso terrestre', not a paradise out of nature, but the right ordering of man in nature. And this is his 'Cosmos'.
>
> (Moody 1982: 145)

It is evident that the equation of a postulated intelligence in nature with the 'right ordering of man' is the very fundament of fascist ideology. It is also obvious that the material employed to advertise or create this *paradiso terrestre*, language, stands in the way. Signifiers are always in excess of signifieds.[18] Inflation is therefore an in-built feature of signification in the same way as the lacking motivation of signs. Both threaten every artistic production which strives to be more than appearance. The dilemma is summarised by Adorno and Horkheimer in the caustic remark, 'the word knows that it is weaker than the nature it has deceived' (Adorno and Horkheimer 1979: 69).

Consequently, *The Cantos* try first to gather language in as many of its manifestations as possible (this includes, for example, hieroglyphs and even musical notation). Then they attempt to paralyse these fragments by fixing them in their own unexplained and inexplicable structure. The 'right ordering' they acquire in the process eliminates their evocative metaphorical potential much more thoroughly than any translation could do. The text turns into a monolithic block which ceases to relate to other texts in its attempt to become the ultimate text. Barthes calls this paralysis a form of suicide. Language plays dead to avoid transformation and eventual obsolescence (Barthes 1973: 144; also Adorno and Horkheimer 1979: 60). This, however, throws *The Cantos* back into the essential impasse of Pound's poetry: its stress on vitality while being completely submerged in the dead. The massive shape and solid structure of *The Cantos* are the external expressions of the dilemma. Their incompleteness can be regarded as the revenge of language for the attempted murder.

7. THE ORDER OF *THE CANTOS*: ARCHIVE AND *PERIPLOUS*

Although *The Cantos* avoid a central narrator or even recurring protagonists, their ordering structure relies on two basic modes of dealing with their rich material: exploration and archive.

The archivist tendency of the poem is expressed in the addiction to all forms of cultural heritage preserved in written language[19] and in the (albeit highly idiosyncratic) ways of ordering them. Yet – unlike *The Waste Land* – *The Cantos* do not aim at integrating the reader into a common cultural heritage. On the contrary, they gain their authority from their inaccessibility. They force their reader to become an academic researcher – and thus to identify closely with both the ordering principle of the text and its creator, Pound. The representation of Sigismundo Malatesta, an obscure Renaissance character, in the poem is typical. Dug up from the archives by Pound himself, he is either portrayed with quotations from manuscripts, or his actions are summarised in the manner of a medieval text. The summary itself gains the status of a document in the poem's attempt to appear unpoetic. An impression of authenticity is created which transcends the fragments. Despite its characteristically artificial appearance, the poem makes the reader believe that it incorporates reality. One is made to forget that the documents cited in it – authentic as they may be – only ever contain fictions themselves. The signal is set once more for the transformation of history into nature, the creation of myth.

The archive as a major ordering device of *The Cantos* has its model in Dante's *Divine Comedy*. Its counterpart and competitor is a very different organisation of traditional knowledge: Homer's *Odyssey*. Both works describe the journey of a courageous individual, and both of them collect established stories from their respective cultural backgrounds. Yet there are crucial differences in their organisation that clash in *The Cantos* where both models are employed simultaneously. Dante's first-person narrator does not become involved in any of the stories he encounters. These remain events of the past, lives of other individuals whom he meets in hell, purgatory, or heaven, where they have ended up as a result of their deeds. What he comes across are stories, other texts that he collects. He is the prototypical archivist. Odysseus, on the other hand, undergoes all the perils of his journey. He is the reverse of Dante's narrator, since he himself describes his adventures to an audience, the Phaiakians. He is the producer of texts, the active principle which Pound endorses.

Nonetheless, as impersonations of phallic activity both Odysseus's journey and his personality are something of a problem. *The Odyssey* is characterised by the absence of a map: Odysseus's journey is a *periplous*, a coastal journeying with uncertain outcome. His eventual return to Ithaca is not his achievement, but a favour granted by the gods who have used him as their toy all the time. Despite his masculine actions he remains a passive victim. His personality is no match for his fate, and very often this fate is represented by women. 'Wandering holes', as they are indirectly alluded to in canto XLVII (237), they still exert considerable control. Circe is the most obvious example and characteristically also the one who appears at the very outset of canto I. When Odysseus and his crew set sail in manly fashion, when *The Cantos* start their exploration and (re-)construction of cultural history, both follow Circe's instructions. She is only one among many powerful female characters, goddesses, historic personalities, or mere unidentified girls in the poem, all of whom are assigned a dangerous and destructive sexuality. Canto XXXIX contains an overt example of this ambivalence:

> When I lay in the ingle of Circe
> I heard a song of that kind.
>   Fat panther lay by me
> Girls talked there of fucking, beasts talked there of eating,
> All heavy with sleep, fucked girls and fat leopards,
>
> (193)

The danger inherent in the female principle is formlessness, the loss of definition and identity. Yet the denial of identity is exactly the survival strategy adopted by Odysseus and by *The Cantos* themselves. Odysseus masters one of his adventures, the defeat of the Cyclops, by keeping his name secret, by punning on the phonetic similarity of 'Odysseus' and *outis*, meaning 'no man'. Dante's protagonist, too, lacks a name. His journey, however, is clearly mapped out and follows the doctrines of Christian faith, an 'Aquinas-map', as Pound calls it. Those guidelines are no longer valid in *The Cantos.*[20] They try to undertake a journey without a defined protagonist and without reliable orientations. This continually throws *The Cantos* back into their own system. The text becomes monadic, self-sufficient, and ends up in an ahistoric isolation that obscures even the history of its production. 'No man made me' is the message of the text, as Maud Ellmann points out (Ellmann 1979: 26). This could also be a self-applied label of many other modernist texts which try to present themselves as *machines célibataires*, created impersonally out of themselves.

The idea that being named endangers one's identity and makes one susceptible to change (one of the standard premises of magic) forces *The Cantos* to shun stable and identifiable representations of identity. Yet the complementary belief that to name and erase is the power of textuality (Ellmann 1987: 189–90) provides the basis for the poem's main stunt. It not only becomes its own history, but suggests that it is much more than the history of a poem: actual history, indeed the only conclusive history of civilisation. In the development from the painful discovery that words no longer describe reality adequately, Pound's poem goes all the way and, although claiming to be interested in 'the thing' only, actually abandons the notion of a reality outside the text. It declares the text to be reality. *The Cantos* are not an account of history, culture and language; they are history, culture and language *in language.* A 'poem including history' is Pound's description of the project.[21] The trick eliminates both personality and competitive mythical fragments in its construction. What it creates instead is an all-inclusive meta-myth that is identical with the text itself and an all-powerful identity that neither requires justification nor has to fear fate.

8. SELF-INFLICTED BLINDNESS AND THE POWER OF MODERNISM

Both the arrangement of its material in paratactic and consequently illogical order, and the careful abstinence from narratorial voices which invite identification by the reader and open the text to interpretation, transform *The Cantos* into a solid block of language. William Carlos Williams saw this accurately in his review of *A Draft of XXX Cantos*, in 1931, where he describes them as 'a closed mind which clings to its power – about which the intelligence beats seeking entrance' (Davenport 1983: 102). *The Cantos* are indeed shaped like a modern mind, or rather like *the* modern mind. Their insights and charges are no longer personal; they aspire towards universal significance.

This impersonal yet universalist nature of *The Cantos* calls for a thorough look at its political and ethical premises. In this respect it is important to see that Pound's poem is primarily an elaborate piece of cultural criticism. Its attention is almost exclusively fixed on the past. Although Durant overstates the case by characterising the poem as peopled by gods, heroic demi-gods and evil spirits, but leaving hardly any part to ordinary men and none to modern man (Durant 1981: 50), it is true that all positive examples offered by the text are drawn from history. The few contemporaries who get a positive mentioning – such as Mussolini – are treated as modern versions of classical values.[22]

Most of those past role models, however, are losers themselves. Sigismundo Malatesta is again a good example: he fell from grace through his political manoeuvrings, ended up in exile and even had his effigy burned. It is apparent that despite their uninhibited restorative tendencies the object of reconstruction in *The Cantos* is far from clear. Alexander calls it Pound's 'Hellenic Zion' and – consciously or unconsciously – fuses Pound's internal contradictions in that term. For neither an unproblematic coexistence of Hellenic and Jewish culture nor Zion have ever been realised. The latter has always remained a utopian promise. Pound would also hardly welcome a Jewish influence in his *paradiso terrestre*. Anti-Semitism is a recurring theme of *The Cantos*. Jews as well as women act as the defamed Other of the text; abuse for them is coupled in the telling term 'intravaginal warmth of / Hebrew affections' in canto XXXV (172–3). Yet in fact the text cannot do without either women or Jews. Its archivist tendencies as well as its endless circulation of economics indeed add a strong 'Jewish' element to it. The same contradiction appears in the propaganda for phallocentrism and the rejection of its opposite, the softness and possible formlessness of the vaginal and anal. Again, rejection mutates into obsession, and the faecal excesses of the 'Hell Cantos' display a degree of *jouissance* that would have pleased Roland Barthes, but undermines the purity of Pound's poetics radically.

The most important of these contradictions affects the very textuality of *The Cantos*, their heart and soul (if they can be granted one), or perhaps rather the folds of that gigantic mind, if one follows W.C. Williams and implies at the same time that, despite their stress on vitality and elemental urges, *The Cantos* remain an example of rationalism driven to an extreme, an embodiment of *logocentrism*. The central term of usury, trickery and inflation, used so broadly to condemn many aspects of culture is also the one that infects *The Cantos* with the disease it describes. As Kenner observes, the term is inextricably connected with Pound's other major concern, that for exact definition: 'The whole key to Pound, the basis of his *Cantos*, his music, his economics, and everything else, is his concern for exact definition' (Kenner 1974: 37). Yet from its introduction in canto XII onwards, the term usury spreads like an epidemic over the entire poem, until it dominates at least cantos XLV, XLVI, L and LI, LXXXV to XC, and XCVI to CIX (Alexander 1979: 132). While condemning usury, *The Cantos* themselves commit the crime. Their inflation of discourse forever repeating the same themes and their excessive use of sign systems fail to arrive at *the* proper expression. Instead they create layers of translation (Smith 1983: 54) and introduce through the back door the polysemy that they strive to overcome. Kearns tries to describe the dilemma in positive terms:

> As always with Pound, we have an enriching conflict of impulses. Gestures towards an infinite opening into textuality, the undecidable, the free association (via play, puns, fanciful etymologies, fortuitous homophones, superimposition of images, texts and languages) is

> balanced by an unwavering longing for 'the total sincerity, the precise definition'.
>
> (Kearns 1989: 12)

The more aggressive the assertions of *The Cantos* become, the more their internal weakness is laid bare. But this does not make them less dangerous. In the absence of firm concepts of belief, order, religion even, the text draws on an impossible equation. The concepts it employs, internal and external nature, had been problematic since their introduction in the Enlightenment. They were discredited by the very crises that spawned modernism. Once more A.D. Moody summarises the equation neatly: '*The Pisan Cantos*, and *The Cantos* as a whole, cohere as things cohere in the process of nature and in the natural process of the mind' (Moody 1982: 136). This is, of course, a premise which eventually justifies everything, because it is based on the interaction of two poles that are neither separate nor separable. Its simplifying nature makes it attractive in times of upheavals. Indeed, as has been stated above, the vacuous formula which employs two dangerously universal concepts of nature is one of the bases of fascism. It acts as a post-Enlightenment myth as discussed in Horkheimer and Adorno's *Dialectic of Enlightenment*. Hans Blumenberg describes its soothing function in terms easily applicable to *The Cantos*: 'History says that some monsters have already disappeared from this world which were worse than the ones responsible for the present state of things; and it says that things have always been exactly or almost exactly as they are now. This makes times of rapid changes anxious for new myths, for re-mythification' (Blumenberg 1979: 41; my translation).

The synthetic consciousness of *The Cantos* unveils a major deficiency of modernism: it does not and cannot contain an element of self-awareness, an inbuilt critical distance to its own assertions. Wolfgang Hildesheimer calls this the lack of a theory of cognition (Hildesheimer 1974: 640), Maud Ellmann an enforced blindness towards its own features (Ellmann 1987: 164). The knowledge of *The Cantos* claims universal validity because it is 'simply there' and has no origins in either a personality or a history. When factual history catches up with the text in the shape of the Second World War, when the creator of *The Cantos* becomes a prisoner of the United States, the poem answers with a structural gap. Two missing cantos, LXXII and LXXIII, create a 'real break or seismic rift' (Moody 1982: 137).[23] The only point in the text where an element of self-criticism could come in through the momentary cease in the flow of discourse is an absence. A weaker echo of this is the exchange of human language for music, the least referential sign system, in canto LXXV. The title of the sixteenth-century composition *Chant des Oiseaux* (Cookson 1985: 78) even hints at the substitution of language for the unconscious voices of birds. The self-inflicted blindness of *The Cantos* hides an extremist rationalism which purges the text from any weakening traces of personality by giving it the status of an all-encompassing consciousness. The text itself becomes the meta-myth of modernism.

NOTES

1. The ritual is indeed incomplete and thus ironically 'impotent' too; see Chandran 1988: 681–3.
2. All quotations from Pound's poems (excluding *The Cantos*) are taken from his *Collected Shorter Poems* (1968). The original title of the first edition of the collected poems published in 1952 was – characteristically – *Personae*, although this caused confusion with his collection of poems of 1926 with the same title. Obviously, Pound wanted to stress the importance of the persona technique.
3. Yet troubadour poetry also encompasses religious and political verse – and among the more than 450 known troubadours there were at least twenty women, the best-known Beatritz de Dia. See Tuchel 1942: 11–30 (11).
4. The famous remark appears in the foreword of a reissue of his earliest poetry *A Lume Spento and Other Poems* (New York, 1965), p. 7. See Harmon 1977: 66.
5. The poem appeared in *A Quinzaine for this Yule* and is reprinted in Link 1984: 24.
6. Ezra Pound, *The Spirit of Romance* (London: Dent, 1910), p. 8; quoted by Harmon 1977: 4.
7. This is what Harmon claims for the early poems by stating that they exhibit four 'positive qualities that deserve preservation throughout time: fame, magic, art, love'; Harmon 1977: 65.
8. Pound also knew Velázquez and this painting. He mentions them, for instance, in canto LXXX, and Velázquez again in canto LXXXI.
9. Which, again, is not astonishing, since his 'knowledge' of the lives of the troubadours is mainly fictional. See Tuchel 1942: 29.
10. The oft-quoted Imagist 'rules' given by F.S. Flint in *Poetry* of March 1913 (they are actually an excerpt from a larger corpus) are:

    (1) Direct treatment of the 'thing' whether subjective or objective.
    (2) To use absolutely no word that did not contribute to presentation.
    (3) As regarding rhythm: to compose in sequence of the musical phrase not in sequence of a metronome.

    (Reprinted in Jones 1972: 18)

11. Quoted from the 1960 reprint, p. 92, in Kenner 1972: 146.
12. The essay appeared in *The New Age*, 16, no. 13 (1915). Quoted in Link 1984: 53.
13. Iser 1966: 374–5.
14. Pound probably conceived the idea for them as early as 1904 or 1905 in a conversation with his Anglo-Saxon teacher, Professor Ibbotson. See Kenner 1972: 354–5.
15. A tendency that provoked once more Wyndham Lewis's criticism in *Time and Western Man* (pp. 85–6): 'Pound is that curious thing, a person without a trace of originality of any sort. It is impossible even to imagine him being anyone in particular of all the people he has translated, interpreted, appreciated . . . Ezra is a crowd; a little crowd' (Quoted in Ellmann 1987: 137).
16. The dubious etymology of the term *cheng ming* is repeated in Kenner 1974: 38. A more critical view can be found in Jung 1984: 211–27.
17. Discussions of phallocentrism and anality are in Smith 1983: 52–5; Ellmann 1987: 185 and 189; also in Durant 1981: 130 and 138ff. They are central issues in Rabaté 1986 and in the Pound chapter in Larrissy 1990: 31 and 43–6.
18. See, for instance, Derrida 1978: 290: 'The overabundance of the signifier, its supplementary character, is thus the result of a finitude, that is to say, the result of a lack which must be supplemented.'
19. In this respect, it remains a mystery why some critics still stress the particular oral and aural qualities of Pound's poetry. See, for instance, Nänny 1973.
20. 'Aquinas-map; Aquinas *not* valid now', Pound writes in *Selected Letters*, p. 323 (quoted in Kearns 1989: 6).
21. It derives from the description of the *Odyssey* by its translator Andreas Divus. See Kenner 1972: 360–1.
22. Canto LXI compares his tax policy to that of the Chinese emperor Yong Tching. See Kenner 1972: 435.
23. The missing cantos are included in the 1987 Faber & Faber edition. They are in Italian and praise German–Italian resistance behind Allied lines. They were first published in early 1945 in an Italian newspaper and reprinted in a small edition for copyright reasons in 1973 (Kearns 1980: 287). See also Ackroyd 1981: 82–3.

CHAPTER FIVE

Modernist Poetry as a Universal Compensation Strategy

1. INTERNAL PROBLEMS AND LOST OUTSIDES

Modernism in English poetry starts from the experience of a fundamental instability. It develops through various experimental stages in which attempts are made to overcome this instability – and culminates in the apparent triumph of the tactics: a stable synthetic consciousness is created which resolves all possible tensions between reality, experience and the medium connecting both: language.[1]

Yet if the eventual result of the compensation process, the concrete block of language embodied in Pound's *Cantos*, is accepted for what it tries to present itself as, *the* modern consciousness, the analyst has become the victim of the self-mystification that accompanies all stages of the development. What has started as a process of substitution, as a defence against the lost grip of poetry on any form of external reality, eventually presents itself as total victory. The 'lost outside' matters no longer, because now everything is and happens 'inside': the work of art becomes its own world. This is not at all similar to aestheticist tendencies that denounce reality in favour of art. Aestheticism finds reality revolting and chooses the artistic realm as its abode instead.[2] Modernism – after a long period of struggle with reality – does not present itself as anti- or counter-realism, but as an ultimately sophisticated form of realism that no longer knows a reality outside its works. This achievement obscures both the processes undergone to arrive at the complete autonomy of the work and – equally important – the traces that every stage of the development inevitably leaves in modernist poems.

Consequently, the aim of this summarising chapter will be threefold.

It will present again in condensed form the strategies with which modernist poetry fights its basic instability, its lack of orientation in a reality outside the works. Secondly, it will outline the consequences of these strategies. Thirdly, taking strategies and effects together and examining them from the outcome of the modernist poetics, ways of assessing the modernist project in English poetry will be discussed. These should still be based on its structures, but without being caught in the greatest structure of all, the modernist myth of itself. They will then determine the second part of the present study which discusses the limits of modernism in English poetry.

2. STRATEGIES OF STABILISATION

The analysis of Hopkins's poetry shows that the basic instability at the heart of modernism is not simply definable as a change of external reality, the context of the poems. The themes and topics of Hopkins's poems remain firmly within the conventions of their time. The same applies to the majority of Yeats's works, and – to a lesser extent – even those of Eliot and Pound. The threat to Hopkins's poems is internal: language no longer fulfils its task of signification; the connection between signifier and signified is lost.[3] The consequences of this loss are manifold. The poems are deprived of their mimetic potential, but also of any external point of reference that could control their imagery. The effect is an increasing artistic freedom: daring combinations of images become possible. Yet this liberation also entails an eventual futility. No matter how ingenious the poems become, the threat is continually felt that within their established autonomy they remain meaningless.

This danger is most noticeable in the central aspect in Hopkins's poetry: the assertion of an identity in the face of a transcendental Other: God. Both this identity and its necessary counterpart become increasingly contradictory and evasive in the development of modernist poetry. Still their interchange and mutual challenge remains crucial. It represents the survival of the Romantic heritage, the continual presence of an identity that is forced to establish and defend itself all the time.[4]

In Yeats's poetry these Romantic roots are even more pronounced. The starting-point of his poems is always the individual – artistic –

self fighting for its position in an environment that denies permanence to the self and its works. History is experienced as a succession of creation and destruction that denies the individual an active part. The only way of coping with this flux is its aesthetic reification. Yeats transforms history into an esoteric cycle in which both man and historic events fulfil passive functions. The leaning of this model towards fatalism and myth is evident.

The tendency of reifying experience is even stronger in Eliot's works. Not only history and events are transformed into objects with the help of metaphors and metonymies. The procedure does not stop when faced with people or even the speaker(s) of the poems themselves. One could argue that reification is indeed a way of dealing with external reality in a text, i.e. claim that this tendency proves – contrary to what has been said above – that the connection between language and reality is still unbroken. If that is the case, language itself has changed its status radically. If it is not to be seen as a paradoxical mechanism that transforms experience into something that is neither experience nor language, it must also be regarded as an object. This would entail the reification of language itself. Not the growing internalisation observed in modernist poetry, but a complete exteriorisation would be the eventual outcome of its development.

The apparent contradiction disappears when one abandons the notion that the relation (or non-relation) between language and its exterior in modernist poetry is a mimetic one. The language of modernist poems is not merely an effect, much less the depiction of an external reality, nor is the reality of modernist poems completely modelled on the features of its material: language. A dialectic tension between the two poles caused by their separateness is a more adequate description of their relation. Both language and reality become fluid concepts that undermine and transform each other continually. The two most radical outcomes of this interaction are indeed the complete objectification of language and the complete internalisation of reality. They can be found in their most refined forms in the works of Ezra Pound, especially *The Cantos* which can be described in both terms and therefore demonstrate the internal similarities of the seemingly antithetical developments.

The underlying strategies of these developments accompany modernism from its very beginnings. They can be labelled reduction and expansion. In most cases, the techniques go hand in hand. The effect thus created is alienating and distorting. Hopkins's compounds which fuse images and his strings of nouns and adjectives are illustrations of their interaction. The goal is clearly contact with a reality the poems try to describe. Yet the belief in the existence of an outside and the mimetic approach towards it already clash with an awareness of the poem's own constructive aspect: form and possible 'content' can no longer be reconciled.

The internal ambivalence of Hopkins's poems concerning their own act of creation, which – if it was successful – would prove the complete autonomy of poetry, leads to self-destructive mechanisms creating and destroying images simultaneously (as in 'The Windhover'). Although this distrust of the potentials of poetry is closely linked with Hopkins's religious beliefs, it can be regarded as an early manifestation of the observed schizophrenic rift within modernism. It undermines the attempts to compensate for the lost grip on reality by the creation of its own with a constant fear of futility, or – in Hopkins's and Eliot's case – hubris.

Yeats's early works seem more at ease with their own position because they do not try to come to terms with real life, but prefer to remain within their Victorian conventions or rely on well-trodden Romantic settings. This addiction to symbolic systems, be they established ones or idiosyncratic, never really leaves Yeats's works. It represents a shift of the problem of text versus a possible outside. Now the point of reference of the poem is no longer reality, but another text. The signifieds of symbols remain opaque and thus powerful. Yet this confidence in an inherent autonomy of the textual does not make Yeats's poems immune to an intrusion from the conveniently ignored outside or problems created by the texts' internal mechanisms.

The former enters the poem in the shape of history and in the equally important suspicion that the reliance on symbols and symbolic settings is incapable of dealing with the concerns of an actual subject (in Yeats's case, Yeats himself and his tortured private life). The latter are generated by Yeats's symbolic technique itself: the use of symbols as an intertextual device fills the poems to the brim with additional associations, paradigms and subtexts. Up to a certain degree this procedure enriches them. But when it becomes dominant, the texts lose their direction. In some cases their capacity of expression disappears completely, and only the impression of chaos remains. This can still be productive (as in 'The Valley of the Black Pig' which deals explicitly with apocalypse). In most cases it is counterproductive and leaves the reader with a jumble of disconnected images.

Again, the additive technique that piles up layer upon layer of symbolic references is countered by a reductive one. The exotic imagery of Yeats's earliest poems and the Irish fairy-tale settings are replaced by personal recollections or images drawn from nature. Yet both substitutes quickly become symbolic themselves. Once a symbolic approach has been chosen, it transforms all images into elements of a symbolic network. Thus Maud Gonne becomes Pallas Athene in 'Beautiful Lofty Things', and seemingly innocent nature images – such as the swans in 'The Wild Swans at Coole' – are charged with symbolic potential.

Yeats's poems only overcome their addiction to symbolism by submitting to an even more universal system, that of myth.[5] His last poems openly discuss their indebtedness to symbols. Poems such as 'Long-Legged Fly' and 'The Circus Animals' Desertion' depict an unbroken reliance on them, yet with the crucial difference that the speaker is now able to discuss this attachment. This capacity is the result of a superhistorical attitude (to use Nietzsche's term) which is nothing but the elevation of the individual through his or her submission to myth.

Addiction to symbols or myths is not the first thing to come to mind in the discussion of Eliot's poems. Indeed, he is the first among the poets in the present study to introduce what appears to be 'realistic' imagery drawn from the 'urban experience' so crucial in most assessments of modernism.[6] The distaste for 'real life' that is so evident in most of Yeats's works seems to have been replaced by a craving for reality. Eliot's poems no longer rely on intertextuality to create a convenient intermediate plane that facilitates (or prevents!) an interaction between text and its exterior.

Two contradictions are, however, instantly provoked by the preceding statements: if Eliot's poems refrain from using intertextuality, why are so many of them supplied with classical epigraphs? And if they aim at grasping 'real life', why do they employ complex metaphors for its depiction? Apparently, Eliot's 'realism' is not a simple one, if it is one at all. His use of daring metaphors – metaphors whose signified hovers between the poles of distant signifiers – hints at an attempt to recapture certain capacities of language that have apparently been lost. If T.E. Hulme's statement is correct and 'abstract words are merely codified dead metaphors',[7] then Eliot's fusion of abstract terms into daring metaphors is an attempt to revive the metaphoric potential of language.

This metaphoric potential has implications which transcend mere linguistic capacities by far. As Kittay points out, cognition and the creation of metaphors are interrelated procedures. Eliot's struggle with metaphors therefore also reveals problems concerning the cognitive handling of experience.[8] His poems are indeed psychological landscapes, but not in the simplistic autobiographic sense. They depict the problems within the interaction of experience, cognition and language that accompany modernism like a birthmark. His increasing use of metonymic structures is an attempt to come to terms with the distorted relation between those poles – and not merely a mimetic reaction to a fragmentation of reality.

Eliot's crucial concept of the 'objective correlative' points at the reification of experience that goes hand in hand with the use of metonymies. It is an endeavour to bridge the gap between language and reality in the arena of their interaction, the realm of cognition. Both his radical tactics of questioning the validity of knowledge in *The Waste Land* and the conservative move that stresses the importance of traditional knowledge in *Four Quartets* are such reifying strategies. The former reifies sensual impressions, i.e. experience, in disconnected images. The latter reifies knowledge, i.e. established symbolic systems and thus forms of (meta-)language.[9]

Eliot's reification of the two poles that constitute cognition and knowledge, experience and language, is radicalised by Pound.[10] His extensive use of personae takes the histories of (imaginary or real) characters – which are nothing but reified experience – as filters to create and support the structures of his own poems. The same applies to the manipulation of mythical fragments.

Language itself is reified when Pound's attention turns towards the materiality of his works. The nature of language is apparently the problem. After the gathering tendencies of the explorer (the random move) and the archivist (the structured assembly of language), Pound's works soon detect the danger of being overwhelmed by their own material. Its paradigmatic aspect which constantly brings in new associations and contexts is the crux – and, on an even more basic level, again the lacking motivation of signs. Pound's poems always fear that, in spite of their attempts at economy, they are invaded by meaning that they do not want to produce, the discourse of tradition for example. The danger of inflation that is eventually directly attacked in the endless sermons on usury in *The Cantos* hints at the peril that every text has to face: the risk of being superfluous.

Pound's poetry in and for an age in which – as Paul Valéry points out – literature has become 'as obsolete and as far removed from life and practices as geomancy, the heraldic art and the science of falconry' (Wilson 1961: 225) (and one should add: not willingly so) has indeed trouble justifying its own existence. The declared Mallarméan intention of purifying the dialect of the tribe must be seen as a macrocosmic endeavour to reshuffle the dominant epistemes, the accepted knowledge, of Western culture. It is at the same time a microcosmic attempt to streamline – and thus to justify – poetry itself.

The radical moves of complete internalisation and total externalisation are consequently most overt in Pound's works. The latter appears as tactics of transforming poetry into formulas (as in Imagism). The 'mathematisation' of language is designed to exempt the texts from temporality and possible corruption. The exact counterpart of the 'simple' formulas of Imagist poems is the 'world formula'[11] of *The Cantos* which tries to include all of history and civilisation. Both strategies simulate a superhistorical position of the work of art and are thus essentially mythical procedures. Yet although they return to myth as the most comprehensive of all structures of language, they are born of the same bewilderment that generates Hopkins's poetry. They cannot come to terms with the basic feature of language: the arbitrary nature of the sign.

3. APPROACHING THE LIMITS OF MODERNISM

The structural description of modernism in English poetry shows how the instability of one of the basic elements of language triggers off various compensation strategies. Each of these strategies is superseded by or incorporated in an even more radical procedure when its shortcomings become obvious.[12] The deficiencies of the tactics are always unveiled when the texts are faced with that which highlights the instability of the sign: the exterior of language, its referent. Whether it confronts the poems in the shape of history or identity, it always acts as the Other of the texts whose repression grants them temporary omnipotence, yet whose inevitable re-emergence not only unveils them as limited, but questions their status and eventually their right to exist.

The modernist yearning for its outside thus reverberates back on its internal justifications. Both the tendencies towards superhistoricism and impersonality can be interpreted as radical attempts to overcome the problem by eliminating its cause. The strategies seemingly succeed when developed to their utmost, when the poems are either everything – or nothing, no thing, apparitions without subjective centre or historic position. The first stance is a radical expansion of the potentials of the poetic material: everything is (in) language – language is everything. The second one is a radical reduction: language is only language.

Both are paradoxical, and their paradoxes are easily uncovered. If everything is in language, then language itself is nothing, nothing, that is, which is separable from reality. But if language was not different from what it talks about, it would not communicate, not even signify. A sign is only a sign because it stands for something that it is not.[13] The presentation of the text as a self-sufficient monadic entity also contradicts the basic rules of communication theory: meaning is only achieved by difference. Signs as well as complete texts achieve their meaning by not being other signs or texts. To signify, signs as well as texts must belong to a system.[14]

The limits of the modernist poetics are exposed by the possibility of analysing their mechanisms, by the capacity of the reader to assume a position which is (a) outside the text (although the text presents itself as an all-inclusive myth) and (b) a discursive one (even though the poem pretends to be non-discursive, an object, the purified 'thing' of Pound's poetic theories). The lost outside – which in its radical formulation includes the reader, the analyst of the text – returns with a vengeance.

Making limits obvious, however, does not explain them. If the present study aims at understanding the motivations, structures *and limits* of modernist poetry, it must broaden its approach to escape the tendency of modernist poetry to present itself as all-inclusive. Yet it must remain attached to those points that have been unveiled as impasses in the analyses of the four poets and the interrelated structures of modernist poems. These areas of tension are the subject – which surfaces in the various futile attempts to give it a permanent and convincing representation – and objective reality 'outside' the texts that confronts them at various points and continually threatens their structures.

The subsequent chapters try to capture the impasses behind these poles by using related disciplines as a point of comparison and as 'lenses' through which the particular problems of modernism in poetry will present themselves as facets of the impasses of the entire 'modernist project'. Psychoanalysis will provide the concepts for an evaluation of the problematic constitution of the subject. Language philosophy will supply some approaches to the connection of language and reality. An 'economic' model will cover the middle ground: the mechanisms of exchange, evaluation and distribution at work in modernist poems. The broadening of the view will eventually enable the present study to survey the attempts of modernist poetry in the light of a general theory of aesthetics. There, the particular aesthetics of modernism will present themselves in a radical light that places particular demands on works of art.

NOTES

1. The term 'synthetic consciousness' derives from an unpublished paper by Michael Bell (University of Warwick) with the title 'Odysseus Bound: Joyce, Nietzsche and the Myth of Modernism' presented at a conference on 'Myth and Modernism' in Meschede, Germany, in November 1990. It will be published in a collection of essays edited by Michael Bell entitled *Modernism and Mythopoeia: Belief in the 20th Century* (Cambridge University Press).
2. Aestheticism as a step in the development from Victorianism to modernism is discussed in Faulkner 1977: 4. He mentions the interest of modernism in ordinary experience as a distinguishing factor (16). Bürger 1984 describes modernism as firmly based in aestheticism. The crucial difference is seen in the modernists' attempt to organise a new life and practice from a basis in art (49).
3. Richard Sheppard describes this loss as follows: 'That which links thought with language; language with the external world, and man with man has disappeared. Like the mock tennis game in Antonioni's *Blow-up*, all language games are felt to have become absurd because the ball, that which guarantees communication between subject and object, is lost' (Bradbury, McFarlane 1976: 328).
4. The Romantic poles of self and world are still present, although their identity is no longer possible. See Faulkner 1977: 51.
5. See James McFarlane:

   > Within the situation of fluidity, 'myth' . . . commended itself as a highly effective device for imposing order of a symbolic, even poetic, kind on the chaos of quotidian events, and offering the opportunity – to use a phrase of Frank Kermode's – to 'short circuit the intellectual and liberate the imagination which the scientism of the modern world suppresses'.
   >
   > (Bradbury, McFarlane 1976: 82)

6. Malcolm Bradbury describes its importance in the following terms:

   > And if modernism is a particularly urban art, that is partly because the modernist artist, like his fellow-men, has been caught up in the spirit of the modern city, which is itself the spirit of a modern technological society. The modern city has appropriated most of the functions and

> communications of society, most of its population, and the furthest extremities of its technological, commercial, industrial and intellectual experience. The city has become culture, or perhaps the chaos that succeeds it.
>
> (Bradbury, McFarlane 1976: 97)

7. T.E. Hulme, *Further Speculations*, ed. Sam Hynes (Lincoln: University of Nebraska Press, 1962), p. 11. Quoted in Schwartz 1985: 57.
8. In Schwartz's words:

   > Language is another mechanism for arranging practical experience. Words like concepts are designed to facilitate practical transactions but only at the expense of immediate experience. They do not so much express our thoughts as condition them. Most of us fail to realize the extent to which language shapes the very way we register impressions.
   >
   > (Schwartz 1985: 28)

9. Schwartz rightly traces this idea back to Nietzsche (Schwartz 1985: 77). This connection will be further explored in Chapter 8, which deals with language philosophy.
10. Schwartz stresses the '"tensional" relationship that mediates between the desire to recover suppressed experience and the desire to project new forms that reshape the world around us' in Pound (Schwartz 1985: 114).
11. The allusion to Heisenberg and quantum physics is intended. The modernist 'project' finds its expression in a multitude of disciplines.
12. This should not be misread as a claim for a linear progression of modernist techniques. As the discussions of the four poets has shown, some techniques prove more addictive than others, and modernism is, after all, not a depersonalised development – despite its claims for impersonality.
13. This is a pragmatic simplification of the problem. For an overview of linguistic positions concerning the referentiality of signs see Barthes 1967b: 35–8.
14. See, among many others, Derrida 1978: 292: 'The presence of an element is always a signifying and substitutive reference inscribed in a system of differences and the movement of a chain.'

CHAPTER SIX

Modernist Poetry and Psychoanalysis

No, non ho madre, non ho sesso,
ho ucciso il padre col silenzio
[No, I have neither mother nor sex,
I have killed father with silence]

(Pier Paolo Pasolini, '*Lingua*' [Language])

1. POETRY AND PSYCHOANALYSIS: INTERSECTIONS OF THE MODERNIST PROJECT

Despite the antagonism the study of the psyche had to face when it emerged as a science from about 1850 onwards and more pronouncedly with the works of Freud after the turn of the century, it could always rely on one ally: literature. The two disciplines instantly established a relation resembling family ties. As Lionel Trilling puts it (his remarks refer to poetry, but can be applied to other genres, too):

> For, of all mental systems, the Freudian psychology is the one which makes poetry indigenous to the very constitution of the mind. Indeed, the mind, as Freud sees it, is in the greater part of its tendency exactly a poetry-making organ. . . . Freud has not merely naturalized poetry; he has discovered its status as a pioneer settler, and he sees it as a method of thought.
>
> (Lodge 1972: 287)

Yet the relationship also worked the other way round. Psychoanalysis happily appropriated both the subject-matter of literature, stories and myths, and made literary terms elements of its own vocabulary. Freud's central concepts of narcissism and the Oedipus complex are the most prominent examples. Whether he applied his ideas to Jensen, Goethe, E.T.A. Hoffmann, or Dostoevsky, he had no problems seeing a close relation between literature (and art in general) and psychological dispositions, a connection discussed in depth in his essay 'Creative Writers and Daydreaming' (Freud 1973–86, vol. 14: 129–41). C.G. Jung – whose works paralleled Freud's before he abandoned individual psychology to concentrate on general anthropological patterns of the psyche – used fairy-tales, folklore, and eventually Eastern mysticism as the material of his inquiries. Jacques Lacan, in many ways Freud's successor, returned to Shakespeare's *Hamlet* for a discussion of desire and its interpretation (Felman 1982: 11–52).

In the terminology of psychoanalysis, the term 'symbol' quickly achieved considerable prominence. It is crucial in Freud's *The Interpretation of Dreams*, but also appears in Jung's theory of archetypes, when he explicitly discusses their symbolic nature as opposed to the notion that they might be allegories (another literary term):

> All the mythological processes of nature, such as summer and winter, the phases of the moon, the rainy seasons, and so forth, are in no sense allegories of these objective occurrences; rather they are symbolic expressions of the inner, unconscious drama of the psyche which becomes accessible to man's consciousness by way of projection – that is, mirrored in the events of nature.
>
> (Jung 1959, vol. 9: 6)

> An allegory is a paraphrase of a conscious content, whereas a symbol is the best possible expression for an unconscious content whose nature can only be guessed, because it is still unknown.
>
> (6, note)

Two other Freudian concepts, condensation and displacement, bear crucial resemblance to metaphor and metonymy. They will be discussed in depth below. Lacan eventually goes all the way in relating psychoanalysis and literature by describing psychic phenomena in terms of textual ones. His claim that the unconscious is structured like a language marks the merging point, while his theory of desire as displacement on the chain of signifiers brings psychoanalysis's attachment to literature back to the basic element of language, the sign.

Yet this seemingly happy and untroubled union of the two disciplines obscures some questions that are glossed over in simplistic equations. The most fundamental one concerns the compatibility of the related elements. Is it at all possible to treat a neurosis, its symptom(s), and its analysis as the equivalent of the meaning of a text, the text in its material manifestation, and the interpretation of the latter? The devaluation that the term 'meaning' has undergone in recent years already hints at some discrepancies. It does not require much effort to identify both tripartite schemes as variants of the classicist model outlined by Foucault: commentary, language (i.e. the utterance), and the underlying 'original text' as the creator of the utterance. In both cases the division is highly problematic: commentary as well as 'meaning' (Foucault's 'original text') only manifest themselves once more in language. In a neurosis, the symptom may appear in somatic, i.e. bodily, shape. But it only gains significance when seen as a sign that is interpreted within the code of the analysis.

Both bodily symptom and the material artefact of the text are nothing but different manifestations of texts. Into the category of textuality slide the underlying neurosis and the analysis of a symptom as well as the assumed 'meaning' of a literary text and its interpretation. In the latter case, it is indisputable that one could not exist without the other. In the case of psychoanalysis, Freud's suspicion that the analysis is not simply a catalyst that helps the neurosis to emerge, but an element in its development, is expressed in his crucial concept of *transference*. It signifies the projection of libidinous impulses of the patient on to the analyst – and also the other way round.

Thus, psychoanalytic treatment and the reading of texts assume the same initial position. While the symptom of a psychoanalytic case only achieves its status through the analyst who identifies it as a sign of something else – the neurosis – the literary text only gains its status when it is perceived as one by its reader. This act of perception, which is the beginning of every reading process, the first stage of the interpretation, is always based on the premise that this text does not stand for itself, that 'underneath' it lurks something the text represents and hides at the same time. More than that: in the same way that the psychoanalysis creates the analyst, the reading of the text creates its reader. The seemingly independent poles of both processes are creators and creations in a dialectic interrelation of textuality and interpretation. They are analogous to the triadic model of the sign in Peirce: signified (trauma)/signifier (symptom)/sign (neurosis).

The stimulus of the operations of psychoanalysis and textual interpretation as well as their stumbling-block is the temporal and spatial distance to their origin which symptom and text bear as birthmarks. They invite attempts to bridge the gap – and signal that the endeavour will be in vain. What the psychoanalyst can hope for is the narrated recreation of the traumatic event that has engendered the neurosis, never the capture of the original situation.[1] What the reader or interpreter of a text produces is also another text. In this respect, Harold Bloom is right in stating that 'the meaning of a poem can only be a poem, but *another poem – a poem not itself*' (Bloom 1973: 70).

On these similarities of interpretation and transference that Freud himself acknowledges will the analysis of the present chapter be based. It will emphasise their common ground in text production rather than simple equations of particular structures. Following the internal logic of this study, the evaluation will work its way backwards from the largest structure of the poetic text, the synthetic consciousness of myth, to the smallest one, the individual sign. During this analysis, certain problems will continually present themselves. The most prominent one arises directly when psychoanalysis and literature are brought into a relation not so much of similarity but of causality: if a psyche is the origin of a text, i.e. if the text is the representation of a self, what is the status of the self of the text, the textual identity? Can it simply be regarded as a secondary identity, a kind of plaster cast of its creator? Or does the question become obsolete when both creating and textual identity are uncovered as fictions, as texts?

2. POETRY'S SYNTHETIC CONSCIOUSNESS AND PSYCHOANALYTIC CONCEPTS OF THE SELF

The tendency of simultaneous expansion and reduction is one of the dominant strategies of modernist poetry. It also has its counterpart in psychoanalysis. There it finds its expression in the drift towards universal holistic concepts of the psyche while simultaneously smaller structures, delineations and borderlines are introduced. Freud's original model of the psyche, the twofold compound of consciousness and unconscious, still adheres to the Platonic distinction of appearance and reality. The unconscious is granted greater power and authenticity. It influences one's individual life – and consciousness – drastically. At the same time it remains inaccessible and only permits occasional glimpses of its contents in dreams, slips of the tongue, or jokes. The consciousness, on the other hand, is – disturbingly – an awareness that is not quite aware, a controlled and self-conscious thinking, evaluating, and judging which is itself controlled by the uncontrollable unconscious.

In modernist poems various similar relations claim attention. The shaping but ungraspable outside of natural phenomena (their 'inscape') and also the layers of the self which constantly frustrate attempts of the text to mirror or deal with them in Hopkins. Yeats's endeavour to handle history, both personal and impersonal, with artefacts that are in turn threatened by the very history they are meant to represent. Eliot's 'objective correlatives', designed to depict mental states, but continually unfaithful to their task. Eventually Pound's striving for a purified 'dialect of the tribe' that is continually polluted by usury, the unwanted exchange of values and meanings.

In all these examples an unsuccessful reification happens whose object becomes increasingly sophisticated, because more universal and more fundamental at the same time. In Hopkins it is still unmediated experience that forms the starting point of the process. In Yeats this experience is already channelled into a dominantly linear experience of history whose continuity is constantly endangered but eventually finds its refuge in the stable linearity of the cycle. Eliot narrows the focus of experience even more and transposes it into the individual, thus creating psychological landscapes with their own landmarks and time schemes. Pound eventually attempts the reification of the most fundamental element in the process of experience, language. This makes his strategy the narrowest and yet most universal of the above.

Although most evident in Pound, in all cases the reification has to face an economic problem (which, paradoxically, also triggers off the reification). 'Economy' is here used in a broad sense, encompassing everything from the distribution of 'energy' and 'tensions' in Freud's early physiological model of psychic activities (Freud 1973–86, vol. 11: 35–44) to Deleuze and Guattari's questioning of Freud's basic assumptions in their *Anti-Oedipus* and Lyotard's sophisticated but controversial merger of psychoanalysis and economy in his *Économie Libidinale*. What concerns the present study is the recurring problem of the adequacy of representation, the origin of the modernist impasses and its strategies of compensation.

As an economic model, Pound's *Cantos* are remarkably successful and a complete failure at the same time. If the most important feature in a working economic system of an advanced nature is the successful transformation of goods and services into a unified symbolic system (i.e. money), *The Cantos* are a masterpiece. Their capacity for integrating diverse material into their own symbolic structure is certainly unsurpassed. But although the resulting construct is impressive, indeed massive and monumental, the process of incorporation (transformation is not the correct term, since *The Cantos* are eager to retain the individuality of their fragments) also engenders internal tensions. These appear as ruptures on the surface of the work. The most obvious 'cracks' are the beginning of the poem, its incomplete end, and the missing cantos in the poem's final section.

The open beginning cannot be considered a serious rupture since it links the text to its dominant model, Homer's *Odyssey*, already with the first word 'And'. The missing cantos, however, and especially the unfinished state of the entire poem are a different issue. They show the intervention of history on the formation of the text. But they are more than that: they are the acknowledgement that the internal arrangement of the poem is flawed. 'Control' and 'ownership' are the issues raised in a rather panicky way in one of the last cantos (CXIV; 792). 'To make Cosmos' has ended up in 'errors and wrecks' (CXVI; 795–6). The 'Notes for CXVII *et seq.*' talk of loss and destruction – and surprisingly also of guilt, very personal guilt after the poem's continual attempts to be impersonal:

> I have tried to write Paradise
>
> Do not move
>   Let the wind speak
>   that is paradise.
>
> Let the gods forgive what I
>   have made
> Let those I love try to forgive
>   what I have made.
>
> (802)

The 'world formula' has unravelled itself and lays bare the same chaos it set out to criticise and overcome – and a personality that was meant to be raised to the status of an impersonal Nietzschean superman.

What is the reason for this failure? What interferes with the creation of Pound's *paradiso terrestre*, designed to represent a coherent synthetic modern consciousness capable of incorporating *and making sense of* the wreckage and fragmentation of culture in the twentieth century? The reason for the eventual failure of *The Cantos* is spread visibly over their surface. It is the text itself, its textuality, that is responsible for its internal problems. In a revealing (because uncontrolled and certainly disconnected) moment, in a late fragment from 1966, the text gives itself away:

That her acts
Olga's acts
of beauty
be remembered.

Her name was Courage
& is written Olga

These lines are for the
ultimate CANTO

whatever I may write
in the interim.

(815)

My emphasis highlights the problem of textual production that is shown as endangering the text's attempted constitution of a stable message. Writing continues – and by continuing blots out and changes what has been said before.

In Freud's writings, the problem of closure appears in his difficulties to state exactly when an analysis is finished. The notion of a complete 'cure', still very verbal in his earlier studies, shifts increasingly into the background. The analysis engenders layer after layer of translation in its effort to arrive at a truth. Its discovery would transpose the suppressed unconscious into consciousness, thus eliminating its power. Yet the point where translation ends and 'the original text' is uncovered is never reached. Worse than that: the translation is not unilateral, it does not lead in one direction only. By acts of transference without which an analysis could not take place, the libidinous impulses of the unconscious enter the translation process, change its direction, and trouble the desired clarity.

To accommodate these contradictory impulses, Freud introduces a threefold distinction in place of the binary poles of unconscious and consciousness: the *id* (which represents the libidinal drives of the unconscious), the *ego* (a substitute for the consciousness, yet with the crucial distinction that in it the struggle of the hostile forces takes place), and the *super-ego*, sometimes also called 'ego ideal' or 'censor', which controls the interaction between *id* and *ego* and is responsible for repression.[2]

Applied to a complex poetic text like *The Cantos*, the problem of arriving at an essence is equally poignant and leads to the imposition of various strata of narratorial strategies (although these need not be connected with identifiable characters). When the discourse of the text seems anonymous or depersonalised, as in many fragments, when the employed texts are seemingly controlled by the poem rather than in control, one must suspect its mechanisms of suppression at work. For, as has been demonstrated, the textual fragments which form *The Cantos* are more than mute props on a stage designed and arranged by the 'super-ego' of the poem, its – hidden yet all-pervasive – textual identity. The areas in which their uncomfortable paradigms clash with the arrangement of the whole, the *egos* of the text, are the protagonists and personae of the poem. (In its attempt to be impersonal it again multiplies rather than reduces the number of its mouthpieces.)

The complex coexistence of voices and patterns, clear intentions and contradictory associations is the result of a discovery similar to Freud's insight that the translation process is neither undisturbed nor unilateral. When *The Cantos* discuss economy, this includes their own as well, even if this is not made explicit. Thus, the poem shifts from what Barthes calls the 'readerly' perspective (where the reader-controlling aspect is dominant) to a 'writerly' one in which its own construction is under scrutiny. This internal change of perspective provides possibilities for the exploration of important dimensions such as the ethics and the politics of *The Cantos*. It is their tragedy that these passages remain unexplored. The refusal of the text to question its own structures leads to the observed blindness concerning its own procedures. In a blatantly brutal move, the poem reasserts the traditional readerly view by filling the conceptual gaps with aggressive rhetoric.

In Freud's terminology, the *super-ego* of the text re-establishes its dominance. The shift of the most basic paradigms of text production in these moments of maximum poetic complexity signals that *The Cantos* approach the limits of modernism. But only when poems abandon both the ideal of conclusiveness and monosemy (unambiguous statements) can the readerly of traditional poetry be superseded by the writerly. In Freud's writings, this desire for abandon (which is for him ultimately related to the assertive drives of the *super-ego* as well as the chaotic libidinal ones of the *id*) is called the *death instinct*. Aptly, its introduction marks the point when Freud eventually abandons (though not explicitly disclaims) his tripartite scheme of the self in 'Beyond the Pleasure Principle' (Freud 1973–86, vol. 11: 270–338). Parallels of the death instinct in modernist poetry will reappear throughout this chapter and form part of its conclusion.

At this initial point, however, one can already suspect that it is related – or indeed the antidote – to a crucial impasse of modernism's attempt at perfecting itself: the potential endlessness of the utterance.

3. THE WRITER AND HIS DOUBLES

Hugh Kenner refers to the threatening double nature of personae and masks which are so important in Pound's works (and also in Yeats's and – to a lesser extent – Eliot's): 'That personae are donned as masks we learn from the etymology of the word and from much of Pound's early poetic practice . . . . That personae may also possess the way spirits do is a truth somewhat obscured by Pound's characteristic stress on expertise' (Hesse 1969: 331).

Personae, in the first instance a handy guise for the subject of the utterance (it does not matter at this point whether an actual person or a textual construct), possess certain frightening or even destructive characteristics. Like Freud's *uncanny*, they are simultaneously familiar, thus controllable, and alien, and thus in control. The etymology of *das Unheimliche* refers to its ambivalent aspects: alien and uncanny, but also *heimlich*, 'secretive', and in nineteenth-century German the same as *heimisch*: familiar. Both alien and familiar, concealed and outspoken, this uncanny – which even in Freud appears closely related to the double (in his famous analysis of E.T.A. Hoffmann's *Der Sandmann*, the sandman is quite clearly the double of the father) – can be identified in modernist poetry as tradition. The texts utilise past or fictional characters to constitute their own message. Yet in a move reminiscent of the fatal personality split in *Dr Jekyll and Mr Hyde*, these characters assume a life of their own and shift the text in directions that disturb its constitution. This achievement of an individual life is of course only possible in language and – as will be shown – also generated *by* language. The introduction of complex foreign associations through this procedure distorts the economy of a text like *The Cantos* which is, after all, primarily concerned with this very economy.

Equally important – considering Pound's 'make it new' doctrine – is the question of the creator and owner of texts which employ foreign material in such a way. At this point one should remember the concern for 'control' and 'ownership' expressed in the final canto,

CXIV. The insecurity of *The Cantos* – which amounts to hysteria in many passages – is rooted in an uncertainty concerning the right to particular utterances, eventually the right to language in general. The poem's manic attempt to gather every available form of written communication is a move against the ever-present threat that this language is only borrowed. The story of the Australian demigod Wanjina in canto LXXIV illustrates the issue. He creates the world by naming it, but is punished for this unauthorised action by his father with the removal of his mouth. The parallels are clear: the making of cosmos with words – and the fear that the institution granting these powers (the father, tradition, eventually language itself) could take revenge for their abuse by imposing a castrational punishment on the creator (Ellmann 1987: 190). The images of carnivorous women and the frequent impotent characters in Pound and Eliot's poetry are connected to this primal fear of the poet: the loss of poetic potency. Line 339 of *The Waste Land* supplies an illustration: 'Dead mountain mouth of carious teeth that cannot spit' (76).

The escape from the shadow of tradition which accompanies every production of language is paradoxically but not unexpectedly attempted with language itself in *The Cantos*. This is yet another variant of the modernist tendency of complete internalisation. In a passage in canto XC that discusses the clash of the compulsion to say something with the knowledge that this always links the utterance with the past, the poem introduces an interesting equation:

> to the room in Poitiers where one can stand
> casting no shadow,
> That is Sagetrieb,
> that is tradition.
> Builders had kept the proportion,
>
> (605)

What appears opaque at first glance – where is the connection between a perfectly designed room and the compulsion to perpetuate tradition? – becomes clear when it is related to the uncanny double that the use of (always preformulated) language brings with it as the shadow of the punishing father. Only the perfect work of art can escape his revenge and create something truly new.

The threatening shadow of tradition can assume very concrete shapes. In Pound's *oeuvre*, *Homage to Sextus Propertius* reveals a shift of attitude from reverence to parody which Eliot, in his introduction to Pound's *Selected Poems* of 1928, characterises as 'not a translation, it is a paraphrase, or still more truly (for the instructed) a *persona*' (Brooker 1979: 152). What happens in *Homage to Sextus Propertius* is in fact a mutilating appropriation. *Hugh Selwyn Mauberley* is an even stronger attempt to exorcise the ghost of tradition – who in this instance is most uncanny, because an exact double of the author of the poem. '*Vocat aestus in umbram*' [the heat calls us into the shadow] (186) is its revealing epigraph. The poem abounds with images of death, of traditions as well as of a generation of young men in the trenches of the First World War. The most surprising of these appears at the very beginning of the poem – or indeed even before it starts. What it presents to its reader is already the sepulchre of the poet E.P. Disposed of and appropriately buried, tradition, here Pound's personal poetic past, becomes controllable as part of a poetic argument. In a different disguise, that of M. Verog, this past undergoes another grotesque reification. It ends up

> Among the pickled foetuses and bottled bones,
> Engaged in perfecting the catalogue,
>
> (193)

Concerned 'exclusively with the dead' (Wyndham Lewis's characterisation of Pound), but at the same time engaged in one of the dominant activities of Pound's later poems, the work of the archivist, Verog is the bogey man easily discarded as a relic of the past. He is busy dreaming of the great of the last generation: Galliffet, Dowson, the Rhymers' Club, and Lionel Johnson. Yet his disposal as 'out of step with the decade, / Detached from his contemporaries' is not entirely condescending. 'Neglected by the young, / Because of these reveries' (193) ends the poem and strikes a sympathetic and pitiful note.

This ambivalent attitude towards tradition is another hint at the double nature of the ghost of one's past. It is both distant and alien and all too familiar, threatening and comforting. Its exorcism by calling it dead is therefore no more a proper elimination than the burning of an effigy – like that of Sigismundo Malatesta, one of the 'heroes' of *The Cantos*. The attitude combines negation and reverence and can be characterised as blasphemy, as will be remembered. It immobilises and controls, but simultaneously internalises and worships what threatens it. It therefore supports the main theorem in Freud's *Totem and Taboo*. The initial murder (and cannibalistic devouring) of the oppressive father institutionalises his control as a totem (Freud 1973–86, vol. 13: 71–131). In modernist poems, this totem can be an actual poet, the artistic model that the text must deal with, tries to integrate and perhaps to overcome. It can even be, as in Pound's case, the shadow of the poet's own past. Julia Kristeva describes the artist's dilemma in the following way:

> A hardy explorer of the same psychic landscape, the artist pours or spends the identificatory symptom into original discourse: into style. Neither subservient like the believer, nor subjected to somatic conversion like the hysteric, but sometimes both of these, he constantly produces multiple identifications, but he *speaks* them. Hypothesis: because more than any other he is in the grip of the 'father in the individual prehistory'. Contrary to the widespread myth of the artist subject to the desire for his mother, or rather in order to defend himself against this desire, he takes himself . . . not for the phallus of the mother, but for this ghost, the third party to which the mother aspires, for the loving version of the third party, for a pre-Oedipal father 'who loved you first' (say the Gospels), a conglomerate of both sexes (suggests Freud) . . . 'God is *Agape*'.
>
> (Collier, Geyer-Ryan 1990: 171–2)

In Eliot, who appears to have fewer problems with tradition (a fact perhaps explained by the restricted amount – and thus greater control – of his poetic output), this totemic ghost appears explicitly very late in his career. The compound spectre encountered in 'Little Gidding', the last part of *Four Quartets*, is such an echo of the past. Stylistic similarities, such as parentheses and 'passages of less intensity' (Eliot 1957: 32) which are abundant in the last three *Quartets*, hint at the identity of the ghost. It is Yeats that Eliot has to deal with eventually. As Sabine Roth points out, Eliot employs Yeats in a complex way to explore some basic issues that are also prominent in the work of the latter, notably the problem of wisdom and age, the by now familiar problem of achieving a stable and valuable message in the continually changing framework of language.[3] Roth explains how Yeats becomes the ghostly double of the speaker of this part of *Four Quartets*: 'So I assumed a double part, and cried / And heard another's voice cry: "What! Are *you* here?"' (217). The speaker of 'Little Gidding' himself initiates the doubling. Also it is not Yeats proper who appears as a stylistic spectre, but a deliberate misrepresentation – or rather a multiple representation, a double (or indeed manifold) double, 'both one and many'. It is Yeats reread or misread through his own works, especially the two 'Byzantium' poems, and the way in which he is interpreted is not a positive one. Yeats's esoteric model of purification of the artistic spirit is perceived through another dominant model of this part of *Four Quartets*, Dante, and found lacking when confronted with the latter's overtly Christian doctrines.

The procedure of reading through the (distorting) eyes of another is, of course, nothing but the reversal of the personae approach analysed in Pound's early poetry. While the arrangement of masks – like a system of lenses – is an appropriating move to achieve increased authority by the bundling of various perspectives, the (mis-)reading of poets and poems through the eyes of other authors and texts disseminates the view. It devalues as much as it creates distance. The complex cut through the layers of tradition follows the same initial mechanisms of appropriation and distancing. They also represent the Freudian notion of dismemberment, cannibalism and totemisation.

The surprisingly personal engagement with tradition in 'Little Gidding' is unique in its cathartic directness in Eliot's *oeuvre*. However, it is not the only instance in which his works deal with the powers of the past, and explicitly those of texts. The first part of *The Waste Land*, 'The Burial of the Dead', and especially its rather confusing final section, expresses the poem's ambivalence concerning the plethora of texts to which it alludes. The poem is permeated by intertextual references which – 'elegant' and 'intelligent' like the Shakespeherian Rag – create a metatext underneath the distorted surface of the poem that, as Maud Ellmann points out, is very much the authoritarian canon of Western civilisation (Ellmann 1987: 95–6). The effect of this technique of simultaneous subversion (mainly by a metonymic scattering of the references that will be discussed in greater depth below) and institutionalisation as a ghostly counter-text is twofold. A feeling of loss and nostalgia is created, which can be interpreted in ideological terms as a conservative or even reactionary feature. It also functions in the same way as the mechanisms of mourning and melancholia, which Freud describes in his essay of the same title (Freud 1973–86, vol. 11: 245–68). Mourning is always coupled with a feeling of relief – in the first instance that someone else has died and not the mourner – and, more important, with suppressed aggression which forms the subtext of mourning: the unconscious wish that the beloved person should die (Freud 1973–86, vol. 13: 132–58).

An object cathexis is replaced by an identification: that which can no longer be had is incorporated into the mourner. This mirrors exactly the modernist technique of continually gathering cultural fragments. Melancholia and depression are regarded in a similar way by Freud as a distorted form of aggression. The aggressive impulse is directed against an object found guilty of refusing the melancholic the attention, sympathy and love that he or she requires.

The analogy to the authoritarian canon of civilisation is evident. Every new text finds itself outside the canon, by its very nature rejected and 'unloved' because of its otherness. Tradition must be made disposable, so that the new utterance can assert itself. This is achieved either by declaring its death (a common move in the history of literature, art, philosophy, etc.) or by its more subtle integration and cannibalisation. A poem like *The Waste Land* which – unlike *The Cantos* – is aware of its mechanisms, even though it cannot escape them, transforms tradition into parts of its own imagery. The title of its first section already introduces the topic. Who are the dead that are buried in the section? Of course they are 'memory and desire' from a personal past. But the explicitly dead are those in the crowd on London Bridge in its final section. The speaker's surprise at their number, 'so many, / I had not thought death had undone so many' (65), is the realisation how many lives have preceded his, more precisely, how many utterances ('Sighs, short and infrequent, were exhaled' (65)) were made before his. This is a common insight for writers and everyone concerned with literature.

The suspicion implicitly arises that perhaps everything has been said already. In a time when access to artefacts from most distant cultures and periods became possible, when the progress of communication technology and the media created a focusing of voices and utterances on the Western mind, this question became poignant indeed. An original statement must have seemed almost impossible. The notes that accompany *The Waste Land* are an indication of what Foucault describes as the inevitable participation of every statement in 'networks and fields of use' in which it 'is subjected to transferences or modifications, is integrated into operations and strategies in which its identity is maintained or effaced' (Foucault 1972: 105). Every utterance is intertextually related to earlier ones. There is no text without its ghostly shadow. In that respect, Eliot's curious note to line 68 of *The Waste Land* concerning the church of Saint Mary Woolnoth whose bell rang 'With a dead sound on the final stroke of nine': 'A phenomenon which I have often noticed' (81), is both an ironic inclusion among all the learned references, and also an assertion that at least this observation is an original contribution.

One original note, however, is not enough to counterbalance the permanent influence of the dead and buried, the suppressed voices of the past. These voices need not even impose themselves on the speaker of *The Waste Land*. Their attraction is so strong that he searches for them (another hint at their combined character as taboo and totem). He discovers a character named 'Stetson' and identifies him as one who was with him 'in the ships at Mylae' (65). The paradoxical coupling of the American name and the incident from classical history is telling:[4] it creates a cultural brace which unites the archaic starting point of Western culture with its contemporary limit. It is not unimportant that this 'end' of culture is located in America, both Eliot and Pound's origin and the country that mirrored Pound's 'making it new' doctrine pragmatically in its 'melting pot' ideology. Yet not even this attitude produces a shadowless present. The buried past can sprout and bloom, although it is uncertain what kind of flowers it will produce. The suppression of cultural origins only leads to their re-emergence in uncontrollable shapes – just as the suppression of libidinous impulses cannot get rid of them but makes them mutate into the symptoms of neuroses. Eventually, the suppressed will be dug up again – and pester the present with its festering stench.

Some 'censoring' significance might also be traced in the image of the unearthing dog in 'The Burial of the Dead'. Curiously capitalised and attributed with 'nails' rather than the more common claws, 'he' (not 'it') provokes interpretation as an anagram. Dog equals God, i.e. Christ nailed to the cross, who will eventually – as the most radical cultural *super-ego* – judge every action, thought, and feeling. If this interpretation is not too far-fetched anyway, it still has to be taken with a pinch of salt. The arrangement of irreconcilable elements in the first part of *The Waste Land*, each with its own paradigmatic shadow, devalues every possible meaning and taints it with irony. By stressing both its metonymic collage and its multi-layered structure, the text cautiously avoids a fixed point of view, a textual identity. Like echoes in a complex building, the effect makes the speaker always seem somewhere else. Every utterance becomes equally inauthentic, a mere quotation.

This removal of textual identity on to the same plane as allusions is characteristic of modernist poetry. It is usually in a rather helpless fashion called irony. Although superficial, the characterisation points at the simultaneously innovative and traditional aspect of the technique. Although textual identity appears destabilised – which in turn leads to a decentring of the texts which offers new opportunities for the authority of statements – a textual identity remains nonetheless, and one that is even more powerful than the firm voice of readerly texts. Irony always requires a point of view. The impossible complete negation of identity encountered in connection with impersonality reappears magnified in the problem of textual surface and the layers 'underneath'. Only texts that transcend the aesthetics of modernism manage to overcome this impasse. Although in many cases just as much constructed out of quotations, they no longer create the illusion of layers in which an identity plays hide and seek. They become polysemous yet single-layered, surface only that no longer knows or needs an identity. The problem of inside and outside disappears.

4. METAPHOR, METONYMY, SYMBOL AND THEIR PSYCHOANALYTIC COUNTERPARTS

> It is not a rich and difficult germination, it is a distribution of gaps, voids, absences, limits, divisions.
>
> (Foucault 1972: 119)[5]

In *The Interpretation of Dreams* Freud describes the dominant mechanisms in the creation of dream images, condensation and displacement, in terms that also apply to metaphor and metonymy. The characterisation of condensation is 'compression' (Freud 1973–86, vol. 4: 383), 'loop-lines or short-circuits' (385) 'brought about by omission' (386). Displacement, on the other hand, is described as a mechanism that

> '. . . extract[s] from the dream-thought fragments of speeches'[6] and 'deals with them in the most arbitrary fashion. Not only does it drag them out of their context and cut them in pieces, incorporating some portions and rejecting others, but often puts them together in a new order so that a speech which appears in a dream to be a connected whole turns out in the analysis to be composed of three or four detached fragments. In producing this new version, a dream will often abandon the meaning that the words originally had in the dream-thoughts and give them a fresh one. . . .'
>
> (545)

Freud's reluctance to draw an explicit parallel is a symptom of his recurring refusal to admit the intricacies of language which are so central to his theories. Far from naming names, Freud constantly slides into metaphors himself, 'switch-words' as he calls them in 'A Case of Hysteria' (Freud 1973–86, vol. 8: 100 note). '*J'appelle un chat un chat*' (I call a pussy-cat a pussy-cat), Freud's defence of his seemingly frank attitude in the same case study gives the problem away in its (unintentional?) pun on the colloquial term for the female genitals and also in its distancing through the French language (Freud 1973–86, vol. 8: 82). Therefore, when the characteristics of displacement are summarised, again an objective comparison rather than a more convincing literary or linguistic parallel is employed: 'Thus speeches in dreams have a structure similar to that of breccia, in which largish blocks of various kinds of stone are cemented together by a binding medium' (Freud 1973–86, vol. 4: 546).

It was up to others to point out the obvious. Roman Jakobson, the Russian structuralist, described the dominance of metaphor and metonymy as functions of poetic language, first without reference to Freud, but in very Freudian terms in his essay on Pasternak's prose in 1935, later in his seminal essay of 1956 entitled 'Two Aspects of Language and Two Types of Aphasic Disturbance' (Jakobson 1971: 239–59).[7] This in turn had repercussion on other structuralists, such as the anthropologist Claude Lévi-Strauss and, full circle back to psychoanalysis, Jacques Lacan (Holenstein 1976: 192).

Of interest for the present study are not the obvious structural parallels of condensation/metaphor and displacement/metonymy, but the question whether the structures – which have been shown to be dominant in Eliot's works – can be related to what has been said above. Is there a connection between the shadow of language, the double of the utterance, and the techniques of paradigmatic condensation and syntagmatic displacement? What happens in the 'gaps, voids, absences, limits, divisions', and what is the material of Freud's breccia, the 'binding medium'?

The poems themselves lead the way into their analysis. So obviously caught in the tension of birth and death, Eliot's works display their entanglement in the dialectic of absence and presence. Once a textual identity is established, the interplay becomes one of disclosure and hiding. 'Pray for us now and at the hour of our birth' (114), the last line of 'Animula', and 'Pray for us now and at the hour of our death' (96), the more orthodox version of the 'Hail Mary' at the end of the first part of *Ash-Wednesday*, bracket the central issue of Eliot's poems from *The Waste Land* onwards. 'Because the beginning shall remind us of the end' (118) (in 'The Cultivation of Christmas Trees') returns as the haunting refrain of 'East Coker': 'In my beginning is my end' (196). What reminds us of the inextricable connection of creation and destruction is again elaborated tentatively in the *Ariel Poems* to be perfected in *Four Quartets*. 'Journey of the Magi' talks about the issue in Christian terms (the magi realise the inadequacy of their religion and their threatening spiritual death when faced with the newborn Christ):

> Birth or Death? There was a Birth, certainly,
> We had evidence and no doubt. I had seen birth and death,
> But had thought they were different; [. . .]
>
> (110)

When applied to the text's self-reflective enquiry into its own temporality and register on the scale of tradition, however, the passage acquires a slightly different meaning. Every utterance is placed on the syntagmatic scale of literary history where it is born and dies almost simultaneously. Worse than this instant death (in its negative form ignorance or forgetting, in its positive shape institutionalisation) is that even in its flash of existence the literary utterance does not occupy a realm of its own. There are already other utterances it relates to. There will inevitably be new utterances in turn relating to and covering it, until it becomes merely the hidden layer of a palimpsest. The covering text can be interpretation, as the example of *The Waste Land*, hardly visible under the critical studies it has engendered, shows. 'A Song for Simeon' refers to this agonising insight in two of its final lines:

> I am tired with my own life and the lives of those after me,
> I am dying in my own death and the deaths of those after me.
>
> (112)

The metaphor embodies the creative principle of poetry. Its invigorating aspect is its in-between status, its merger of two signifiers that creates or points to a signified that appears to be new. Yet metaphors can and do die. Furthermore, they become poetic set-pieces which are recycled, distorted, and fragmented by other texts, over- or rewritten and transformed into a mere layer of the tradition from which they originally emerge as different and alienating. This points to the ambiguity of the metaphoric principle itself. Although it creates something new both on the textual and cognitive level and therefore becomes a moment of significatory expansion, it is essentially a retentive technique. Creating meaning between signifiers, it retains this meaning in the locus of its creation. Although potentially polysemous, the poles of the metaphoric creation (at least try to) bar the way for the unreliable and sliding signification. A hint at this ambivalence can be found in the line from 'A Song for Simeon' quoted above: 'I am dying *in* my own death . . .' (my emphasis).

The complex daring metaphor of poetic and sexual creativity in *The Waste Land* is another case in point: 'Dead mountain mouth of carious teeth that cannot spit' (76). 'Dead mountain' is in itself not very meaningful, yet evokes its opposite, a living mountain, a volcano. Into this image the mouth and its edges (the broken teeth) can be integrated. 'Cannot spit' hints at the inactive state of the volcano which, in its active form, represents ceaseless, senseless and destructive distribution, coupled with 'mouth' the production of language. Yet the 'cannot' is more than a tautological doubling of the 'Dead' of the beginning of the verse. It is not so much a 'cannot spit any more', but implies an (at least underlying) reluctance – in the manner of Hopkins's 'cry *I can no more.* I can' in '(Carrion Comfort)' (99). Its status is that of the analysand's 'no' in the psychoanalytic process, the refusal to give away that which constitutes the core of his neurosis, but which in a complicated but crucial move also becomes a fetish of his desire. Julia Kristeva calls this complex that hovers between subject and object and becomes crucial because of the contradicting urges to expel and keep it, the *abject* (Kristeva: 1984). While this fetish must remain secret, the act of refusal to unveil it, the analysand's 'no', the impotences, cuts, dead ends and silences of modernist poems, are the stylisations of the refusal, a secondary betrayal. As Abraham and Torok state for Freud's Wolf-Man:

> For the Wolf-Man – we understand why – a return of the repressed in the waking state through symbolization, for example, is out of the question. The single exception concerns the expression of *the very act of the retention of telling*, well expressed hysterically by tenacious constipation. But whatever might be the *object* of telling is so deeply buried behind words never to be uttered that its emergence, when it does take place, occurs not in the form of a symbol or a symptom but of a delirium such as that of the nose or later of the cut finger, and finally of the erogenous fantasy itself.
>
> (Abraham, Torok 1986: 21)

The transformation of the first significant production – as Freud calls the faeces – or, in the case of poetry, the utterance itself and the act of its creation into a fetish also features strongly in a form of poetry already discussed. Imagism, although not essentially a metaphoric technique and indeed opposed to merely ornamental uses of metaphors, displays striking similarities to the characteristics described above. When an Imagist poem is seen as a generator, the creation between two signifying poles becomes obvious. The 'apparition' is formed by the interaction of perception and object. In the same way as longer poems (such as Eliot's), Imagist texts refuse to give away the secret of their creation in their attempt both to be impersonal and to refrain from narrative.

Imagism is an exceptional literary movement, because it coincides with the establishment of its own rules. It becomes a perfect *machine célibataire* that keeps its creation and eventual death inside its own realm. Complete self-sufficiency is achieved by its refusal to communicate, become external and open: constipation. Thus the importance of 'THE LIST OF DONT'S' of Imagism:[8] do not use the potentials of language! The object, 'the thing', so central to modernist poems, from Eliot's 'objective correlative' to Pound's *res*, preferably sculpted by the poet himself, is therefore not a utopian goal, outside and new, but the embodiment of a thing of the past, a loss:

> It is in this sense that we are going to call this erogenous image, this good-luck charm fantasy, this magical taboo dodger: *a fetish*. Beneath the fetish, the occult love for a word-object remains concealed, beneath this love, the taboo-forming experience of a catastrophe, and finally beneath the catastrophe, the perennial memory of a hoarded pleasure with the ineducable wish that one day it shall return.
>
> (Abraham, Torok 1986: 22)

This desired return is also at the root of the modernist quest, both of Eliot's *The Waste Land* and the Odyssean detours of Pound's *Cantos*.

But what is the 'experience of catastrophe' which becomes 'the perennial memory of a hoarded pleasure'? This is an area in which psychoanalysis remains opaque exactly when it is most talkative. Of course it abounds with eventually unveiled traumatic situations, some more conventionally shocking, others quite banal. Still neither does a pattern evolve out of them, nor do they answer the question why neuroses develop in some people and not in others. The analysis of literature is both easier and more difficult, because unrestricted, in this respect. The textual nature of its 'symptoms' can hardly be overlooked. Texts can be considered in isolation or in any context that interests the reader, because the 'end' of the analysis is equally evidently another text without implications for an actual person.

As the discussion of the refusal strategies of modernist poems has shown, it is not the refusal itself that forms the core, the origin of the textual mechanisms. Yet if one takes these mechanisms of refusal, retention and internalisation as expressions of a shared modernist anxiety, one can hardly overlook the various indications that pinpoint the main source of the tactics – at least with regard to poetic production – in the simultaneous destruction and (re-)construction of identity. One can speculate that the reason for cherishing the trauma in a neurosis is its radical threat and thorough highlighting of the personal identity of its victim. There are many instances of this in Freud's studies: the discovery of the missing penis of the mother threatens the little boy's world-view, but also gives him a feeling of superiority; the exposure to sexual misdeeds of the father shatters the role model of the ego-ideal, yet offers a chance of independent development; etc. Lacan eventually draws attention to the first instance in which loss and gain for the personal identity are painfully exposed: the discovery that one is a separate being (analysed in his seminal paper on the 'mirror-stage').[9] Lacan and Julia Kristeva link the dialectic of loss and assertion of identity with language. They draw the line between the imaginary stage, a realm of unconnected impressions, and the symbolic stage where impressions are metonymically severed and given names, and reality achieves an order. For this stability, however, the newly established subject has sacrificed the feelings of wholeness and belonging.

It is possible to reject these assumptions. It is difficult, though, to ignore some striking parallels in modernist poems. Unsuccessful or negative instances of identity constitution through retention have already been pointed out. Yet there are just as many positive ones, sometimes in texts displaying retentive features at the same time. Pound's essay on the Imagist 'Image' has already been quoted in relation to myth. It is quoted again at this stage to highlight the psychological overtones in this particular act of poetic creation, the function that 'the fetish of the word-object', as Abraham and Torok call it, fulfils:

> An 'Image' is that which presents an intellectual and emotional complex in an instant of time . . . . It is the presentation of such a 'complex' instantaneously which gives that sense of sudden liberation; that sense of freedom from time limits and space limits; that sense of sudden growth, which we experience in the presence of the greatest works of art.
>
> (Pound 1954: 4)

Apparently, the 'presence' of this magical object helps to overcome the limits of the self, and these are very clearly described as those of its body in the 'freedom from time limits and space limits'. Once more the dilemma of birth and death is addressed here. Just as those poles of human existence are only seemingly binary, the function of the 'greatest works of art' is twofold and contradictory: it liberates and it expands. Liberation from the constraints of one's (physical) self is nothing but the regressive wish never to have been born, to be ejected as a solitary being into a potentially hostile reality. The 'sense of sudden growth' is the move in the opposite direction – but to the same end: the desire to transform the isolated and dislocated self into its own universe that encompasses (and controls!) every aspect of reality. The starting point and end of modernist poetry are re-encountered in psychological terms: the isolating feeling of a loss of mimetic connection between language and its outside, any conceivable form of reality, and the compensation technique of constructive expansion that eventually leads to the modernist myth of itself as an all-encompassing reality *inside* the text.

Yet again, the positive description of the metaphoric word-object implies negatively the threat that the fetish embodies once it is established. Already in the repetitive formulas of Pound's description lies a hint at its stifling power, the suspicion that it offers only a momentary liberation and immediately creates new limitations. Therefore the recurring terms presents/presentation/presence; instant/instantaneously; sense/sense(/pre*sence*). The ambivalent nature of the metaphor as creative and petrifying is encountered again. Turning the final clause of Pound's description upside down produces a much more common characterisation of 'the greatest works of art': they make their beholder feel *small*. Again, the potentially original utterance, the great work, both establishes identity (of its creator and its percipient – who seemingly become one in the reading process) and immobilises and threatens it. In the shadow of the rebellious act of creation lurks the punishing law of the father.

It is ironic and yet paradoxically consequent that the escape from this overpowering double nature of the metaphor is sought in exactly the strategy that embodies the initial problem: repetition. The shift towards metonymies observed in Eliot's works is an attempt to break up the instantaneously petrifying nature of the metaphoric *hapax legomenon*, the singular unique utterance,[10] to break through the echoes of the authority of the past, 'the father in one's own personal prehistory', by the creation of another echo. For, in spite of its nature as fragmentation or mutilation, the metonymy is always also a reconstruction, a reconstitution of the fragmented and mutilated, albeit with a changed character. As has been pointed out, the metonymy stresses this simultaneous destruction and reconstruction as well as the textual identity responsible for it, contrary to the metaphor which hides it. If the metaphor equals retention and refusal, the metonymy is a spouting out, an overspilling, seemingly the ceaseless unveiling of that which the metaphor suppresses. Yet just as the metaphoric retention is not a meaning in itself, the metonymic overflow is not the simple equivalent of an unleashed libidinal flow, the eventual giving away of the guarded secret. Its apparent submission is merely the continuation of the pleasurable hide-and-seek game – and ultimately connected with the paradoxical constitution and preservation of identity through the very act of endangering it.

> The Wolf-Man's hope was depositec the word whose secret lover he was. This word, his Object, he kept in his possession for an entire lifetime. Initially and by vocation, the word was addressed to someone. As an Object of love, it had to be removed from everyone's reach so that it would not be lost. Saying it without saying it. To show/hide. Walk around with a rebus and pretend it is undecipherable. Repeat tirelessly to one and all, especially to his analyst: 'Here is nothing, hold it tight.' Inaccessible, wending his way alongside the unattainable. To love without knowing, to love desperately, to love loving the analyst endlessly.
>
> (Abraham, Torok, 1986: 22)

Abraham and Torok's surprising conclusion which suddenly brings the analyst back into the game is linked with the problem of transference. Yet is also concerns the relation of text and reader in modernist poetry. A famous passage in *The Waste Land* is the perfect illustration of their idea: 'I will show you fear in a handful of dust' (line 30; 64). 'Here is nothing, hold it tight.' The idea of the love-affair which – through the word-object – connects analyst and analysand will be taken up again in the concluding part of the present study. There, the view will be reversed: what is the effect of reading modernist poems on the constitution of identity of their reader? More bluntly, why is modernist poetry read – or, more realistically, why is it read so rarely and reluctantly?

Although metonymies in modernist poetry must – like those in the tales of the Wolf Man – be seen as 'not a *metonymy of things* but a *metonymy of words*' (Abraham, Torok 1986: 19), their material often consists of images. Their treatment follows the same pattern of reification as the construction of metaphors. By the act of naming or evocation between the poles of signifiers, an act of appropriation takes place that makes its object controllable and places it simultaneously *outside* the creative identity of the text and *inside* its creative universe. While this act strives towards singularity in the metaphor and tries to ban its object inside the created 'apparition', the metonymy is a compulsive return to the dismembered object, a re-enactment of its mutilation. It mirrors the totemisation of the overbearing and eventually cannibalised father in Freud's *Totem and Taboo* (Freud 1973–86, vol. 13: 203). It is analogous to the magic ritual that tries to ban its object, as Ellmann rightly points out, by using imitative magic (based on similarity – like that of a voodoo doll or an effigy) in the metaphor, and contagious magic (working through contiguity) in the metonymy and its variant, the synecdoche (Ellmann 1987: 72).

The object attacked in modernist poems is often the human body. As the arena in which the initial traumatic loss in the constitution of identity is inscribed, its central importance is not surprising when this original loss is repeated on a much larger, namely impersonal and universal scale. The simultaneous threat to both identity and meaning through signification endangers these two basic symbolic gains that the initial loss of the coherence of the imaginary stage has procured. Therefore the return to its focus, the body, with the mixture of hatred and desire characteristic of ritualist obsession.

Four examples from Eliot's works will illustrate the ways in which the metonymy bans and invokes, disintegrates and recreates simultaneously. In 'Whispers of Immortality' two complementary metonymies are at work. The first one, the skeleton, represents the body *ex negativo*: skull (rather than head), breastless, lipless, empty sockets where the eyeballs should be, no flesh, only bones. The second metonymy, which depicts the woman Grishkin, complements the first one positively. This does not imply that the description is favourable. On the contrary: Grishkin's ambiguous features have become famous. Yet no matter whether her presence is pleasant, a presence it is, the *Da* [there] to the skeleton's *Fort* [gone].[11] She has eyes. They are even emphasised. Contrary to the 'breastless creatures', she has more than her share of a 'friendly bust'. Where they live 'underground', she has a maisonette, and in general she counters their lifelessness with the larger-than-life presence of an attractive, dangerous, and smelly jungle animal, the jaguar. Freud discusses the split into ideal and horror image in a paper called 'Repression' (Freud 1973–86, vol. 11: 139–58, 150). In 'Whispers of Immortality', the counterpointing, again of death and life, creates desire, the only immortal thing in the poem, in the irreconcilable contradiction between abstract metaphysics and the irreducible sensual experience of its last lines. Once more, Eliot's poem creates the loss it laments. The primordial feeling of pleasure and shelter, the warmth of its finale (clearly linked to the image of breasts with their promise of 'bliss') is fragmented and rearranged in metonymic description and infused with its counter-terms.

The ritualist procedure re-enacts the 'loss of innocence' through intellect. The *vanitas* motif of the skeleton signals the mind's awareness that the end of all bodily pleasure is death. The stress on the dominant creative and perceptive mind of modernism is there, but its power is undermined by the very images it creates. The metonymic woman does not remain fragmented. She rhizomatically grows together again through paradigmatic extension and even manages to infuse the consciously mental images of the skeleton metony (whose references to Donne and Webster stress their intellectual rather than sensual character) with her vitality. The self of the text, so much master of its allusions in the poem's first half, is literally brought to its knees, reduced to a nameless member of a species. The 'our lot' of the poem's penultimate line also includes the reader.

> But our lot crawls between dry ribs
> To keep our metaphysics warm.
>
> (56)

There are still traces of ironic detachment in the humorous final line, but the general impression is that of a preventive ritual turning into the danger it tries to ban, a danger that is also its desire: the return to the mute bliss of the primordial shelter. 'Mute' is important here. Grishkin does not speak and hardly seems to think, whereas Webster has his vision, Donne even knowledge, and the anonymous speaker of the poem his suppositions. Grishkin merely *is*. That makes her so powerful as an undermining imaginary force even in fragmented form. As the goal of desire she represents the death of the poetic utterance which is created exactly out of the experience of *not being*. The modernist circle closes itself again. The utterance that regrets its birth strives to die, but its act of striving keeps it alive, although in fragmented and mutilated form. This is the implication of Abraham and Torok's idea of the endless love-affair of analysand and analyst. Foucault refers to it in his paper on the utterance fighting its own death (Foucault 1963b). Leo Bersani's excellent study of psychoanalysis and art makes it its central point in the discussion of the ultimately masochistic nature of libidinal drives which also finds its expression in the creation and reception of works of art (Bersani 1986: especially 45–7).

The close link between body, ego, and the poetic utterance is discussed by various critics. Robert Rogers' study of metaphor in psychoanalytic terms, although sometimes reductive in its views on poetry, offers an interesting collection of case studies illustrating particular analogies (Rogers 1978). Two cases of fragmented body imagery produced by a schizophrenic girl are particularly interesting when compared to the already discussed Eliot prose poem, 'Hysteria'. They are attempts to overcome symbolically the rift between unity and individuation, expulsion (of the child from the womb, of faeces, and of language) and incorporation (feeding and devouring as well as being devoured, the swallowing of (imaginary) others and the cannibalisation of discourse):

> ... g Milner [a psychoanalyst whose case studies ... cusses appears to her as a picture of a cavity, 'not ... cavity which has some kind of sentience, since ... features of a profile face on its inner boundary ... as teeth-like forms all around it. In fact, could ... ttempt to depict the idea of an anus–vagina as a ... organ; or, to put it in another way, is there not here a pri... itive conception in which mouth, vagina, and anus are all undifferentiated?' . . . . 'Alternatively, the eyes in the middle of the two ovals can be seen as the nipples of two breasts.'
>
> (Rogers 1978: 98)

In the picture of the schizophrenic as well as in Eliot's poem metonymic fragmentation is at work. In both cases, however, the initial fragmentation gives way to a growth of new connections, whose effect in Eliot's poem is not as positive as the analyst's interpretation of the girl's picture suggests. The animated fragments in 'Hysteria', far from being controlled by their percipient, deprive him of identity. He succumbs to the regressive desire to become part of his opposing Other, 'lost finally'. The effect of this loss of identity is a further fragmentation of perception and mutilation of images. The metonymy produces its own echoes and eventually takes over. The seemingly reasserted identity capable of claiming 'I decided that if the shaking of her breasts could be stopped, some of the fragments of the afternoon might be collected, and I concentrated my attention with careful subtlety to this end' (34) is ironic and consequently highly dubious. The conditional form of the statement ('could'/'might'), the hint at limitation ('some of the fragments') and some blatantly contradictory claims (where does concentration and subtlety come in after the literal hysteria of the preceding lines?) disqualify the seemingly collected 'I decided' completely.

This effect of the metonymy is more obvious when it is not presented by an apparently coherent narrator who reifies an Other, but affects the speaker him- or herself. The figure of the possibly raped woman in 'The Fire Sermon', the part of *The Waste Land* that is closely connected with sexuality, is a case in point. As in 'Whispers of Immortality', two metonymies interact, diffuse each other and consequently intensify the metonymic displacement. In this case, the topographic metonymy depicting London as 'Highbury', 'Richmond', 'Kew', and 'Moorgate' (before the image is carried to Margate by the connecting River Thames) is coupled with that of an apparently female narrator (or three voices sharing the same point of view, if one sees them with Eliot as the 'Thames-daughters' analogous to Wagner's *Rheintöchter*) submitting to the sexual advances of an anonymous 'he'. This time, the effect of fragmentation is clear. It leads to the loss of the self: 'Highbury bore me. Richmond and Kew / Undid me' (74). The connection with destruction unveils its violent nature. With what is perhaps a cruel echo of Yeats's line from 'He wishes for the Cloths of Heaven', 'I have spread my dreams under your feet; / Tread softly because you tread on my dreams' (Yeats 1983: 73), the speaker refers to her shattered identity: 'My feet at Moorgate, and my heart / Under my feet' (Eliot 1974: 74).

The metonymy has its counterpart in the imaginary self-destruction of the schizophrenic: 'She saw a figure with arms and legs all over the place, kind of floating, and a breast somewhere' (Rogers 1978: 98). This is analogous to Lacan's descriptions of the 'fragmented body' produced by the individuation of the mirror stage:

> This fragmented body – which term I have also introduced into our system of theoretical references – usually manifests itself in dreams when the movement of the analysis encounters a certain level of aggressive disintegration in the individual. It then appears in the form of disjointed limbs, or of those organs represented in exoscopy, growing wings and taking up arms for intestinal persecutions.
>
> (Lacan 1977a: 5)

In 'The Fire Sermon', the metonymy again produces its own echo: 'I can connect / Nothing with nothing' (74). This outcry also slyly alludes to the constitutive principle of the device itself: the syntagmatic connection of distant signifiers (no things). The metapoetic closure, however, excludes the speaker's identity, and after a final 'Nothing' her utterance ceases for good.

The dislocated voice speaking its own destruction, thus asserting itself in its dissolution and vice versa, identity as its own limit, is a recurring feature of modernist poetry. It will be re-encountered in the philosophy of Heidegger. A final example from Eliot's works will highlight this metapoetic aspect of the metonymy while simultaneously leading to the final trope to be discussed in psychoanalytic terms, the symbol. Tiresias, one of many voices in *The Waste Land*, has, as Maud Ellmann points out, only 'a single walk-on part'. Yet, she continues, he indeed represents the 'osmotic force that makes all the voices of *The Waste Land* melt into one another' (Ellmann 1987: 97). He blurs the borderlines of textual identity while simultaneously asserting it in a complex new shape. In

Tiresias, identity strives towards an all-encompassing paradoxical double nature as absence and presence. For, indeed, as Eliot claims in his notes to the poem, 'What Tiresias *sees*, in fact, is the substance of the poem' (82). Nothing, that is, for Tiresias is blind. He is the representative of all the decentred voices of the poem, decentred because revolving around absence. In his 'personage', as Eliot prefers to call him, the negative effects of the metonymy leave 'nothing'. Tiresias is both metaphor (the act of fusion), metonymy (displaced and fragmented voice), and symbol as the concrete representation of an abstract concept. He represents the modernist impasse, the incurable rift between language and reality that makes him unable to see anything. Yet he sees a lot in the prophetic metaphoric sense, so much that the vision becomes painful, even more so because the gaze is always directed backwards (the internalising strategy is again at work) and inevitably discovers the shadow of the past in the present: 'And I Tiresias have foresuffered all' (72). The utterance continues *ad infinitum*, but only ever repeats what has already been said. Pound's Cino defines his position between 'I have sung' and 'I will sing'. One adds 'forever the same old song' and gets Eliot's Tiresias.

Tiresias' multiple function as an unceasing purveyor of nothing is also reflected in his physical description. Both man and woman, he is not at all the perfect Platonic union. The halves do not complement each other, but only unveil each other's incompleteness: 'throbbing between two lives' (71). In *The Waste Land* Tiresias is already more than old. What the reader gets is a *post-mortem*. The seer has already 'walked among the lowest of the dead' (72). Interesting is the recurring stress on his female breasts. Their connection with distribution, giving, and spilling out, their role as the source of language has already been discussed. Also their fetish-character as the ultimate goal of desire, because they are the primordial means of its fulfilment. In Tiresias' case, the breasts are wrinkled and no longer capable of production. They are even called 'dugs' once. The coupling of attraction and repulsion characteristic of the fetish is evident once more. Potentially a symbol of the union of displaced subject and its bisexual ego-ideal, 'the father in the personal prehistory', Tiresias fails abysmally. Only a shadow himself, and a rather unimpressive one, he indicates that the way back to primordial wholeness is blocked. If *The Waste Land* is a complex question looking for an answer, Tiresias is the hapless Oedipus who knows that the sphinx has no secret. As Ellmann points out:

> Now *The Waste Land*, like any good sphinx, lures the reader into hermeneutics, too: but there is no secret underneath its hugger-muggery. Indeed, Hegel saw the Sphinx as a symbol of the symbolic itself, because it did not know the answer to its own question and *The Waste Land*, too is a riddle to itself.
>
> (Ellmann 1987: 92)

The radical enquiry into the constitution of the self with the help of a symbolic fetish who has no problems in stating his identity (the triple 'I Tiresias' certainly has the character of a productive charm here) is already a wide-reaching, structural step in modernist poems. As the analysis of the poetry of Hopkins and Yeats has shown, often the completion of the second part of the formula 'I –' leads to severe problems. The symbol helps to overcome some of them. By its nature a compound signifier like the metaphor, but one that – unlike the metaphor – transfers and locates meaning directly from one signifier to another, it manages to stabilise the flow of signification at least to some extent. The symbol therefore becomes a more reliable device than metaphor and metonymy, the first necessarily imprecise, the second one unstoppable in its repercussions. Moreover, a symbol is always part of a symbolic system which adds further stabilising weight to a construction employing it.

Tiresias is a symbol in various respects. He represents the merger of masculine and feminine. Furthermore, he stands for the crossing of the barrier between life and death, therefore also for the inevitable return of the past, the dead and suppressed. Related to this, he also embodies the connection and communication between ordinary reality and a higher sphere. He represents the symbolic system of Greek mythology where he is an established character. In an even more archaic sense he is the prototype of the seer (who is often blind), the magician, and the trickster (the latter, as anthropological studies show, often attributed with blurred gender characteristics). The combination makes him a powerful symbol and indeed a practicable point of orientation in the osmotic sliding of signification in Eliot's long poem, although not quite an identity, as Eliot's description as 'not indeed a "character"' indicates.

Yeats also employs symbolic characters to deal with complex issues which in his poetry usually combine personal and general problems. These characters display a strong tendency towards archetypes. Some already possess inherent archetypal status, such as the heroes of Irish mythology, Cuchulain, Oisin, etc., who are part of an established cultural heritage. Other characters are geared towards this mythical status, such as the ubiquitous 'Lover' of Yeats's earlier poems and his counterpart, called 'he' in a move that makes him both anonymous, impersonal and universal.

The 'set forms within the reader's mind' (Riffaterre 1978: 39) that are the locus of quotation and cliché are also the realm of the archetypal symbol. It facilitates identification by the reader. The shadow of tradition, far from threatening, is here a necessary constitutive factor both for the textual identity and for the reader who establishes his position in the act of recognition. Jung puts this as follows:

> The necessary and needful reaction from the collective unconscious expresses itself in archetypally formed ideas. The meeting with oneself is, at first, the meeting with one's shadow. The shadow is a tight passage, a narrow door, whose painful constriction no one is spared who goes down to the deep well. But one must learn to know oneself in order to know who one is. For what comes after the door is, surprisingly enough, a boundless expanse full of unprecedented uncertainty, with apparently no inside and no outside, no above and no below, no here and no there, no mine and no thine, no good and no bad. It is the world of water, where all life floats in suspension: where the realm of the sympathetic system, the soul of everything living, begins; where I am indivisibly this *and* that; where I experience the other in myself and the other-than-myself experiences me.
>
> (Jung 1959, vol. 9: 21–2)

'Death by Water', the shortest section of *The Waste Land* (75), is a perfect illustration of Jung's ideas concerning individuation and loss of identity as interrelated procedures. Tellingly 'Fear death by water' (64) is also the advice of clairvoyante Madame Sosostris to her anonymous customer in the poem. Eliot's long poem is aware of the drastic implications of this self-destructive modernist concept of identity.

Jung is convinced that the collective unconscious is a factual entity which provides the stimulus for the creation of archetypal images and eventually unveils them as inadequate, so that new ones are continually sought (12–13). A similar stimulus will be re-encountered in Nietzsche's drive to create metaphors. The validity of Jung's claim is immaterial for the present study, but not the economic principle embedded in it: the urgency to create images which represent something both personal and universal, and the eventual dissolution or petrifaction of these images when faced with their source and eventual goal. In this process the move of signification from the imaginary to the symbolic manifests itself.

In terms of textual economy, the creation and perfection of symbolic networks eventually leads to their toppling through self-reflection and self-destruction. This happens when the systems reflect back on themselves and question both their material and their premises, in the case of poetry language and textual identity. If one described the archetypal move in Freudian terms (and I would suggest considering the Jungian concept a substructure of the Freudian system rather than a complementary one), the impersonal collective unconscious is the projective wish for the wholeness of the maternal womb. It is the source of all signification – out of whose security the phallic power of the symbol emerges. The perfect universal symbol would be the phallic mother, and just like her it proves unattainable.

If the metaphor corresponds to retention and hiding and the metonymy is the equivalent of distribution, dissolution and speaking out, the symbol combines features of both. Structurally a stable metaphor, so to speak, it is one that blatantly displays its meaning. In contrast to the 'anal' metaphor and metonymy, it is indeed the proudly displayed phallus of signification. In this respect, it is telling that its exhibition is often coupled with hints at its possible removal: castration. The dialectic of absence and presence does not spare the structure that claims the strongest presence of those hitherto discussed.

Yeats's early poem 'The Cap and Bells' employs the archetypal characters of jester and young queen as its protagonists. The jester represents the masculine, but his position as a sexually active being is curtailed by his role. He occupies a position similar to children, madmen and eunuchs. His social status is inferior. The young queen, on the other hand, is both sexually mature and in an unattainable position of power. These two symbolic characters are metonymically dissolved into smaller symbolic units. The jester first becomes his soul, then his heart, eventually the central symbol of the poem, his cap and bells. The latter is the most evident depiction of what the more abstract descriptions hint at. Rising upward and standing straight, red and quivering, they describe an erection. The cap and bells are a symbol of the male genitals.

The young queen is in turn described by metonymically employed symbols relating to her body and, more and more explicitly, her genitals, too. The settings connected with her are garden and house, conquered wilderness and epitome of civilisation, inhabited in the Victorian imagination by woman, but governed by man. The queen, half-asleep, is first implicitly equalled with the garden 'fallen still' (64) (note the promise in the ambiguity of the verb). Then the masculine symbol approaches the first vaginal threshold, the windowsill, but is rejected. Her genital symbols, suddenly solid and magnified into 'heavy casement' with 'latches' (64), bar the way. The jester's second attempt, this time directed at the more conventional, yet equally vaginal door, is also defeated, this time with a fan, an object whose folded shape resembles the female genitals.

Only the – again archetypal – third attempt is successful. Three is a traditionally masculine number referring to the male genitals; the symbolic network of the poem is very dense indeed. The queen permits the masculine symbol access to her body. The barred thresholds open, and sexual intercourse is clearly implied in 'her red lips sang them [the cap and bells] a love-song / Till stars grew out of the air' (65). Eventually the poem ends in the post-coital calm of 'the quiet of love in her feet' (65) which forms a symbolic bracket with the initial erotic fantasy of the jester, the 'quiet and light footfall' (64).

This admittedly crude survey of the symbols in Yeats's poem helps to highlight features of psychoanalytic interest which ultimately relate back to the poem's textuality and act as metapoetic devices. To make these pieces fit, two central issues of the text that have so far been ignored must be added to its discussion. The most important one is the ambiguity of the jester's conquest: he achieves his aim through his destruction. He sacrifices his cap and bells and then dies. His castrational death may also be read in a positive light, 'die' as an ancient euphemism for orgasm. It indicates nonetheless that the possession of the phallus is the necessary prerequisite of identity. This, very importantly, is also the precondition of the poetic utterance. For the second hitherto ignored feature is the curious description of the masculine symbols: both soul and heart (traditionally the twin realms of identity) are endowed with a (once more phallic) tongue. Their intrusion is that of an utterance; the erection is that of a symbolic system – which in turn refers to the poem itself. Paradoxically, though, the aim of the phallic symbolic system is exactly its own destruction, its loss in the embrace of the Other. The symbols' aim and end lies in the womb of the imaginary. The identity of the jester reaches its (literal and metaphoric) climax when his song is taken over by the Other and melts into what Kristeva calls the undifferentiated *chora*, the relics of the imaginary in the symbolic sphere:[12] 'They set up a noise like crickets, / A chattering wise and sweet.' In Lacan's words, the subject is constituted by the desire *of* the Other (with all the ambiguity inherent in the preposition), or: 'The Other is, therefore, the locus in which is constituted the I who speaks to him who hears, that which is said by the one being already the reply, the other deciding to hear it whether the one has or has not spoken' (Lacan 1977a: 141).

The creation of symbolic systems out of archetypal images which then, in turn, become threatened by dissolution into the imaginary again is a recurring feature in Yeats's works. It has already been discussed in the analysis of 'To the Rose Upon the Rood of Time' with its ambiguous lines

> Come near, come near, come near – Ah leave me still
> A little space for the rose-breath to fill!
>
> (31)

The issue is even more explicit in 'Fergus and the Druid' where 'knowledge' eventually means the annihilation of symbolic certainty and sliding into the chaos of the imaginary. Its result is the loss of identity: 'But now I have grown nothing, knowing all' (33). Jung believes this to be the essential danger of human consciousness:

> The unconscious no sooner touches us than we *are* it – we become unconscious of ourselves. This is the age-old danger, instinctively known and feared by primitive man, who himself stands so very close to this pleroma. His consciousness is still uncertain, wobbling on its feet. It is still childish, having just emerged from the primal waters. A wave of the unconscious may easily roll over it, and then he forgets who he was and does things that are strange to him. Hence primitives are afraid of uncontrolled emotions, because consciousness breaks down under them and gives way to possession. All man's strivings have therefore been directed towards the consolidation of consciousness. This was the purpose of rite and dogma; they were dams and walls to keep back the dangers of the unconscious, the 'perils of the soul'.
>
> (Jung 1959, vol. 9: 22; 'perils of the soul'. English in the German original)

If this is a primitive notion, it is also one that pervades the most sophisticated expressions of human creativity both as desire and fear. As Foucault states: 'Perhaps language delineates the realm of experience in which the speaking subject, rather than expressing itself, exposes itself, thrusts itself against its own temporality and finds itself referred back to its death with each word' (Foucault 1963a: 768; my translation).

Exposing rather than expressing, showing oneself in symbolic shape as one's phallus in order to rise from the chaos of the imaginary – only to be reminded of one's inevitable dissolution in the same – is a formula that fits Yeats's poems as well as modernist poetry in general.

The impossible utterance refuses to die, but in order to prevent this, death only ever produces mirror images of death's grinning face. The distancing that keeps fear of old age and mortality at bay in external depictions, such as the 'battered kettle' (194) in 'The Tower' and the simultaneously phallic and morbid 'tattered coat upon a stick' (193) in 'Sailing to Byzantium', as well as the desperate hyperbolic formulas 'Now shall I make my soul' (199) (in 'The Tower') and 'Man has created death' (234) (in 'Death') are such symbolic mirrors.

They are the *Fort* [gone] move in the *Fort-Da* game of symbolic representation. But as every *Fort* provokes yet another *Da*, so the poems cannot escape the shadow of their own destruction, which is nothing but the echo of their creation. While characterised by a disillusionment concerning symbolic certainties, modernist poems never completely abandon symbolic systems, one of which is that of symbolic identity. Jung describes this impasse as follows:

> Is it becoming a problem today? Shall we be able to put on, like a new suit of clothes, ready-made symbols grown on foreign soil, saturated with foreign blood, spoken in a foreign tongue, nourished by a foreign culture, interwoven with foreign history, and so resemble a beggar who wraps himself in kingly raiment, a king who disguises himself as a beggar? No doubt this is possible. Or is there something in ourselves that commands us to go in for no mummeries, but perhaps even to sew our garment ourselves? . . . Anyone who has lost the historical symbols and cannot be satisfied with substitutes is certainly in a very difficult position today: before him there yawns the void, and he turns away from it in horror. What is worse, the vacuum gets filled with absurd political and social ideas, which one and all are distinguished by their spiritual bleakness.
>
> (Jung 1959, vol. 9: 14–15)

Yeats discusses the dilemma of the symbolic technique in poems like 'The Circus Animals' Desertion', in which symbols are uncovered as what they are: set-pieces employed as mirrors by a textual identity that needs them for its own constitution. Yet not even exposing their status overcomes their influence and impasses. The uncovering agency, the textual identity, is a symbol itself. Its dissolution would affect the poetic utterance radically. It would indeed be the end of a coherent and closed articulation. Although permanently caught in the dialectic of absence and presence, *Fort* and *Da*, identity in its tensional and liminal state is never completely abandoned. The cord connecting the playing child and the reel representing the mother becomes a borderline of the poetics of modernism.

5. SIGNS OF DESIRE / THE DESIRE OF SIGNS

> *Le Sexe est un charnier de Signes.*
> *Le Signe est un Sexe décharné.*
> [The sex is a grave of signs. The sign is a skeletised sex.]
>
> (Baudrillard 1976: 154)

If the initial catastrophe of individuation spawns both the ego as the isolated body and the sign, their nature as twins is reflected in their similar structures as well as their unceasing attempts to reach for each other, for the one to inscribe itself in its counterpart.[13] Their birthmarks are absence, lack, and the desire for its completion. But just as the body cannot return to its (either prenatal or preconscious) wholeness, the sign never manages to establish a stable connection between its components, signifier and signified. The effect of the body's attempt to recover totality is narcissism. In textual terms, the striving to stabilise the 'two non-overlapping networks of relation' that signifier and signified represent (Lacan 1977a: 126) only ever leads to the production of new signifiers in a process that defers rather than establishes what it tries to achieve: coherence, meaning, and identity.

Hopkins's poems, with their strategy of lining up signifier after signifier in their attempt at an impossible connection with an evasive signified, are examples of this futile yet essential urge of signification.

> Earnest, earthless, equal, attuneable, ' vaulty, voluminous,
> . . . stupendous
> Evening strains to be tíme's vást, ' womb-of-all, home-of-all,
> hearse-of-all night.
>
> (97)

The beginning of 'Spelt from Sibyl's Leaves' illustrates this urge to return to – explicitly – the womb. Here, as in Yeats's 'The Cap and Bells', the appeal of the mother appears in Oedipal guise, the mother as a phallic one.

> Her fond yellow hornlight wound to the west, ' her wild
> hollow hoarlight hung to the height
>
> (97)

The play on 'horn' and 'hoar' (which phonetically resembles 'whore'; note also its vaginal adjective 'hollow') is evident. But the lines also exhibit stylistically the struggle they depict. The seven adjectives of lines 1 and 2 fail to describe the 'Evening' they precede. 'Strains' is the first of many verbs in the poem representing painful activity met with resistance. The list continues with 'wound', 'hung', 'overbend', 'steepèd', 'páshed', 'Disremembering', 'dísmémbering', 'whélms', 'wind/Off', 'grínd'. They all describe the Sisyphean labour of signification

> . . . which proves never to be resolved into a pure indication of the real, but always refers back to another signification. That is to say, the signification is realized only on the basis of a grasp of things in their totality.
>
> Its origin cannot be grasped at the level at which it usually assures itself of the redundancy proper to it, for it always proves to be in excess over the things that it leaves floating within it.
>
> (Lacan 1977a: 126)

[. . .] Lét life, wáned, ah lét life wind
Off hér once skéined stained véined varíety ' upon, áll on twó
   spools; párt, pen, páck
Now her áll in twó flocks, twó folds – black, white; ' right,
   wrong; reckon but, reck but, mind
But thése two; wáre of a wórld where bút these ' twó tell, each
   off the óther [. . .]

(98)

'Spelt from Sibyl's Leaves' represents what Lacan calls 'the congenital gap presented by man's real being in his natural relations, and by the resumption, for a sometimes ideographical, but also a phonetic, not to say grammatical, usage, of imaginary elements that appear fragmented in this gap' (Lacan 1977a: 127).

Yet in this gap, 'Where, selfwrung, selfstrung, sheathe- and shelterless, ' thóughts agaínst thoughts ín groans grínd' (98), identity finds its only possible realm of constitution. The self that cannot come into being without being called by an Other cries out for the attention of this Other, but only hears itself: 'self ín self steepèd' (97). The self that is not quite itself strives towards itself. In Freud's terms, *Wo Es war, soll Ich werden*, not, as the English translation suggests, 'where id was, there ego shall be', but in Lacan's more adequate interpretation: 'it is my duty that I should come into being' (Lacan 1977a: 128–9) with all its paradoxical implications. The modernist self desires its own end, as the various attempts at impersonality show. But to achieve this end, the self has to constitute itself first. Self-destruction falls together with self-creation, modernism's *machine célibataire*, Pound's hammering of the phallic self, Eliot's sibyl surviving into the present by repeating her death wish, Yeats's creation of both his soul and its death, and

Hopkins's recurring references to the death of the nuns in *The Wreck of the Deutschland* as birth.

This realm of creation and destruction of the self is language, as *The Wreck of the Deutschland* indicates when it introduces – seemingly only superficially motivated – the feast of the immaculate conception which follows the night of the shipwreck in stanza 30:

> But here was heart-throe, birth of a brain,
> Word, that heard and kept thee and uttered thee outright.
>
> (61)

The word as creator refers to the beginning of the gospel according to John, but also to the creation *sui generis* of modernist poetry. Easily overlooked, however, is the self-destructive implication of the lines: the 'Word, that heard' must be one that is – at least momentarily – silent, i.e. not a word at all. It is first an absence, then a retention ('and kept thee'), finally a distribution ('and uttered thee outright'). It unveils the contradictory yet also complementary strategies of modernist poems. But if this locus of the constitution of the I – Lacan's Other – 'extends as far into the subject as the laws of speech' (Lacan 1977a: 141), it is also subject to the rules of speech and its pitfalls: arbitrariness, ambiguity, and the possible failure of communication. 'Me? or me that fought him? O which one? is it each one?' (100) asks Hopkins's '(Carrion Comfort)', unable to answer the central question concerning its own textual identity – which nevertheless makes this enquiry.

Hopkins's poems abound with desperate appeals addressed to an Other, all of them unanswered. The tragedy is brought to a point in one of the 'Terrible Sonnets', 'I wake and feel the fell of dark, not day':

> [. . .] And my lament
> Is cries countless, cries like dead letters sent
> To dearest him that lives alas! away.
>
> (101)

Christ, imaginary lover, or both, the addressee is the Other whose desire, expressed in a reply, would ensure the constitution of identity, but whose silence leads to its incompleteness and eventual loss:

> The lost are like this, and their scourge to be
> As I am mine, their sweating selves; but worse.
>
> (101)

The insight that the subject is characterised by lack, yet the way to the appropriation of the Other – necessary for the completion of this self and guarantee of the reality of the signs it employs –

is barred, marks the essential crux of both identity and the sign in modernist poetry. Out of this basic deficiency evolves the desire of modernism for wholeness, control, and totality, because, as Lacan reminds us, 'the signification is realized only on the basis of a grasp of things in their totality' (Lacan 1977a: 126). The greatest endeavour of modernism merely reflects its attempt to control its very basis. Yet the control it simulates is only that of the signifier. 'The signifier alone guarantees the theoretical coherence of the whole as a whole' (126). The adjective 'theoretical' is crucial here. Adding signifier to signifier only creates a layer of *text*, the plane of the 'signifying quest' in which 'I dedicate myself to becoming what I am, to coming into being. I cannot doubt that even if I lose myself in the process, I am in that process' (Lacan 1977a: 165–6). Modernist poetry, caught between the refusal of its own material and the desire for what it cannot attain, true being, constitutes identity negatively as a continual absence along 'the rails', as Lacan puts it, 'eternally stretching forth towards the *desire for something else*' (Lacan 1977a: 167), the rails, that is, of its own never-ending utterance.

NOTES

1. In Murray M. Schwartz's words: 'The analyst's wording ("spelling out!") of this experience simultaneously articulates a difference and makes a difference. The patient can then perceive a difference for the first time. Even so simple an interjection as, "I see!" implies both difference and distance. The interpretive wording bridges the gap between subjectivities by symbolizing their relationship. The past becomes present to consciousness for the first time as it becomes consciously past for the first time. The interpretive words are a real illusion; they create what is there by substitution' (Hartmann, 1978: 9).
2. 'The ego ideal is therefore the heir of the Oedipus complex, and thus it is also the expression of the most powerful impulses and most important libidinal vicissitudes of the id. By setting up this ego ideal, the ego has mastered the Oedipus complex and at the same time placed itself in subjection to the id. Whereas the ego is essentially the representative of the external world, of reality, the super-ego stands in contrast to it as the representative of the internal world, of the id. Conflicts between the ego and the ideal will, as we are now prepared to find, ultimately reflect the contrast between what is real and what is psychical, between the external world and the internal world' (Freud 1973–86, vol. 11: 376).
3. The central ideas concerning the role of Yeats in Eliot's *Four Quartets* derive from Sabine Roth's essay 'Eliot Comforted: The Yeatsian

Presence in *Four Quartets*' (1993).

4. The *Concise Oxford Dictionary* explains 'stetson' as 'slouch hat with very wide brim and high crown [f. J.B. Stetson, Amer. hat-maker d. 1906]'. Mylae is the site of the battle between the Romans and the Carthaginians (260 BC) in the First Punic War (Southam 1968: 77).
5. I am using Foucault's description of discursive formations somewhat illicitly here to describe in a slightly provocative way the formation of the identity of texts.
6. Or images. The passage is taken from a section entitled 'Speeches in Dreams' (Freud 1973–86, vol. 4: 544–53).
7. A useful discussion is in Holenstein 1976: 143–51.
8. 'The immediate necessity is to tabulate A LIST OF DONT'S for those beginning to write verses' (Pound 1954: 4).
9.

> This development is experienced as a temporal dialectic that decisively projects the formation of the individual into history. The *mirror stage* is a drama whose internal thrust is precipitated from insufficiency to anticipation – and which manufactures for the subject, caught up in the lure of spatial identification, the succession of phantasies that extends from a fragmented body-image to a form of its totality that I shall call orthopaedic – and, lastly, to the assumption of the armour of an alienating identity, which will mark with its rigid structure the subject's entire mental development.
>
> (Lacan 1977a: 4)

10. The *Concise Oxford Dictionary* reveals its paradoxical nature in the definition 'word of which only one instance is recorded'. The recording, of course, instantly doubles the utterance.
11. The 'Fort–Da' game was observed by Freud as the ritual of a little boy who used it as a means of coping with the inexplicable absences and returns of his mother. He threw a reel out of his cot and babbled words that Freud interpreted as 'Fort' (gone). When he recaptured the reel with the string attached to it, he expressed pleasure with a sound resembling 'Da' (there). Freud took this ritual to be a model of both individuation and relationships (Freud 1973–86, vol. 11: 283–7).
12.

> I believe that this archaic semiotic modality that I have referred to as infantile babblings, in order to give it clearer definition, is a modality which bears the most archaic memories of our link with the maternal body – Of the dependence that all of us have *vis-à-vis* the maternal body, and where a sort of self-eroticism is indissociable from the experience of the (m)other. We repress the vocal or gestural inscription of this experience under our subsequent acquisition and this is an important condition for autonomy.
>
> (Kristeva in Rice, Waugh, 1989: 130)

13. Michel Foucault's work studies the ways in which the body acts as a writing-board for cultural discourses, from his early *Discipline and Punish* onwards to his final work, *The History of Sexuality*. The present study is concerned with an aspect of the other side, the sign, and the ways in which features of the body and the self are mirrored in it.

CHAPTER SEVEN

Towards an Economy of the Modernist Poem

> *Nous n'avons qu'une ressource avec la mort: faire de l'art avant elle.*
> [We only have one means of coping with death: to make art before it.]
>
> (René Char)

1. THE TEXT AS AN ECONOMY OF MEANING

Little could be less obvious than a close relation between poetic texts and economy. So apparently designed to be non-pragmatic, non-functional in an everyday sense, poems can in very few cases claim to be statements on distribution, exchange, and value.

The impression changes, however, when the poems are viewed internally as a system that establishes a relation between its elements, a structure of equations and disjunctions, comparisons and incompatibilities. In this respect, poetic texts work like economic systems. They display surplus and shortage, place value on certain aspects and devalue others, shift the balance of significance, and transform elements without intrinsic value – words – into symbolic value in a similar way to that in which advanced economic systems transform labour into money or its equivalents.

The comparison of modernist poetry and psychoanalysis has revealed comparable features, although these concerned the identity of texts, mirror-images or counter-concepts of a psyche whose shortcomings and internal ruptures found equivalents in textual mechanisms. If the above discussion covered the illocutionary aspect of modernist poetry, i.e. the question 'what do the texts convey about their own conception, their own "selves"?', the seemingly more abstract enquiry into their economy is interested in their perlocutionary attitude. What do the texts try to achieve as texts? In this respect, the comparison of the techniques of the four authors covered by this study will reveal a consequent development of some economic theorems. These can be detected in the analysis of economy as an underlying theme of poems, a view which eventually merges with an evaluation of economy as *form*, following one of the fundamental ideas of the present study, that of the transformation of form into theme in modernist poems. The results of their economic strategies will present themselves as borderlines of the aesthetics of modernism.

2. THE STABILITY OF THE MIRROR

Hopkins's poems display the modernist tensions between a mimetic approach and a growing awareness of construction. Starting from the assumption that the endless variety of natural phenomena cannot adequately be grasped in language, i.e. from an idea of scarcity of poetic means, the power of signification shifts increasingly into the focus of his works (see 'Spelt From Sibyl's Leaves'). It simultaneously introduces a notion of entropy affecting reality, a draining away of its force, essence, and value. Even those of Hopkins's poems which display few signs of self-reflection can be regarded as complex discussions of 'economic' issues. Economy is here related to the polarity of appropriation and distancing observed in the analysis of the sign in Hopkins's poetry.

A pair of related sonnets, 'The Lantern Out of Doors' and the later 'The Candle Indoors', illustrate the central mechanisms of subject–object relations whose adequate description is one of economy. In 'The Lantern Out of Doors', the reader is faced with an impersonal situation and a vague setting in a 'Sometimes' which is hardly made more specific as 'along the night'. It only takes two more lines, however, to make the text both concrete and personal. Via the possessive 'our' the poem focusses on a narratorial 'I'. It also introduces the crucial setting 'outside versus inside' which reappears in reversed form in its companion piece.

Sometimes a lantern moves along the night,
That interests our eyes. And who goes there?
I think; where from and bound, I wonder, where,
With, all down darkness wide, his wading light?

(71)

The speaker is inside, watching the light of a lantern outside, until it is seemingly lost in the darkness. The second quatrain of the poem transforms the beam of light produced by the lantern into a symbol of man's physical and spiritual beauty.[1] It penetrates ordinary reality (described in the negative terms 'our much-thick and marsh air') like rain.

Men go by me whom either beauty bright
In mould or mind or what not else makes rare:
They rain against our much-thick and marsh air
Rich beams, till death or distance buys them quite.

(71)

The poem's concern with values becomes apparent when the adjectives 'rare', describing men of quality, and 'rich', which accompanies the beams, contrast with the worthlessness implied in 'marsh' (indicating land of no value). The paradigm is then extended with the unusual formula 'till death or distance *buys* them quite' (my emphasis). Apparently, human qualities are not simply lost in the baseness of ordinary life; they are sold, exchanged at too low a price. Thus the insistence on consumption that the poem displays by repeating the formula in slightly altered shape:

Death or distance soon consumes them: wind,
What most I may eye after, be in at the end
I cannot, and out of sight is out of mind.

(71)

The lines can be read as autobiographical statements.[2] Yet they are also related to the ambiguous role of distancing and loss in Hopkins's poems. As has been pointed out in the discussion of distancing as a mode of signification, it is a necessary prerequisite of textual identity which thus becomes part of a dialectic resembling the Freudian *Fort-Da* game. Put in a simplified formula: I exist, because there is something outside of me, distant (temporally and spatially) and eventually lost. Its implications for identity as a liminal state have been discussed in the preceding chapter. The detected desire for completion through the Other is depicted accurately in Hopkins's lines 'What most I may eye after, be in at the end / I cannot'. They also describe the wish of the speaker to belong, to 'be in', although this is exactly the place where he is, at least physically. The verb 'wind', attached to death and distance, hints at the physical intensity with which this separation of subject and Other is experienced.[3]

But how does the poem respond in economic terms when faced with this loss that cannot be prevented? It refuses to accept it and invokes Christ who rescues those nearly lost and gathers them in his care. This reflects the Christian – and specifically Catholic – doctrine that all evil is outbalanced by God's grace which is granted indiscriminately of personal merit.

> Christ minds: Christ's interest, what to avow or amend
>   There, éyes them, heart wánts, care haúnts, foot fóllows kínd,
> Their ránsom, théir rescue, ánd first, fást, last friénd.
>
> (71)

Care and responsibility belong to a medieval concept of economy which is closed and non-expansive. Redistribution happens hierarchically. All goods are loans, and their use is granted in exchange for services and dependency towards their owner: the aristocracy for material goods, God and His representative, the Church, for spiritual ones.

Although Hopkins's poem follows this religiously motivated pattern, the terms employed in its description stem from a different period and economic background. They are those of mercantilism.[4] Christ's 'interest' is in the centre of the poem. To secure it, he must be a clever investor with explicit demands and a sometimes unpleasant presence ('care haunts'), paying the necessary 'ransom'. Even though 'The Lantern Out of Doors' tries to present a spiritual ideal untainted by materialist or even (proto-)capitalist notions, it cannot help but display a knowledge of the dominant economic principles of its time. This becomes a problem when Hopkins's poems have to position themselves inside an economic model.

'The Candle Indoors', the companion piece to the above poem, is an example of a text reflecting its own status, its value. Now the speaker, clearly present from line 1, is outside, exposed to 'night's blear-all black'. The tempting light is inside, a candle in a window.

> Some candle clear burns somewhere I come by.
> I muse at how its being puts blissful back
> With yellowy moisture mild night's blear-all black,
> Or to-fro tender trambeams truckle at the eye.

By that window what task what fingers ply,
I plod wondering, a-wanting, just for lack
Of answer the eagerer a-wanting Jessy or Jack
There / God to aggrándise, God to glorify. –

(81)

Once more the distance helps to identify the position of the speaker more clearly. In spite of being in the dark and, one assumes, in a much less comfortable position than that inside the house, he knows where he stands and has time to muse. Even 'plod' indicates, besides laborious work, that he has a task. The bright window, on the other hand, is 'somewhere', the candle 'some', i.e. non-specific, without a clear identity.

Nevertheless it is again its light that is attributed with positive qualities. 'Clear', 'blissful', 'mild', and 'tender' are its characteristics, while the speaker is, as in 'The Candle Out of Doors', 'a-wanting', suffering from an outspoken lack. In a complex act of deferral, the speaker's lack, his desire to know who or what is inside the brightened window, is projected on to the woman or man he suspects there and becomes the wish that they worship God in the same way he does. In psychological terms, a sublimation happens which fulfils libidinal urges by integrating the desired object into the desiring subject, by making it like him in an act of eventually narcissistic identification. In economic terms, a potential loss is prevented by channelling the expenditure (once more of light as the equivalent of human value) into the transcendental resources of God which are thus 'aggrándise[d]'. Yet the poem does not end there. In a dramatic reversal, a voice suddenly appears which, apparently from inside the house, calls to the person outside and asks him in. Or is it the speaker himself who turns his wish that people worship God into action and starts sermonising – using various biblical allusions for his argument?

Come you indoors, come home; your fading fire
Mend first and vital candle in close heart's vault:
You there are master, do your own desire;

What hinders? Are you beam-blind, yet to a fault
In a neighbour deft-handed? Are you that liar
And, cast by conscience out, spendsavour salt?

(81)

If the first assumption is correct, an act of self-criticism happens which places the speaker's value, his 'fading fire', against the 'clear' candle, i.e. weakness and exhaustion versus moral brilliance. It shows that behind the missionary zeal of the speaker of the first half lies a personality uncertain of its merits. If the second interpretation is more adequate, a rift appears within the speaker's attitude. It shows that the apparent attraction of the light disguises some ambivalence: fear that it may unveil his imperfections, or a contradictory nature of the light itself which brightens the night, but is also capable of blinding. (One ought to remember that in Hopkins's poem 'To what serves Mortal Beauty', beauty also distracts and endangers.)

Although 'The Candle Indoors' favours the first reading (the 'plod' of its first half and the 'fading fire' of the second, among other hints, point at the identity of the addresser of part one and the addressee of part two), the text offers no definite solution. This, together with the sheer aggressiveness of its final accusations, creates a sombre ending which, in economic terms, opens up the neat enclosure of its first part and hints at the possibility of total exclusion and loss. 'Spendsavour salt', a reference to the Sermon on the Mount (where, significantly, the image of the 'salt of the Earth' is followed by that of the 'light of the world'), Matthew 5: 13 (MacKenzie 1981: 120), indicates utter worthlessness. What has started as an orthodox exclamation turns back on itself. In the final consequence, the poem accuses itself of self-righteousness and thus moral depravity. In the context of the entire corpus of Hopkins's works, where the problem of artistic production as hubris is continually present, this outlines a crux which marks the beginning of a new, namely the modernist aesthetic. There, the work of art tries something it cannot achieve, knowing that by its failure it admits its superfluous status, but by succeeding it destroys the premises of its own production.

What Hopkins's poems discuss in their imagery and the miniature dramas of their plots corresponds to their structural premises, the way they deal with and estimate their material. Language is still regarded as essentially mimetic, as capable of depicting reality. Ideally, there is a one-to-one relation between the phenomena of reality and the terms language provides to illustrate and mirror the former. This perfectly outbalanced system is never abandoned as an ideal in Hopkins's works. It denotes a stable economy without one-sided increase and, even more importantly, without any waste either. The most elaborate example of the force with which his poetry clings to it is 'That Nature is a Heraclitean Fire and of the comfort of the Resurrection'. This poem counters possible expense ('Man, how fast his firedint, ' his mark on mind, is gone!' (105)) with the absolute stability of the 'immortal diamond' (106) representing Christ. It strikes today's analyst as traditionalist in its religious implications, as naïve and anachronistic even in Hopkins's age. Yet the analysis of the evolution of modernist poetry below will reveal that in its most refined developments a return to a very similar system of stability takes place.

When faced with the danger of producing works that fall visibly short of their ideal, works in which either the constructive principle takes over or the construction is unveiled as deficient compared to God's grandiose creation, as waste, Hopkins's poems opt for silence, the termination of the poetic utterance. His seven years of poetic inactivity before the writing of *The Wreck of the Deutschland* can be seen in this light. The inevitability of this outcome is already sketched in his earliest works. 'The Habit of Perfection', for instance, illustrates in rather paradoxical eloquence the need for ultimate renunciation and reduction which entails the abstinence from poetic production:

> Elected Silence, sing to me
> And beat upon my whorlèd ear,
> Pipe me to pastures still and be
> The music that I care to hear.
>
> Shape nothing, lips; be lovely-dumb:
> It is the shut, the curfew sent
> From there where all surrenders come
> Which only makes you eloquent.
>
> (31)

'The Alchemist in the City' is an even more interesting case in point. Alchemy, the transformation of base metals into gold, is a potent symbol of artificial creation. As will become evident in the following section, this creation – in textual terms of symbolic reality or realities – is one escape from the impasses brought to the surface when the mimetic model collapses and the rift between language and reality becomes unsurmountable. In Hopkins's poems, however, the alchemist produces nothing. Static in the face of an ever-changing world, he is aware of *wasting* his life by attempting an impossible discovery.

> My window shews the travelling clouds,
> Leaves spent, new seasons, alter'd sky,
> The making and the melting crowds:
> The whole world passes; I stand by.
>
> They do not waste their meted hours,
> But men and masters plan and build:
> I see the crowning of their towers,
> And happy promises fulfill'd.
>
> (24)

He is a strange alchemist who knows that the teachings of his profession are unsound, and one cannot help but wonder what keeps him locked in his tower, tied to a thankless task, when all his desire is the freedom of the wilderness and eventual death.

> And then I hate the most that lore
> That holds no promise of success;
> Then sweetest seems the houseless shore,
> Then free and kind the wilderness,
>
> Or ancient mounds that cover bones,
> Or rocks where rockdoves do repair
> And trees of terebinth and stones
> And silence and a gulf of air.
>
> There on a long and squarèd height
> After the sunset I would lie,
> And pierce the yellow waxen light
> With free long looking, ere I die.
>
> (25–6)

The question can be answered if one takes the alchemist to be an allegory of the poet on the borderline of a new aesthetic, aware of the collapse of the old certainties of his craft, yet unwilling to leave them behind.

3. ARTIFICIAL CREATION: SYMBOLIC VALUES

Talking of religion with reference to Yeats is a thankless task. His poems offer a hotchpotch of beliefs, an eclectic mixture of faiths and fibs. Yet the intellectual climate that influences his *oeuvre* and determines its attachment to and struggle with symbolism rests on premises which can ultimately be traced back to the Reformation.

In its attempt to fight the increasing worldliness of faith, Protestantism separated reality and the sacred and denied an access of the first to the latter. Saints, relics and holy images had to go, and the main principle of Catholicism, the belief in the transubstantiation, the actual transformation of the host into Christ's body through the sacramental formula, i.e. *language*, was denied. This liberated everyday life from religious constraints and made, most importantly, the development of capitalism, the uninhibited creation of wealth independent of religious scruples, possible (Tawney 1926; Weber 1930; Bataille 1988: 124–7). Yet it also robbed language of its power to partake in a transcendental reality and reduced its status thoroughly (Weber 1930: 104–5, 117, 149). This remained acceptable as long as the products of language, literary works, found an alternative realm in the bourgeois world of commodities. But only as long as this world provided coherent explanations of its premises, an unbroken set of paradigms. This started displaying cracks when from the mid-nineteenth century onwards the ever-increasing speed of industrial capitalism continually removed those traditional principles that were in its way. Furthermore, the scientific developments that preceded or followed in its track shook the established certainties of the ruling bourgeoisie. Darwin, Marx and Freud are the unholy trinity in this respect.

Literature, hitherto only a more or less ornamental means of underlining accepted doctrines, was suddenly called for as a rescuing force which had to provide alternative truths. Artificial production, already the long-established mode of capitalist economy but frowned upon in the arts, became not only acceptable but a necessity when the toppling of truths created a desire (and a market) for artificial ones. Phenomena such as the rise of spiritualism and occult sciences, but also the renewed interest in Catholicism, the vogue for everything Oriental and exotic as well as the search for mythical Germanic or Celtic roots can be seen in this light. In this intellectual climate the works of W.B. Yeats matured.

At first introduced in a subtle way that still adheres to traditional models, the early poem 'The Lover tells of the Rose in his Heart' illustrates the shift from a mimetic approach to one that detaches language from reality. It literally dreams up a better reality inside subjective imagination and thus ultimately in language.

> All things uncomely and broken, all things worn out and old,
> The cry of a child by the roadway, the creak of a lumbering
>   cart,
> The heavy steps of the ploughman, splashing the wintry
>   mould,
> Are wronging your image that blossoms a rose in the deeps of
>   my heart.
>
> (56)

The comparison between sordid reality and the better variety found in love is an old literary topic. The decisive shift in the above poem is its professed aim to *remake* reality inside its own sphere in the shape of a symbol:

The wrong of unshapely things is a wrong too great to be
  told;
I hunger to build them anew and sit on a green knoll apart,
With the earth and the sky and the water, re-made, like
  a casket of gold
For my dreams of your image that blossoms a rose in
  the deeps of my heart.

(56)

The 'casket of gold' is an early example of Yeats's symbolic representations of the work of art. Its implications are threefold and determine the significance of the symbol throughout Yeats's career. They also apply to every form of symbolic approach in modernist poetry. First, gold represents unquestionable value. The consequent implication that the work of art, here the poem, is valuable, should not be taken for granted. As has been stated, redefining the status of the work of art is one of the aims of the symbolic approach. Secondly, gold stands for immutability. Faced with the collapse of certainties, value must be sought in things which do not change, do not succumb to the seemingly arbitrary shifts of reality. This becomes even more evident in the artificial (and also golden) nightingale in the much later 'Byzantium' poems. There the production of the steadfast symbol is motivated by a rather different emotion from romantic love: fear of death.

The third implication of the 'golden casket' shows the economic ideal of the symbol: it is still an economy of keeping together, one that knows no expenditure. The extended paradigm of 'casket' includes both the money-box and the coffin. It provides the possibility of creation of wealth, of increase. At the same time it keeps its creation in its own realm. The analogies to metaphor and symbol in a psychoanalytic view are obvious. While being the proudly displayed symbol of value, the casket is also the metaphor inside which creation takes place, but which keeps the created in its place, prevents a significatory overflow, expense and loss. If one accepts the undertone of death in 'casket', one could argue with Derrida that the metaphor keeps even its own end in its enclosed sphere: 'Metaphor, then, always carries its death within itself' (Derrida 1982: 271). It will become evident below that this multiple face of the modernist symbol mirrors the capitalist myth of creation of wealth out of nothing (the economic *machine célibataire*) as well as its repressed borderline, Bataille's *part maudite* (Bataille 1967), what he calls the ultimate luxury and waste: death.

To sum up: a shift takes place that devalues objective reality and in turn reinvests language with 'eternal' merit in the shape of subjective imaginary creation. Two major problems that Yeats's later poems have to tackle are produced by this move. First, although reality is downgraded, it still acts as the source of inspiration. The mimetic model is not entirely overcome. Reality is only 're-made', not created as autonomous and new. Secondly, the stress on individual imagination brings with it a tendency to passivity in the face of external change – which the above poem treats ambivalently without taking a clear stand. '[B]uild them anew and sit on a green knoll apart' (56) describes the creative power as well as the contemplative passive isolation of the artist, the 'ivory tower' position. Other poems condemn this passivity as deadening (implications can already be found in the early poem 'The Man Who dreamed of Faeryland') and/or escapist (hints are even in the suggestive images of 'The Stolen Child').

Although never entirely free from the escapist fascination for idyllic fantasy worlds, Yeats's poems become increasingly aware that historic reality demands action. At first this action is sought in writing alone, but eventually even the self-sufficient attitude of the writer is criticised as inadequate (as the discussion of 'Easter, 1916' has shown). The symbolic approach fails to create a self-sufficient stable textual economy. The devaluation/revaluation dialectic swings back on the texts and deals with them in a similar way to that in which they deal with reality, by declaring them 'uncomely and broken, . . . worn out and old' (56): waste.

If the poems themselves eventually get tainted with the decay and futility that has caused their drift into a dubious semi-autonomy from reality in the first place, it is not only because reality proves impossible to keep out of their construction. Although the inevitable intrusion of (personal and impersonal) history is one of the causes of their trouble, as the chapter on Yeats's poetry has shown, their problems are not – as in Hopkins's works – those of a complex and overbearing reality versus a limited language. The partial absorption of this reality into language prevents this simple imbalance. Indeed the poems' impasse derives from exactly the opposite cause: the success of the symbol. It has been claimed in various places in the present study that the perfect symbol leads to the collapse of the symbolic system, therefore to the end of the poetic utterance.

What does this mean in terms of textual economy? The symbolising machinery of the poems perfects itself, runs more and more smoothly, until it runs completely on its own, without the need of input by the subject and reality and – more importantly – without any kind of output that is of use to the creator of the system. Indeed, when faced with the subjectivity of a creator, the poet, two things can happen in symbolic poetry, both of which are highly undesirable. The machinery can exclude this subjectivity altogether and become self-sufficient yet useless. As in the short poem significantly entitled 'Words', words may indeed obey the call of the poet, but produce no effect on reality. W.H. Auden's line 'For poetry makes nothing happen: it survives' from 'In Memory of W.B. Yeats' (Auden 1977: 242) is a shorthand description of modernist poetry in this respect. Words thus become 'poor words', worthless, and are eventually thrown away. The perfect symbolic system is useless for the production of lasting values. This is a long-term effect of the insight that the symbol remains an inadequate representation. Roland Barthes claims that 'in the symbol the representation is analogical and inadequate (Christianity "outruns" the cross)' (Barthes 1967b: 38). There are still two external authorities which cannot be overcome without endangering the poetic utterance: subjectivity and reality. Their presence devalues everything that the text produces.

The second possible fate of the subject in symbolic poetry is the very opposite of its exclusion: internalisation. The symbolising machinery takes its material from a reality it cannot leave behind – and also from the personal reality of its creator. Yet what it produces out of them are forever symbols, fictions which offer temporary escape from reality, but no means of coping with it. The *machine célibataire* does not only produce worthless junk. Much worse: it transforms valuable reality into rubbish. 'The Fascination of What's Difficult' describes this effect in personal terms. Although apparently a lament over the difficulties of running a theatre, it deals with the economic relation of art and its creator.[5] It uses the image of a cart-horse as a sad parody of the mythical Pegasus to indicate that, since divine inspiration is no longer available, all art has become extremely hard and unrewarding labour. After the loss of transcendental certainties the status of art as product is laid bare.

The complaints of artists about the difficulties of their task and their lack of reward are as old as their profession. What is really interesting in this otherwise thematically unremarkable poem is its attempt at a symbolic solution of the problem. In order to escape the restraints of artistic production, the speaker suggests the liberation of the poetic impulse. In a significant double move first its locus has to be found, then it has to be set free. What becomes even more explicit in the late poem 'The Circus Animals' Desertion' is already prefigured here: the symbolic system strives towards perfection, but once it is complete, the only possible continuation of artistic production lies in the collapse of this very system. In structural terms this means the dissolution of symbols into metaphors and metonymies. In economic terms it is the shift of the artificial surplus of symbolic creation either into the stability of reification (Eliot's half-objects, for instance), the equivalent of fixing a – however subjective – price, or the continual devaluation of the metonymy with its echoes of diminishing intensity which describe inflationary diffusion.

These are the options of modernist poetry, and both of them arrive at their own borderlines. The alternative is illustrated in various poems by Yeats. 'The Circus Animals' Desertion' has already been mentioned several times as an assembly of disconnected, 'broken' symbols with strong tendencies towards a metonymic arrangement. 'Lapis Lazuli' represents the alternative solution. It reifies the experience of symbolic overkill into the literally petrified image of a Chinese sculpture meant to express Nietzschean tragic gaiety. In 'To a Friend whose Work has come to Nothing', an even more radical reification in the face of the inevitable collapse of symbolic certainties is recommended. There, the poetic potential itself is petrified in silence. The text advocates an end of texts – yet under one crucial condition: 'like a laughing string', 'Amid a place of stone', the poetic silence survives 'secret' (109) and triumphant in an élitist realm in which – this is important – even in its ultimate zero-state the modernist artistic utterance remains an intact work.

The alternatives, dissolution and devaluation (rather than condensation and revaluation), are easier to accept when they affect not the artistic utterance, but a concrete, everyday object untainted by pretensions of artificial value. 'Upon a House shaken by the Land Agitation' describes the fate of such a building and claims that, in spite of its value as a cradle and shelter of human life, activity and inspiration, it does not constitute a symbolic statement. Yet by putting the issue into verse, 'gradual Time's last gift, a written speech' (96), the poem cleverly contradicts its own claim and immortalises the decaying house. In negative terms this signals that the symbolising activity cannot be stopped. Important is the paradoxical constitution of this gift. 'Wrought of high laughter, loveliness and ease' (96), it is not the stable encoded artefact, but an expression of Nietzschean tragic gaiety which retains an awareness of the elementary contradictions of existence while assuming a position detached from them. Its disappearing echo conveys constitution as well as destruction which, because of its detachment, it can bear with 'ease'.

4. STABLE INVESTMENTS: REIFICATION

If one can accept Jürgen Habermas's assessment that 'greatly oversimplifying, . . . in the history of modern art one can detect a trend towards ever greater autonomy in the definition and practice of art' (Foster 1985: 10), it becomes evident why Eliot's poems fit more neatly into the canon of modernism than those of Yeats and Hopkins. In his *œuvre*, the shift from a polarity of reality and language via the symbolic stage in which reality partly merges with language to a total union of both is completed. The psychological landscapes for which Eliot's works are renowned have no reason to lament their exclusion from an external reality outside of them. Capable of taking in everything, their problem is, on the contrary, that they cannot shut their eyes (and ears and nose – Eliot's poems are very concerned with the senses, a fact often eclipsed by their intellectual treatment of these sensations) to the impressions that bombard them. Like a camera whose shutter is jammed, they become the victim of perception, a passive writing-board of phenomena. Tiresias in *The Waste Land*, who '[p]erceived the scene, and foretold the rest' (72), who has 'foresuffered all' (72), is the embodiment of this condition.

The shift of objective reality into the psyche where impressions undergo a further transformation, an intellectualisation and draining away of their physical force (recalling Derrida's description of the de-colouring of myth by Western philosophy), eliminates the problem of value. There is no longer an outside against which the constructions of the text have to be measured. Even more importantly, the relativistic notion of the poetic work as product is obfuscated. Artistic creation thus follows the same path of mystification with which capitalist economy obscures the origins of capital and surplus.[6] It is evident that modernism always remains entangled in the conditions of society, even when it tries to criticise them. This essential impasse will be re-encountered in Adorno's aesthetics in the final section of the present study.

> Among the smoke and fog of a December afternoon
> you have the scene arrange itself – as it will seem to do –
>
> (18)

starts 'Portrait of a Lady' and describes its own mechanisms.

> The voice returns like the insistent out-of-tune
> Of a broken violin on an August afternoon:
>
> (20)

are two lines from its second part which display the seemingly unstoppable intrusion of external sensations into the text.

This stream of objects entering the poem through the senses puts poetic identity in a precarious position. It is no longer in control, but becomes the hostage of the things it describes. When the portrayed lady of Eliot's poem suggests to its speaker '"Perhaps you can write to me"', he responds with a revealing 'My self-possession flares up for a second' (21). Here, truly, is identity called into being by the desire of the Other in the Lacanian sense, by its command. However, being called into existence in this way (the circularity of the writer created by the reference to writing is a first hint at a textual *machine célibataire*) is no guarantee of a stable textual identity. Already the verb 'flares' hints at the momentary character of the identification. When the end of this 'objective' stimulation is contemplated in the form of the death of the irritating yet captivating woman (Freud's fetish is certainly not far away), the speaker experiences a radical anxiety concerning his own status, his capacity of creating himself out of the transformation and evaluation of impressions:

> Well! And what if she should die some afternoon,
> Afternoon grey and smoky, evening yellow and rose;
> Should die and leave me sitting pen in hand
> With the smoke coming down above the housetops;
> Doubtful, for a while
> Not knowing what to feel or if I understand
> Or whether wise or foolish, tardy or too soon . . .
> Would she not have the advantage, after all?
>
> (22)

Indeed, she would. For the revenge of the objects, as Baudrillard enthusiastically calls it (Baudrillard 1990: 81–99), for their reification is their eventual takeover. The props of the subjective play-actor begin a life of their own and eventually push him off the stage.

> This music is successful with a 'dying fall'
> Now that we talk of dying –
> And should I have the right to smile?
>
> (22)

Even the half-jocular reference to Shakespeare's *Twelfth Night* cannot hide the fact that the speaker is overawed by the sensations that only permit him to come into being after all. In a similar vein, the second line of this stanza, 'Afternoon grey and smoky, evening yellow and rose', presents itself as an almost ritualist invocation of the objective impressions without which the identity of the text could not constitute itself. Analogous references are overabundant in Eliot's poems.

The system has now become watertight. Everything inside it has already been labelled by perception. There is no longer a listing of values of objects in the face of an external measure determining their worth. It is as if one wanted, as Marx suggests, to apply the evaluating principle behind the price of commodities to that against which this price is measured: money.[7] Yet the monetary value of money cannot be determined. The system closes in on itself and becomes tautological. Only on this apparent tautology can arguments which see the modernism of Eliot's works in conflict with their capitalist premises be based. The circular motion of transformation and evaluation that his poetry exercises points at the ultimate emptiness of the process, its lack of both transcendental *and* objective foundation. The conveyor-belt of civilisation's objects (and those include people, too) traversing his poems only describes the ultimate absence of a concept of civilisation. The constitution of identity in Eliot's poems with the help of impressions filtered into the text through exactly this identity (again the tautological machine) highlights the loss of a concept of identity, its more than endangered, indeed already paradoxical status. Maud Ellmann describes this impasse as narcissism (Ellmann 1987: 67–8). Freud's concept of narcissism gives as the four forms of the narcissist's love the love of

(a) what he himself is (i.e. himself),
(b) what he himself was,
(c) what he himself would like to be,
(d) someone who was once part of himself

(Freud 1973–86, vol. 11: 84)

The first three cases hint at the principle of metamorphosis that characterises the succession of speakers in Eliot's poetry. A radical view could indeed call all of them mere variants of a single identity. Yet even when the principle itself is personified – as in Tiresias in *The Waste Land* – the self-reflective view of the speaker is always directed to one, and only one of his states at a time. Freud implies clearly that the narcissist does not love his transformations, but always one particular stage in this metamorphosis. Narcissism is therefore essentially ahistorical and entails the reification of the self by itself.

When Freud's fourth category is slightly expanded to include 'something' besides 'someone', it becomes clear that reification is indeed the way to establish a love-affair between subject and object, yet one that transforms all objects into parts or organs of the subject: 'I am, because I perceive objects who thus become parts of me.' As we have seen, the need for objects to be reified eventually overthrows the order. Entire poems, such as 'Hysteria' and 'Whispers of Immortality', are taken over by reified Others. What has started as a transmutation of the objective into the subjective leads to the reification of the subject itself. The subject becomes (its own) object. The system perfects itself until its internal frictions disappear. Yet still – or perhaps because of this perfection – the value produced by the tautological machine remains nil.

The Waste Land is such a machine that transforms lack into absence and vice versa, indeed – what many critics have overlooked – not only a wasteland but also a land of waste in which all the props on the stage are shown as what they are, the papier-mâché of poetry, empty words. Its addiction to prefabricated discourse, fragments gathered from other texts, is an indication of its attempt to bring value into its system, no matter which means must be exploited. Yet the fragments it has shored against its ruins remain fragments, leftovers and waste. The ruins are not transformed into shiny new palaces. The ivory tower is broken for good. The work of art remains the dump into which it has been turned by history. Even though *The Waste Land* borrows wherever it can (another attempt at sponging on alien genres is its inclusion of dramatic fragments), it fails to increase its value, because even outside of it (and it is important to note that this 'outside' is only ever other texts) nothing valuable can be found. Its seemingly optimistic end, the peace-inducing magic spell of its finale, must therefore be regarded with suspicion. Magic depends on a connection of words and things. Eliot's poems – despite Eliot's concept of an 'objective' correlative – only know a connection of words and words. Thus their modernism and their hopelessness. The seemingly stable economy of the modernist poem is bought at the price of self-declared worthlessness.

'A penny for the Old Guy' (89), the begging epigraph of 'The Hollow Men', prepares for the bleakest example of a discussion of economy in Eliot's poems. The poem is itself a kind of dumping ground: some of the more pessimistic elements removed from *The Waste Land*, for instance the reference to Conrad's *Heart of Darkness*, have ended up there. The economy of 'The Hollow Men' is one of utter bankruptcy.

The poem sets up a dualistic concept. Its 'here' is a dead land (the waste land once more) where the voices of the text identify themselves as hollow, stuffed with straw, quiet and meaningless, i.e. completely devoid of value. They inhabit a reality of reified objects which do not constitute a message, a meaning, and much less worth.

> Here the stone images
> Are raised, here they receive
> The supplication of a dead man's hand
> Under the twinkle of a fading star.
>
> (90)

Worse than the draining of reality of meaning and value is that the speakers of the poem are in no way different from their surroundings.

> Shape without form, shade without colour,
> Paralysed force, gesture without motion;
>
> (89)

describes them as reified or indeed petrified objects. 'Form' refers to the Platonic idea that individual objects are formed according to a universal idea. 'Shape without form' describes the strange hybrid produced by the *machine célibataire*, not only a self-contained system, but a cancerous growth deviating from any original plan, an implication important for the poem's attitude to loss.

The 'there' of the poem is enigmatically called 'death's other Kingdom' (89). This can be interpreted as a reference to sleep and dreaming (in Greek mythology, *hypnos*, sleep, is the brother of *thanatos*, death), a utopian realm of unrealised possibilities and unfulfilled desires. The second section of the poem corroborates this view by renaming the realm 'death's dream kingdom' (90). Secondly, the capitalised 'Kingdom' can be read in Christian terms as a negation of the belief that death has no power over God's Kingdom. Here it apparently has. Thirdly and most slyly, 'death's other Kingdom' implies that not only this negative utopia, but also the 'here' of the poem, its worthless but nonetheless present landscape, is ultimately ruled by death.

Death unsettles the poem (and, one could argue, also provokes it into existence). For in spite of its worthlessness, the 'dead land', 'cactus land' (90) of 'The Hollow Men' is at least, like every good desert, a haven of stability. But why must the poem defend itself against a possible loss, if there is no value to start with? The means of this defence will be discussed in the next section, but the origins of the problem must be sought inside the stable economy of worthlessness. The poem fears that 'reality' and utopian counter-reality could meet.

Let me be no nearer
In death's dream kingdom
Let me also wear
Such deliberate disguises
Rat's coat, crowskin, crossed staves
In a field
Behaving as the wind behaves
No nearer –

(90)

Here is an anxiety very similar to that of Yeats's poems: the fear that the desired perfect symbol could bring about the end of the poem. One also senses a prefiguration of the ghostly encounter with the composite spectre in *Four Quartets* which has been discussed in its psychoanalytic implications. The self-description of the speakers of 'The Hollow Men' also uses the symbolic imprecision of the ghosts in Yeats's 'Byzantium'. Yet there is no symbol here, neither is there a recognisable person. Still, the mechanisms are the same as in Yeats and 'Little Gidding': the potential union of reality and the utopia of everything which might be but is not would topple every notion of existence and therefore also identity. Identification and localisation would no longer be possible, not even as men of straw in a dead land.

That the fear of 'The Hollow Men' is again the fear for the intactness of the poem as work becomes clear when a related aspect of its anxiety is highlighted. It is the suspicion that something has already been lost, namely the capacity for speech, the means of poetic production. 'This broken jaw of our lost kingdoms', the only significantly different variant of the seven-times repeated formula of the kingdom, is an emblem of speechlessness. Worse than the production of nothing is no longer having the means of production. By producing nothing, the poem at least produces itself.

In this last of meeting places
We grope together
And avoid speech
Gathered on this beach of the tumid river

(91)

Marginalised by history ('on the beach of the tumid river'), the poem turns in on itself. Yet there is a world of difference between being silent and being silenced. The struggle of 'The Hollow Men' reveals that inside the value-free economy of modernist poems two residual values have survived that they are not willing to give up. A notion of subjectivity – however thwarted and mutilated it may be

– and the equally strong concept of the poem as work, an artefact that might not have an intrinsic value, yet retains a special status in a world of continual reification.[8] Individual subjectivity and the artistic work are threatened by 'the Shadow' whose negative influence is evoked in the fifth part of the poem. The characteristics of this shadow and possible strategies to infuse the dying conglomerate of work and subject with new life, meaning, and value, ways of rising out of the ashes – or even turning ash into something valuable (as in *Ash-Wednesday*) – will be discussed in the following section.

5. CONSPICUOUS WASTE: LOSS AND DISSOLUTION AS LIMITS OF MODERNISM

Visualised in a diagram, the economic structures of the analysed modernist poems display three distinct phases.

The final phase reveals two areas of tension: the liminal status of subjective identity and the endangered notion of the work of art. Both are produced by the one element that has taken over: language itself. The three phases are analogous to the changing concept of the sign. From binary compound signifier/signified via an opaque signified in symbolism it is eventually reduced to one layer, that of the signifier only.

In Baudrillard's concept of the development of representation, the three phases correspond to what he describes as the 'successive phases of the image':

> (1) It is the reflection of a basic reality.
> (2) It masks and perverts a basic reality.
> (3) It masks the absence of a basic reality.

The oft-mentioned rupture between language and reality happens between stage two and three. The consequent attempts to bridge the gap shape the third phase. The fourth and, so Baudrillard claims, currently most influential stage of the process is

> (4) It bears no relation to any reality whatsoever: it is its own pure simulacrum.
>
> (Baudrillard 1988: 170)

1. *The stable economy of mimesis*

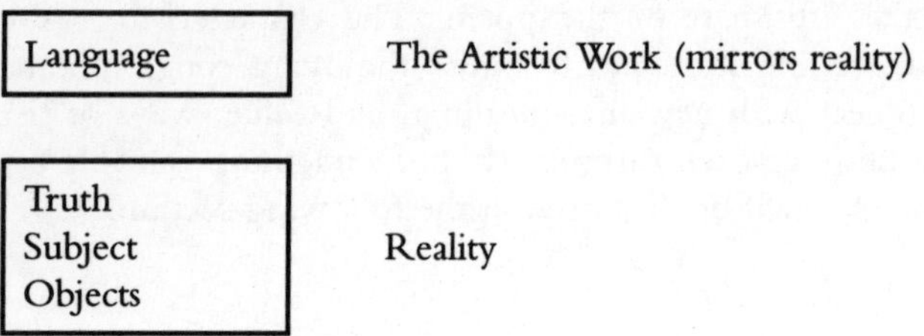

2. *The expansive economy of symbolism*

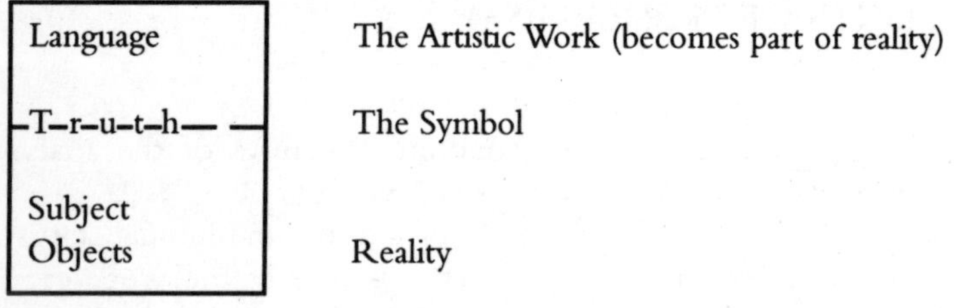

3. *The empty economy of modernism*

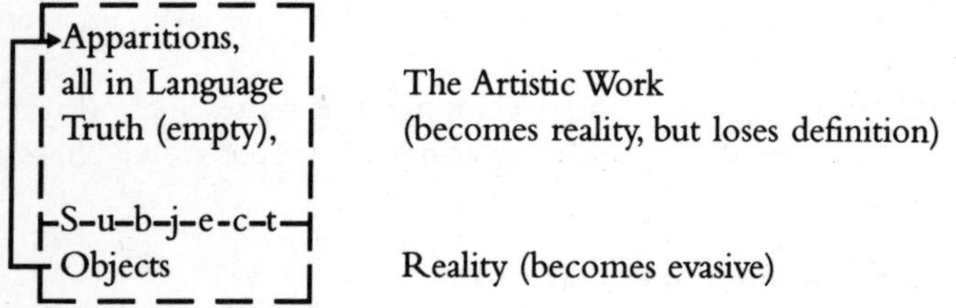

Figure 3

The modernist poem must be located between stage three and this final stage. It is torn between merely acting in the place of an absence, i.e. setting up a machinery that runs empty, and simulating an artificial presence. The conflict leads Adorno, whose aesthetics are determined by an adherence to the specifically modernist work of art, to the following description:

> Art works are things which tend to shed their thing-like quality. The authentic and the thing-like do not form distinct layers in a work of art; spirit is not superimposed on some supposedly solid objective basis. One of the key characteristics of works of art is, on the contrary, their ability to undo their own reified shapes in such a way that reification becomes the medium of its own negation. The two levels are mediated through each other. The spirit of art works evolves from their thing-likeness, and conversely their thing-likeness – i.e. their existence as works – springs from their spirit.
>
> (Adorno 1984: 389)

The attempt to overcome their status as objects is an attempt to escape the symbolic exchange of society which, as Baudrillard points out in the introductory hypothesis of *Pour une critique de l'économie politique du signe*, determines value according to its own rules rather than any intrinsic value (of use, for instance):

> A veritable theory of the object and consumption will not be founded on a theory of needs and their satisfaction, but on a theory of social obligations and of signification.
>
> (Baudrillard 1972: 8; my translation)

> From the moment (which can theoretically be isolated) when exchange ceases to be purely transitive, the object (the material of the exchange) comes into being through the exchange; it becomes reified in the sign. Instead of abolishing itself in the relation that it founds and assuming for itself symbolic value (like the gift), the object becomes autonomous, intransitive, opaque, and starts immediately to abolish the relation. The object-sign is no longer this shifting signifier in the gap between two beings, it is 'part of' the reified relation (as on a different plane goods are part of the reified force of labour). Where the symbol returns to lack (in the absence) as a virtual relation of desire, the object-sign no longer refers to anything but the absence of the relation and the separated individual subjects.
>
> (Baudrillard 1972: 62; my translation)

This integration into the evaluating symbolic exchange system is responsible for the spiritual and aesthetic bankruptcy of the modernist works, and the poems are aware of it:

> Here the stone images
> Are raised, here they receive
> The supplication of a dead man's hand
> Under the twinkling of a fading star.
>
> (63)

Pound's poems are even more outspoken:

An Object

This thing, that hath a code and not a core,
Hath set acquaintance where might be affections,
And nothing now
Disturbeth his reflections.

(63)

His little exercise laments exactly what it undertakes through its own structures: the reification of impressions, objects and people in the modernist work of art – which thus becomes 'An Object' itself.

Pound's 'Portrait d'une femme', in a way a companion piece to Eliot's 'Portrait of a Lady', attacks the woman described because her personality is a mere collection of objects assembled over the years, just as the Sargasso Sea with its lack of currents (to which she is compared in the poem's first line) collects algae and gulf-weed. If she is exemplary of the modern character, this is described in rather straightforward terms as a cross between junk-shop and garbage heap, the realm of valueless objects.

Yet when the poem is compared to Eliot's, some striking differences emerge. Eliot's speaker is passive and almost carried away by his observations. Pound's is in control, capable of taking a stand and indeed attacking his object. But even his position of authority is endangered. This is indicated by the sly reference to the fact that the woman is not the, but 'our' Sargasso Sea. The 'bright ships' that have supplied the vacuous woman with

Ideas, old gossip, oddments of all things,
Strange spars of knowledge and dimmed wares of price.

(61)

are the true spirits of the age, 'Great minds' (61). They are, of course, male in Pound's chauvinist universe which, however, is also that of the other modernists discussed here. The male principle creates; it is responsible for the artificial production of the modernist *machine célibataire*. The female principle collects, devours – or is used as a dump. It does not produce, but turns the glittering artefacts of the male project into useless rubbish, back to earth or the faeces from which the male creators so vehemently distance themselves.

The conspicuous absence of women from the canon of classical modernism deserves a thorough structural treatment that is beyond the scope of the present study. When women actually appeared on the scene, such as H.D. and Amy Lowell, they were quickly excluded as polluters of the modernist project. Pound's attempt to rescue Imagism from becoming 'Amygism' is typical in this respect. Yet the feminine as the antithesis of modernist production lurks everywhere, even inside perfectly masculine works – and their authors. It is Bataille's *part maudite*, the accursed share, as the English translation calls it. For Bataille, it is the inevitable waste and expenditure that accompanies every act of production despite being negated by it.

> Human activity cannot entirely be reduced to processes of production and conservation, and consumption must be differentiated into two distinct realms. The first, which is reducible, contains the minimal consumption necessary for the support of life of the individuals of a society and for the continuation of their productive activity: it is therefore merely a fundamental condition of the latter. The second realm encompasses the so-called unproductive expenditures: luxury, mourning ceremonies, wars, cults, the erection of representative monuments, games, theatre, the arts, perverse (i.e. non-genital) sexuality represent a similar number of activities which, at least originally, have their end in themselves.
>
> (Bataille 1967: 33; my translation)

Bataille later reintegrates this expenditure into what he calls 'general' economy to distinguish it from restrictive economies which simply deny its existence. In a general economy, waste and expenditure create space for new life. This is the link with the modernist attempt to 'kill' tradition. In a world that leaves virtually no room for the poetic utterance, space has to be created – by force, if necessary – to make the poem possible as a 'statement', in Foucault's terminology. As such it includes references to its 'self', its textual identity, as well as its status and value as a work.

When Bataille lists the three most prominent forms of expenditure, one re-encounters the obsessive principles of modernist poetry:

> The eating of one species by another is the simplest form of luxury. . . . generally vegetation is less burdensome than animal life. . . . the wild beast is at the summit: Its continual depredation of depredators represents an immense squandering. . . . Eating brings death, but only in an accidental form. *Of all conceivable luxuries, death, in its fatal and inexorable form, is undoubtedly the most costly*. . . . It continually leaves the necessary room for the coming of the newborn, and we are wrong to curse *the one without whom we would not exist*. . . . The luxury of death is regarded by us in the same way as that of sexuality, first as a negation of ourselves, then – in a sudden reversal – as the profound truth of that movement of which life is the manifestation.
>
> (Bataille 1988: 33–5)

The textual equivalent of eating, cannibalism even, is the recycling of pre-existent discourse, intertextuality, and the palimpsest. The suspension and endangering of textual identity in its shifts between self and Other, subject and object, corresponds to the luxury of sexuality. Finally death finds its alternative shapes in the options of silence, the end of the poetic utterance, and metonymic overspill, the echoing self-destruction of the text.

Needless to say, the texts do not like these forms of shifting themselves into oblivion, even though they are attracted to all of them. They are not capable of seeing that their eventual dissolution is inherent in their structures. Bataille even characterises poetry as the purest form of loss:

> The term poetry which characterises the least polluted, the least intellectualised forms of expressing a state of being lost, can be seen as a synonym of expenditure: it signifies, in fact, most precisely creation through loss. Its meaning is thus close to that of the sacrifice.
>
> (Bataille 1967: 36; my translation)

Concerning the work on the market, it is precisely this in-built character as waste that creates problems for the poetic genre. Poetry is indeed an institutionalised form of waste in the bourgeois sphere, a respected waste of time and energy whose actual market-value is negligible. It therefore indicates that even the streamlined rationalist world of the bourgeois needs its outlet of expenditure. Its present shape, however, is radically different from the great and sometimes orgiastic forms of antiquity and pre-capitalist times.

> Today the great deliberate social forms of unproductive expenditure have disappeared. Yet one should not as a consequence conclude that the principle of expenditure itself has ceased to be the aim of economic activity.
>
> A particular development of wealth whose symptoms are illness and exhaustion leads to an embarrassment of itself and simultaneously to an evil hypocrisy. Everything generous, orgiastic, and boundless has disappeared: rivalries which continue to determine individual action happen only in hiding and resemble an ashamed belching. The exponents of the bourgeoisie choose a more subtle attire: the display of riches takes place only behind the walls of boring and depressing conventions.
>
> (Bataille 1967: 44; my translation)

Yet as part of the private entertainment of the bourgeois, the poetic work is not only submerged in the market, it also becomes the victim of market forces. These eventually push it into a corner whose one angle is kitsch, the surrogate satisfaction of desires, the other an equally false classicism that institutionalises and petrifies it. The twin dangers of kitsch and fake classicism find their expression in Pound's struggle with his own early works. His famous verdict on his early poems, 'stale creampuffs', hints at the first danger, while the confrontation with a classical canon shapes his poetry throughout his career.

The very institution of poetry as a cultural necessity disappears in the late nineteenth century, and poetry finds its realm among the poets only, until it is eventually rescued by the emerging field of literary studies. In order to cope with these changes and ultimately step out of the structures of the market, the poems must overcome their status as works. This, however, they refuse to do.

Eliot's poems register their invasion by the sordid phenomena of reality in the early twentieth century passively. The individual body, the city, and civilisation as a whole merge into one huge metaphor of defilement (Ellmann 1987: 99). In *The Waste Land*, the agents of this defilement are rats, traditionally the spreaders of disease, here symbols of *The Waste Land*'s particular infection which severs words from meanings (Ellmann 1987: 105) and makes language impotent. The ever-widening rift between language and reality is broadened by every attempt to bridge it in the structures of an artistic text, as will be shown in Pound's works below.

Eliot finds an apparent solution to the problem of this continued loss – of value, integrity and existence – in the very structure he employs to describe it. The symbol becomes the lifebelt of his poems, the lid on the unstoppable significatory dissolution. In *Ash-Wednesday*, this symbolic reversal coexists in a paradoxical combination with its own antithesis. The poem renounces all capacity of transformation, reification and vision of language.

> Because I know that time is always time
> And place is always and only place
> And what is actual is actual only for one time
> And only for one place
> I rejoice that things are as they are and
> I renounce the blessèd face
> And renounce the voice
> Because I cannot hope to turn again
>
> (95)

This reduction of the potentials of language (which has analogies in Imagist doctrines) is accompanied by the paradoxical, inward turn already encountered in Yeats:

> Consequently I rejoice, having to construct something
> Upon which to rejoice
>
> (95)

Seemingly the text becomes its only object. Yet at the same time it invokes an external agency exactly when it has been reduced to the smallest possible output of a *machine célibataire*, the mere production of itself. This external force is indeed the greatest available one. The move corresponds to what Odo Marquard calls the replacement of the question of fate:

> Why did just this happen to me, to us, to him, to her, to them? – the question of (as it is now called) 'mastering contingency' – [which] is surpassed in Biblical Christianity and theological metaphysics by the absolute initial question, to which God is the absolute answer: the omnipotent creator alone, and no one else, makes everything and guides everything. This appeal to God – to creaturely contingency and divine omnipotence – brings the career of fate to an end: the one omnipotent God is the end of fate. And the modern world, it seems, merely implements this end of fate, which in essence was already accomplished earlier.
>
> (Marquard 1989: 69)

That this absolute solution is a regression to the symbolic technique which eventually tries to rescue some – however paradoxical – value for *Ash-Wednesday* becomes evident in its second part. It abounds with symbolic images adding up to the hope of resurrection through the intervention of a female figure (Dante's Beatrice comes to mind and, of course, the Virgin Mary). When the third part of the poem then echoes Yeats in its image of the winding stair, it is clear where the journey goes. Against the lost word and spent word with which the poem characterises itself is set the yet unheard Word (note the capitalisation).

> If the lost word is lost, if the spent word is spent
> If the unheard, unspoken
> Word is unspoken, unheard;
> Still is the unspoken word, the Word unheard,
> The Word without a word, the Word within
> The world and for the world;
> And the light shone in darkness and
> Against the Word the unstilled world still whirled
> About the centre of the silent Word.
>
> (102)

The allusion is, of course, to John 1: 1–5. God's word is the only creative one. Economically speaking, the poem tumbles back through the stages in the development of textual economy and indeed reaches the mimetic starting position again. There, truth, reality and subject are firmly in place. There is an address to which the poetic utterance can be directed. Consequently, the prayer with which the poem ends becomes a practicable and adequate form once more.

Eliot's late magnum opus, *Four Quartets*, reveals that this prevention of absolute loss and worthlessness is the very opposite of the development from a restrictive to a general economy that accepts and includes expenditure and waste. Indications are the well-known philosophical speculation on time as an enclosed monadic system (again, no expenditure, no escape) in 'Burnt Norton' and the image of the dance (also important in Yeats) which, also in 'Burnt Norton', is linked with a view of the cosmos as a wheel on which

> Garlic and sapphires in the mud
> Clot the bedded axle-tree.
>
> (190)

The image refers to Eastern religions as well as the Western idea of cyclical time which ultimately leads to an integration of waste in the machinery of production of value. It is 'Garlic *and sapphires*', and although they are 'in the mud', they gain value by being part of an all-encompassing symbolic system, that of a transcendental philosophy.

Even death, the ultimate obstacle, loses its threatening and subversive status as luxury and loss when it is integrated in the vertical, historicist structure of cultural layers. In the first part of 'East Coker', the peasants dancing around a bonfire (again dance symbolises historic inevitability) are described in an archaic English referring to a time when the connection between language and the sacred was still strong. The reference to 'matrimonie – / A dignified and commodious *sacrament*' (197; my emphasis) is therefore not coincidental. The image is used to declare death as merely one layer of life. The poem extends its view to include in the style of Ecclesiastes

> The time of the seasons and the constellations
> The time of milking and the time of harvest
> The time of the coupling of man and woman
> And that of beasts. Feet rising and falling.
> Eating and drinking. Dung and death.
>
> (197)

Death as a kind of fertilizer, that is what the poem tries to convey, thus rescuing reality from loss – and implicitly itself from the possibility of disappearance. The poetic utterance continues, even though this might be in other texts.[9] The poem's self-depreciation is thus more than a little hypocritical:

> That was a way of putting it – not very satisfactory:
> A periphrastic study in a worn-out poetical fashion,
> Leaving one still with the intolerable wrestle
> With words and meanings. The poetry does not matter.
>
> (198)

In spite of its surface humility, the text neither abandons the notion of value nor sacrifices itself when faced with the dissolution of certainties. 'O dark dark dark. They all go into the dark, / The vacant interstellar spaces, the vacant into the vacant,' (199) is countered by 'You say I am repeating / Something I have said before. I shall say it again' (201). The poem refuses to become a victim in Bataille's sense:

> The victim is a surplus taken from the mass of *useful* wealth. And he can only be withdrawn from it in order to be consumed profitlessly, and therefore utterly destroyed. Once chosen, he is the *accursed share*, destined for violent consumption. But the curse tears him away from *the order of things*; it gives him a recognizable figure, which now radiates intimacy, anguish, the profundity of human beings.
>
> (Bataille 1988: 59)

Its destruction would remove the poem from the sphere of commodities which ultimately denies its value. Yet despite its insight into the paradoxical nature of its beliefs, it chooses Christ rather than self-abandonment. Christ's death has a similarly ambivalent character:

> The cults demand a gory wasting of men and animals *as sacrifices*. Etymologically the 'sacrificium' is nothing but the *creation of sacred things*.
>
> This shows that holy things are created through loss. The success of Christianity in particular rests on the importance of the degrading crucifixion of the son of God; it enlarges ordinary human fears to a vision of unlimited loss and humiliation.
>
> (Bataille 1967: 34; my translation; emphases in original)

Bataille fails to observe that this ultimate because Divine expenditure is saved from being one by its integration into the Divine rescuing scheme for His creation. In the re-creation of Christ's sacrifice in the Eucharist the three main forms of expenditure according to Bataille are merged: cannibalism (the congregation eats Christ's flesh and drinks his blood), sexuality (highlighted in Freud's analysis of cannibalism and also spelled out by Christian mystics), and of course death. Still this potential overkill of expenditure is sublimated (in Adorno's sense: removed from the realm of things by the insistence on its thing-likeness) by its connection to the paradoxical idea of eternal life deriving from death.

The structural similarities between the complex position of faith in the twentieth century and the impasses of modernist poetry explain their mutual attraction.[10] Corresponding analogies will present themselves in the analysis of Heidegger's existential philosophy. What the symbiosis *produces* is, however, a utopian concept, one that remains symbolic and thus ultimately chained to language. In Baudrillard's words:

> Only that secret is seductive that does not circulate as a hidden meaning, but as a rule of the game, as a form of initiation, a symbolic pact without a key to its interpretation, without a code that offers itself for deciphering. Moreover there is nothing to uncover. One cannot repeat it too often: THERE IS NEVER ANYTHING TO PRO-DUCE (PRO-DUIRE). In spite of all its materialist endeavours *production remains a utopia.*
>
> (Baudrillard 1987: 57; my translation)

This relapse of the poetic work into a traditional sublime status, despite the disappearance of firm transcendental values, assumes a rather different shape in Pound's works. In the form of Imagism, he also cultivates the reductionist technique making the poem its own object, the perfect enclosed machinery which produces a single apparition only. This apparition may be multifaceted, but never disperses itself. It is never integrated – into an argument or a narrative pattern – and therefore never overwritten and lost. In contrast to some of Eliot's later poems, which subject poetic form to a transcendental system promising value to the work in spite of its obvious worthlessness and failure to produce, Pound's Imagist texts vehemently deny an outside. They are the purest representations of Adorno's idea of the work as a thing moving beyond 'thing-likeness' by stressing its materiality. Pound's poems insist that their creative tactics are the only reality. They turn the reality–art dichotomy upside down and call symbolic production real and reality empty. Examples are numerous. 'Apparuit' is a poem whose title indicates that it discusses an apparition, the transformation of a vision into reality: symbolic production.[11]

Golden rose the house, in the portal I saw
thee, a marvel, carven in subtle stuff, a
portent. Life died down in the lamp and flickered,
caught at the wonder.

(68)

Life significantly dies down under the weight of the apparition and thus unveils its inferior status. The vision, however, continues, and supplies all the elements usually associated with reality: colour, temperature, moisture, etc. The apparition 'drinks in' reality which is thus transferred into the text.

Crimson, frosty with dew, the roses bend where
thou afar, moving in the glamorous sun,
drinkst in life of earth, of the air, the tissue
golden about thee.

(68)

Even a poem more sceptical about the status of art versus reality, such as 'Silet', cannot help but contradict its own argument – the actual event is more significant than its artistic depiction – just when it makes its point:

When I behold how black, immortal ink
Drips from my deathless pen – ah, well –
away!
Why should we stop at all for what I think?
There is enough in what I chance to say.

(59)

The poem replicates the old Platonic idea (explained in the tenth book of *The Republic*) of a hierarchy of diminishing value from idea via concrete objects (which are the impersonations of ideas) to artistic imitations of real objects (which are therefore mere pictures of pictures). Plato uses this model to condemn poetry as the producer of highly imperfect illusions (Plato 1935, vol. 1: 420–35, 440–69). Yet in spite of the protestation of 'Silet', 'It is enough that we once came together' (59) (repeated three times), the poem is there. Its own order – contrary to Plato's – is the actual event, thinking about it, saying it, and eventually 'setting it to rime' (59). 'To plague to-morrow with a testament' (59) is what the poem claims it wants to avoid. It refuses to institutionalise itself as permanent, because this would contradict the momentary character of event, thought, and verbal utterance. It achieves the opposite, though.

It is rewarding to compare Pound's poem 'The Alchemist' with Hopkins's poem on the same subject. The differences could not be greater. Pound's alchemist is not for a moment plagued by doubts concerning his success. Like a well-oiled machine, he is encountered in mid-action, busy conjuring up assisting spirits. The names used in the invocations stem from various sources. There are Provençal-sounding ones, such as Raimona, Tibor, Berangèrë (the poem's shape hints at its Provençal models; its subtitle 'Chant for the Transmutations of Metals' (75) also stresses its claim to authenticity – which is always a dubious one in Pound). Some appear to be Greek in origin (Tireis, Alcmena, Briseis, Alcyon, Phaetona), others seem sheer fantasy creations. The poem patches together its intertextual roots in an attempt to duplicate the alchemy it describes. Its goal is the creation of an authentic poem out of fragments of other texts, gold out of base metal. The 'fire' in the heart of the production process is the poetic force which first fuses the impressive images and colourful allusions to a homogeneous amalgam, then stabilises it in its form: 'Quiet this metal' (76). Again the modernist machinery creates something out of nothing, and then keeps the created value inside itself.

Besides this stress on form, which displays once more the work's reluctance to give up its status and disperse the artificially created value, the poem also foregrounds the second force it refuses to abandon. It is the creative subject which is still in power and control. In the above poem it finds its expression in the speaker. But even in Imagist attempts at impersonality, so central to Pound's own poetic ideas, this subject merely hides behind the apparition it creates. As Ellmann points out, in Pound's doctrine of the 'Direct treatment of the thing', one can discern the intact subjective force in the very term 'treatment'. It simultaneously institutionalises a subject–object dichotomy and disguises the process-character of the formation of the apparition (Ellmann 1987: 143). This process-character is called 'work' (as in 'labour', not 'thing') by Durant who points out that this process is obscured by subject and object, although these are both created by it (Durant 1981: 23).

The concepts of work and creator find a combined expression in *The Cantos*. Among the many themes, stories, and mere lists of this complex text, they are the continuing threads, its lifeline, but also its limit. Its Odyssean attempt to create the voice of Western culture while remaining impersonal forces it to dig deep in the rag-bag of history. What it comes up with is exactly the dilemma which proves fortunate for Odysseus: the similarity of *polumetis* (many-minded) and *outis* (no man). The poem's attempt to transcend history by becoming it, by leaving its own status as product behind in order to become an immortal work, purges it from the restrictions of a clearly defined textual identity. Yet the price for this achievement is both a dangerous blindness through lack of self-reflection, which makes the blatantly misogynist, anti-semitic, and pro-fascistic statements of *The Cantos* possible, and a drifting of its discourse in all directions, a real and sometimes orgiastic overspill.

The Cantos' attempt to purge language from impurity, i.e. waste, is ultimately connected with the text's problem of justifying its own existence. It only leads to the production of more waste, however. This impasse results from the poem's premises, which regard nature as an economy without waste. This applies to external nature and the internal nature of the creative human mind, the distinction – here A.D. Moody is right – has disappeared (Moody 1982: 136). The refusal to think beyond the restrictive economy of the realities of production which surround the text is its eventual downfall. 'The production IS the beloved', exclaims canto CIV. Even the Second World War does not change the text's view of expenditure. Wars, Bataille claims, are a dominant form of organised and sanctioned expense of our age.

Rather than seeing the limits of their major theme of usury, which always adheres to the capitalist structures it criticises, *The Cantos* eventually fall victim to their own taboo. It is not at all Pound's intention which nonetheless pushes the text towards the limits of modernism through its dissolution and fragmentation. In an interview with Allen Ginsberg, he claims that *The Cantos* were 'a mess . . . stupid and ignorant all the way through . . . botched it . . . picked out this and that thing that interested me, and then jumbled them down into a bag. But that's not the way to make . . . *a work of art*' (Brooker 1979: 363). The status as work is never abandoned. Rather than disclaiming the concept of devaluation, Pound shifts planes in a way very similar to Eliot when he suddenly asserts that not usury lies at the root of all evil, but avarice:

> re USURY:
> I was out of focus, taking a symptom for a cause.
> The cause is AVARICE.[12]

The reintroduction of the Christian notion of sin is the rescuing move back to the symbolic when the machinery of the modernist poem threatens to approach its own destruction.

When *The Cantos* implicitly proclaim the end of the work of art in their unstoppable expenditure into the nothingness of history, their inability to keep together and form a whole, they show the way to an aesthetic that might be capable of making statements about its political and social backgrounds, the premises of its own production. In this respect, the indiscriminate condemnation of postmodernism as a mere ploy of the consumer society[13] and the naïve acceptance of the modernist work as a valuable social comment need to be reassessed.

The breaking-up of the work on the border of modernism, which lays bare its internal processes of production, its economy, is analogous to Deleuze and Guattari's concept of the schizophrenic body which symbolically sheds its organs in its realisation that it is not an object, but a process (Deleuze, Guattari 1984: 9–16). In the same way as the schizophrenic refuses to be locked in the Oedipal triangle father, mother, and child, in which all routes lead from father (the father in the personal prehistory) to father (the analyst) (Deleuze, Guattari 1984: 23, 35), a modernist text on the border of its own dissolution like *The Cantos* refuses to be a mere move from the classical works of its tradition to a self-created classical status as work of art. By exposing its own construction, by spilling over and wasting its force, it not so much sublimates itself in the traditional sense, i.e. removes itself on to a higher sphere, but infuses reality – if there is one outside of it – with its contradictory utopian notions. Or if one rejects the idea of an external reality altogether, it forms a temporary surface, Lyotard's *grande pellicule éphémère*, on which the transactions, exchanges, transformations and simulations visibly take place which constitute reality in the twentieth century (Lyotard 1974: 9–55).[14]

NOTES

1. As Marshall McLuhan points out, by a further symbolic shift beauty becomes a symbol of God's grandeur (Kenyon Critics 1975: 15–27).
2. Norman H. MacKenzie interprets 'out of sight . . .' as Hopkins criticising his friends (MacKenzie 1981: 94–5).
3. The underlying religious paradigm of Christ trying to rescue frail mankind in the darkness of their sins does not clarify the situation, since the speaker is already secure, unless one reads his longing as that to follow Christ's sacrifice – with the consequence that the rescue of others is bought at the expense of the self.
4. Tawney 1926: 43–4 defines mercantilism in the following ways: '. . . economic interests are subordinate to the real business of life, which is salvation, and . . . economic conduct is one aspect of personal conduct upon which, as on other parts of it, the rules of morality are binding. Material riches are necessary; they have a secondary

importance, since without them men cannot support themselves and help one another; the wise ruler, as St Thomas said, will consider in founding his State the natural resources of the country.'

5. Since its construction in 1904, Yeats had been involved with the Abbey Theatre in Dublin. In 1910, when 'The Fascination of What's Difficult' was published in *The Green Helmet and Other Poems*, Miss A.E. Horniman, the theatre's main patron, withdrew her financial support. (Mac Liammóir, Boland 1971: 67–9, 132).
6. 'Hence we see that behind all attempts to represent the circulation of commodities as a source of surplus-value, there lurks an inadvertent substitution, a confusion of use-value and exchange-value' (Marx 1982 vol. 1: 258–69, 261).
7. 'As against this [commodities], money has no price. In order to form a part of this uniform relative form of value of the other commodities, it would have to be brought into relation with itself as its own equivalent' (Marx 1982 vol. 1: 188–244, 189).
8. Steven Connor, in a talk on 'Rubbish, Waste, Negativity, and the Avant-garde' (Oxford, February 1991), used the ambiguous connotations of the adjective 'priceless' to indicate the paradoxical status of the modernist work: it wants to remain outside the realm of commodities, yet strives to be called valuable. He has since published some of his ideas in *Theory and cultural value* (Oxford: Basil Blackwell, 1992).
9. In this connection, Harold Bloom's otherwise rather misleading ideas might have some bearing. Texts do indeed sponge on other texts, even though they might not be aware of it, yet the ways in which this happens are determined by plenty of factors and not just the 'greatness' of some authors (Bloom 1973: 5–12, 93–6).
10. A.V.C. Schmidt sees in Eliot's poetry a 'discovery of a homology between religion and poetry, faith and art, which furnishes the basis of the process of "integration"' (Schmidt 1991: 232). Yet his optimistic view of both religiosity and integration prevents him from seeing that the similarity derives from the same structural impasses and that integration can also lead to the opposite of integrity: disintegration.
11. The title is an allusion to Dante's *Vita Nuova* where the line 'Apparuit iam beatitudo vestra' describes the effect of Beatrice's apparition (Brooker 1979: 77–8).
12. Pound wrote these lines in Venice on 4 July 1972 (Pound 1973: 6).
13. Fredric Jameson set the tone with his essay 'Postmodernism and Consumer Society' (reprinted in Foster 1985: 111–25).
14. I am indebted to Iain Hamilton Grant for permission to read the draft of his translation of Lyotard's *Economie Libidinale* (Athlone, 1993). Mr Grant is also the translator of Baudrillard's *L'Échange symbolique et la mort* (Sage, 1993).

CHAPTER EIGHT

Modernist Poetry and Language Philosophy

Willst du ins Innere der Physik dringen, so laß dich einweihen in die Mysterien der Poesie.
[If you want to enter into the depths of the physical world, let yourself be initiated into the mysteries of poetry.]

(Friedrich Schlegel)

1. COGNITION AND LANGUAGE

After having discussed the 'interior' of modernist poems in terms of their problematic identity in Chapter 6 and their 'outside' in Chapter 7, the picture now demands completion by a closer description of this outside. The object of the analysis is far from stable, though. As the attempt to outline the development of poetry in the three diagrams of the preceding chapter has shown, what is or what is *considered to be* outside varies from virtually everything (every *thing* that is, objective reality including the subject) to nothing. The situation is complicated even further if one takes into consideration that what is described as outside is always described in language and therefore already at least partly internalised.

The problems are the same as those of the description of the psyche in its manifestation in or as a text. Once more, what is to be discussed, pinned down, and objectified, is not automatically given as an object. It is always already in a relation which is a textual one. This is a simple insight with wide-reaching implications, one that the first modern linguists were aware of when they formulated the problem of the sign in relation to what it stands for, its *referent*.

Charles Sanders Peirce, the founding father of pragmatics, arrived at what he called 'four incapacities' in three essays on the logical faculties of man published in 1868/69:

(1) We have no power of introspection, but all knowledge of the internal world is derived by hypothetical reasoning from our knowledge of external facts.
(2) We have no power of intuition, but every cognition is determined logically by previous cognitions.
(3) We have no power of thinking without signs.
(4) We have no conception of the absolute incognizable.[1]

Peirce's seemingly unspectacular statements are the result of some of the most radical upheavals in the philosophy of the modern period. Although too complex to be condensed into a mere paragraph of this chapter, it is helpful to keep its main stages in mind. Kant is the one to question the problem of objective reality most thoroughly in his first critique, the *Critique of Pure Reason*. Its main question is whether it is possible to assume the existence of an external reality that is not based on an act of cognition. Is there a reality that is not produced by human consciousness? The question is a very old one and can be detected in the medieval scholastic dispute of universalists versus nominalists – which can in turn be referred back to Aristotle and his 'objective' view of reality versus Plato's theory of apparitions. Kant's provocative demand for a non-reflexive proof of external reality brought the ongoing struggle between idealists and empiricists to a boiling point. Its repercussions can be felt in modernist philosophy up to Heidegger and Wittgenstein. These two, this chapter intends to demonstrate, occupy binarily opposed positions in relation to Peirce's claim that there is no reality which can be proved to exist outside signs.

This has various implications for poetry. It takes away two of its most important points of orientation. First, the external reality the poem depicts, mirrors, even distorts, makes more beautiful or uglier according to its intention, becomes evasive when unveiled as a cognitive construct. Secondly, subjectivity, the realm of this cognition, is also questioned by the scrutiny of objective reality. What is the status of this (self-)reflective organ, cognition and subjectivity, in relation to the objects it perceives or creates? If poetic creation was traditionally seen as hovering between the poles of object(s) and subject, it was virtually left in a vacuum when these poles were forcibly taken away.

Hopkins's simultaneous attempts at appropriation (of a problematic objective 'outside') and distancing (from an equally unstable subjective 'inside') can be seen as an attempt to span the ensuing gap. This double move is then transformed into the dialectic of expansion and reduction which is one of the dominant features of modernist poetry. In Wittgenstein's early philosophy this becomes extension and exclusion, as will be explained below.

At the same time, the weight hitherto attached to Truth, Reality, and the Subject as transcendental entities was shifted on to the material of this problematic cognition which, as Lotman states, is also the *matériel* of poetry: language. The increasing concentration of poetry on its constitutive elements, far from a deliberate craze for experimentation, is a consequence of poetry being burdened with the leftovers of aborted philosophical disputes. Poetry became the dumping ground for spiritual problems from the mid-nineteenth century onwards, and its engagement with these issues is very different from the liberal exercise of ideas in eighteenth-century poetry, for example. It is the struggle to shore fragments against ruins, to create something stable and valuable, truth, reality and a notion of subjectivity, albeit of reduced dimensions, in the waste land that poems were assigned to.

2. NIETZSCHE'S RADICAL REDEFINITION OF TRUTH

> What is truth? A mobile army of metaphors, metonyms, anthropomorphisms, in short, a sum of human relations which were poetically and rhetorically heightened, transferred, and adorned, and after long use seem solid, canonical and binding to a nation. Truth are illusions about which it has been forgotten that they *are* illusions, worn-out metaphors without sensory impact, coins which have lost their image and now can be used only as metal, and no longer as coins.
>
> (Nietzsche 1989: 250)

Nietzsche's radical redefinition of truth in 'On Truth and Lying in an Extra-Moral Sense' turns the Platonic hierarchy of truth, objects and language upside down and focuses on the element most derided by Plato as insufficient and treacherous, language, as the only one at man's disposal. In spite of its radicalism, Nietzsche's doctrine is a reaction. It responds to the continuing secularisation of reality with its epicentre in the Reformation which spawned the mutual independence of theology, philosophy and the sciences, and art – a separation that had not existed before.

By shifting the attention to truth as a human creation, Nietzsche reinvests language with an enormous potential. This applies especially to poetic language with its necessary imprecisions and instabilities. It now becomes the creator of the premises on which our notions of reality are based. Nietzsche's move can therefore be regarded as the second major shift within modernity. The first move is from theology to science and empirical philosophy in the Enlightenment. The second one reacts against this Enlightenment by shifting the emphasis from the false alternative of materialist empiricism and idealism to aesthetics. It is precisely this shift of balance in favour of aesthetics that corresponds to the move from a mimetic approach (which relies on the existence of an objective reality) to the symbolic approach which stresses the inextricable involvement of the subject in the creation of truth. Symbolic truth hovers between a subject it cannot define without endangering and a notion of transcendental Truth it requires as an orientation yet is unable to reach. This oppositional move against the modernity of the Enlightenment with its ensuing instabilities of both identity and statements is the starting point of modernism.

The liberation of language from a subservient status as a mere mirror of objective reality opens up possibilities for the creation of alternative worlds, utopian concepts. The need for these has been explained in the previous chapter as the consequence of the crumbling of established certainties. Their most sophisticated shape can be encountered in Martin Heidegger's attempts to transcend Western metaphysics by establishing a linguistic universe in which language becomes all-powerful. The structure of this realm and its implications and dangers of totalisation will be discussed in a separate section below.

It would be misleading, however, to interpret Nietzsche's essay on 'Truth and Lying' in this one-sided way. As Habermas rightly points out, Nietzsche's works represent a crossroads of modern thinking, and only one of its paths leads to Heidegger (Habermas 1987: 97). The other direction is outlined by a description equally as radical as that of truth which both relates to and relativises the former. For before Nietzsche criticises man's capacity to know, he puts the entire endeavour into a perspective which is more than historical:

> In some remote corner of the universe that is poured out
> in countless flickering solar systems, there once was a star
> on which clever animals invented knowledge. That was the

> most arrogant and the most untruthful moment in 'world history' – yet indeed only a moment. After nature had taken a few breaths, the star froze over and the clever animals had to die.
>
> Someone could invent such a fable and still not have illustrated adequately how pitiful, how shadowy and fleeting, how purposeless and arbitrary the human intellect appears within nature. There were eternities when it did not exist; and someday when it no longer is there, not much will have changed.
>
> (Nietzsche 1989: 246)

The parable illustrates Nietzsche's superhistorical attitude which devalues every human attempt to grasp reality and truth. All these endeavours are restricted by man's actual being – which Adorno calls the subject's thing-likeness: 'For that intellect has no further mission leading beyond human life. It is utterly human, and only its owner and producer takes it with such pathos as if the whole world hinged upon it' (Nietzsche 1989: 246).

While on the one hand opening up possibilities for the creation of truth with and in language, Nietzsche cynically points out the limitations of this creation. It is devoid of any value that transcends human immediacy and can never hope to come to terms with anything outside the human sphere. As Wiebrecht Ries points out, Nietzsche becomes 'the spiritual father of the suspicion that all final constructions of history, morality, and truth are ultimately meaningless' (Ries 1982: back cover; my translation). It would be a misunderstanding, however, to see him merely as the inventor of nihilism (although nihilism can be seen as a misreading of Nietzsche). Nihilism as an institutionalised negation is the very opposite of Nietzsche's continual questioning of the limits of human knowledge. As a matter of fact, he curbs most thoroughly the one human faculty left intact in the creation of certainties, that of the production of language. After separating truth from objective reality, he divorces language from both of them: 'What is a word? The portrayal of nerve stimuli in sounds. But to conclude from a nerve stimulus to a cause outside ourselves is already the result of a false and unjustified application of the law of causality' (Nietzsche: 1989: 248).[2]

Far from actually denying the existence of Truth and objective reality, Nietzsche merely takes away the possibilities of reaching them and leaves the issue in a provocative suspense. Language, declared to be the medium with which man creates truth and reality, is thus simultaneously shown as infinitely lacking, incapable of making exactly those statements that would give a foundation to its creations. This fundamental disqualification of language as the means of establishing contact with an exterior reality, truth even, makes Nietzsche the precursor of Wittgenstein, the early Wittgenstein of the *Tractatus*, to be precise. Wittgenstein's elaborate outline of the impotence of language will be the focus of the following section.

Nietzsche's essay formulates precisely the impasse that is also the locus of modernist poetry. Statements have to be made, not only simple but universally valid ones, yet the only material available for this artificial creation is not up to its task. Forever caught in the realm delineated by its shortcomings, the poetic utterance behaves exactly like Nietzsche's 'knowledge' in the face of its inevitable destruction. It inflates itself until it covers up the abyss above which it hovers. It *becomes* reality and truth, but cannot escape the constant threat of death, the border unveiling its paradoxical status – against which its continual permutations try to erect aesthetic barriers. The modernist poem tries to bridge the gap between phases three and four in Baudrillard's scheme: from merely covering the disappearance of reality, it moves on to create a simulacrum of reality inside its own sphere. This simulated reality tries to exclude death, its own and the death of the paradoxical poetic utterance which produces it. Alternatively it tries to *include* it, which leads to the same result.

Nietzsche is aware that among the limitations and discontinuities of his model of human cognition and its creation of dubious certainties there is one continuity left. He calls it the 'desire for truth' (Nietzsche 1989: 250). It is nothing but the need to invent metaphors in order to give meaning to existence. Nietzsche replaces the thinking thing – Descartes' *res cogitans* – as a philosophical description of man, by the poetic animal. Only from this metaphoric stage do more abstract concepts and schemes emerge.

> Everything that sets man off from the animal depends upon this capacity to dilute the concrete metaphors into a schema; for in the realm of such schemata, something is possible that might never have succeeded under the intuited first impressions: to build up a pyramidal order according to castes and classes, a new world of laws, privileges, subordinations, boundary determinations, which now stands opposite the other, concrete world of primary impressions, as the more solid, more universal, more familiar, more human, and therefore as the regulatory and imperative world.
>
> (Nietzsche 1989: 250).

This urge to create metaphors and out of them terms, schemes, concepts and truths, the discoloured myths that Derrida accuses Western metaphysics of employing, falls together with the human desire to master existence. It is a variant of Nietzsche's will to power. In Wiebrecht Ries's words:

> As a means of self-preservation, the intellect is a *deception* about the direction- and meaningless character of the natural world. But it is a deception which makes human existence possible in the first place with its foundation 'on the mercilessness, the homicidal' of interior as well as exterior nature 'in the indifference of its ignorance'.
>
> (Ries 1985: 26–7; my translation)

One recognises the parallels to the compulsion to produce – perpetually inadequate – poetic utterances. This becomes evident in Hopkins's 'cry *I can no more.* I can' (99), in Yeats's search for a theme in the absence of possible ones in 'The Circus Animals' Desertion', and in Eliot's 'Trying to learn to use words, and every attempt / Is a wholly new start, and a different kind of failure' (202) in part V of 'East Coker'. The compulsion to continue produces the endless poetic utterance in the face of its own impossibility. When the expanding complexity of this utterance eclipses the abyss over which it is constructed, as in Pound's *Sagetrieb* in canto XC (605) (literally 'drive towards uttering', and thus the very concept Nietzsche has in mind), when the human reaction to a hostile nature presents itself *as this very nature*, a reversal of roles takes place. This reversal simultaneously blots out the createdness of the utterance (as in the drive towards impersonality) and institutionalises this utterance as nature, as a myth with all its opportunities of ideological misuse.

Nietzsche admits the necessity of at least a temporary deception of man by his creation in order to permit *Selbstbewußtsein*, literally a consciousness of the self, but also self-assertion that makes action possible (Nietzsche 1989: 252). Yet when the deception becomes permanent, the path is cleared for the establishment of oppressive systems based on fictitious metaphysical distinctions between true and false. Nietzsche regards morality as well as religion and political beliefs as such systems. He is adamant that there is no connection between subject and object save one:

> For between two absolutely different spheres such as subject and object, there can be no expression, but at most an *aesthetic* stance, I mean an allusive transference, a stammering translation into a completely foreign medium. For this, however, in any case a freely fictionalizing and freely inventive middle sphere and middle faculty is necessary.
>
> (Nietzsche 1989: 254)

Poetry which foregrounds the principle of the formation of metaphors is therefore a way to point at the only available 'truth':

the drive to create metaphoric crutches to come to terms with a hostile nature. This nature can only become 'reality' in the same way as the subject comes into existence: by being clothed in inadequate language. In this creative process, language remains at the same time a radically undermining force. It threatens established systems based on metaphysical premises by unveiling their createdness, relativism and arbitrariness. Nietzsche sees both the erection of truths, their eventual dismissal, and artistic creation as symptoms of the same drive towards metaphoric creation:

> That drive to form metaphors, that fundamental desire of man, which cannot be discounted for one moment, because that would amount to ignoring man himself, is in truth not overcome and indeed hardly restrained by the fact that out of its diminished products, the concepts, a regular and rigid new world is built up for him as a prison fortress. It seeks a new province for its activities and a different riverbed and generally finds it in *myth* and in *art*. It constantly confuses the categories and cells of concepts by presenting new transferences, metaphors and metonyms; constantly showing the desire to shape the existing world of the wideawake person to be variegatedly irregular and disinterestedly incoherent, exciting and eternally new, as is the world of dreams.
>
> (Nietzsche 1989: 254)

(The analogies to psychoanalytic distinctions of consciousness and unconscious are obvious. The passage reads like a precursor of Jung's theory of the necessary setting up and eventual disappearance of beliefs.)

When Nietzsche throws truth back into language and even questions the value of the search for truth, yet within his radical destruction sets up the human desire for metaphoric cognition as the only permanent force, and art and metaphysics as its binary and mutually threatening expressions, he implicitly sets aside a special position for the work (of art and philosophy; the distinction becomes fluid) capable of seeing this dialectic. Inextricably linked with the human attempt to master nature and thus part of the will to power, yet at the same time capable of seeing the endeavour and its eventual futility, the work attains a strange orbital position. It is neither detached from human existence nor entirely determined by its needs and therefore blind towards its mechanisms. In Nietzsche's discussion of history in 'On the Use and Disadvantage of History for Life', the superhistorical position would be the parallel (its relation to myth has been discussed in the chapter on Pound). Nietzsche's view of art in a dialectic interplay with the force creating it sets up a far less static and thus more responsible model.

Towards the end of his essay 'On Truth and Lying in an Extra-Moral Sense' Nietzsche describes the not always harmonious coexistence of 'intuitive man' (who represents the endlessly shifting world of metaphoric creation) and 'reasonable man' (who trusts the stability of abstract metaphysical concepts). 'Both desire to master life' (Nietzsche 1989: 256), yet both attitudes are described as deficient. In an attempt to combine what appears as the Dionysian and Apollonian in 'The Birth of Tragedy', Nietzsche claims that his ignorance concerning the necessities of life makes intuitive man incompetent in the face of misfortune, incapable of learning from mistakes because of his rejection of rules. Reasonable man, on the other hand, is not equipped to deal with happiness, indeed unable to experience it.

The strange finale of Nietzsche's essay, seemingly a claim for the superiority of the stoic position controlled by the certainty of concepts, indeed advocates the tangled interplay of art and rationality as the only available option.

> How different stands the stoic person who has learned from experience and controls himself by reason! He who otherwise only seeks honesty, truth, freedom from delusions, and protection from enthralling seizures, now, in misfortune, produces a masterpiece of dissimulation, as the former did in happiness; he does not wear a quivering and mobile human face but, as it were, a mask with dignified harmony of features . . . .
>
> (Nietzsche 1989: 256)

Even the most austere rationalism is suffused with the irrationality of art, just as much as the most fluid artistic expression is caught in the stability of form and can be subjected to rational scrutiny. Modernist poetry, aware of its own mechanisms, expresses this insight in attempts to become metapoetic, to discuss the principles of its own constitution. Yet when it tries to stabilise its mechanisms completely in a rationally determined form (as in Imagism), the metaphoric drive blasts the 'artificial' stability and leads to fragmentation, incompleteness and the dissolution of works. Pound's *Cantos* are once more the most drastic expression of this failure to control the material of poetry.

The alternative danger is to be found in attempts to set up art itself, the artefact, as a substitute truth unrestricted by rationality. Yeats's stone sculpture of the Chinamen in 'Lapis Lazuli' comes to mind, which is intended to represent exactly the Nietzschean concept of tragic gaiety described in the above parable as the serene mask of the stoic. Yet the mask remains external and dead. It has no connection with what goes on underneath – which it only hides, but fails to control. The consequence for a poem relying entirely on its aesthetic function is a depreciation. It becomes an empty ornament, incapable of making statements concerning the reality that surrounds it. The dialectic of art and rationality is developed to its most sophisticated expression by Adorno. His views on the position of the modernist work of art will be part of the conclusion of this chapter.

3. WITTGENSTEIN'S DISTRUST OF LANGUAGE

The space allocated to poetry in Wittgenstein's early philosophy developed in *Tractatus Logico-Philosophicus* (Wittgenstein 1961; henceforth quoted by its subdivisions) is easy to determine. There is none. Concerned with its attempt to outline the limits of language (in the same way as Kant tried to delineate those of thought) in its capacity to make propositions about facts, non-factual language falls outside the realm of investigation and into that of non-sense (4.114–4.116). Wittgenstein neither denies poetry's right to exist nor does he call it deficient in the way Plato does. It is simply concerned with that about which we cannot speak (in a philosophical sense) and about which we consequently ought to keep quiet, as the famous final statement of the *Tractatus* suggests (7).

In its endeavour to cut down the functions of statements to their atomic bases and to eliminate everything that does not derive logically from the resulting elementary propositions, the philosophy of the *Tractatus* relies, as its name implies, on the strict rules of logic. The rule of the excluded middle, the basic logical assumption that something either is the case or is not – with nothing in between (or, in a logical formula, p≠not-p) – is one of those necessary exclusions. It eliminates exactly the locus of the metaphoric, the constitutive principle of poetry as that which is created *between* two significatory poles and continues to hover in this space.

If in spite of this clear demarcation, I use Wittgenstein's early philosophy to highlight further parallels between modernist poetry and contemporary philosophy, this attempt is based on two assumptions which will have to be validated during the comparison. First, it will be demonstrated that, despite its exclusion, the metaphoric invades Wittgenstein's concepts in a subtle, yet decisive way. Secondly, the main impetus of Wittgenstein's project, the purification of philosophy through exclusion and reduction, will be shown as analogous to the aesthetics of modernist poetry – and as deriving from similar sources.

The insight engendering Wittgenstein's *Tractatus* is that philosophy too often concerns itself with questions that do not fall within its competence and whose investigation therefore leads to nonsense. Point 6.53 of the treatise claims:

> The correct method in philosophy would really be the following: to say nothing except what can be said, i.e. propositions of natural science – i.e. something that has nothing to do with philosophy – and then, whenever someone wanted to say something metaphysical – to demonstrate to him that he had failed to give a meaning to certain signs in his propositions. Although it would not be satisfying to the other person – he would not have the feeling that we were teaching him philosophy – *this* method would be the only strictly correct one.

Wittgenstein's early philosophy follows the assumptions of critical philosophy as opposed to transcendental philosophy which, in the broadest sense, tries to point beyond the realm of factual existence. When critical philosophy completes its inward turn and attempts to outline the capacities and shortcomings of its own devices and material, language, it becomes linguistic philosophy. Although the movement of contemporary philosophy appears more self-determined than that of modernist poetry (this might, however, merely reflect a stronger self-mystification), it is evident that the underlying problems provoking the move are similar. The realm of competence, the sphere inside which sensible utterances can be made, is suddenly seen as limited.

First the transcendental is, if not completely lost, at least experienced as unapproachable. Kant's first critique, that of pure reason ('pure' stands for transcendental), tries to compensate for this loss by positing what was hitherto *outside* human existence (God and morality) *inside* the subject as points of orientation in the subject's relation to itself and objective reality. The aesthetic equivalent is the symbolic move which makes the suddenly evasive transcendental sphere (called 'Truth' in the schematic model of the preceding chapter) part of the subjective poetic construct. Both the philosophical and the aesthetic attempt to bridge the gap created by the departure of the transcendental (prompting Nietzsche's claim of the death of God) encounter the same impasse. The two poles employed to set up a compensatory force-field prove inseparable and eventually mutually destructive. Permanence and stability of neither subject nor objective reality can be ascertained.

Wittgenstein's 'negative' endeavour in the *Tractatus* is therefore to arrive at a minimal, an atomic stability. The task is far from simple, since he refuses to assume a position 'outside' discourse as a vantage point of his inquiry. David Pears describes the procedure in a useful image: 'First, he worked back from the skin of the bubble of ordinary factual discourse to its notional centre, elementary propositions. Then using a logical formula he worked outwards again to the limit of expansion of the bubble' (Pears 1985: 56–7).

Once more, a loss of the outside is compensated by a simultaneous reduction and expansion. The attempted purification – here of philosophy, in the case of modernist poetry of the 'dialect of the tribe' – rests, as Pears points out (although he does not use the term), on a structuralist concept of language which assumes that all languages are based on the same foundations, even though these are difficult to figure out (Pears 1971: 85). Point 4.002 of the Tractatus concludes:

> Language disguises thought. So much so, that from the outward form of the clothing it is impossible to infer the form of the thought beneath it, because the outward form of the clothing is not designed to reveal the form of the body, but for entirely different purposes.
>
> The tacit conventions on which the understanding of everyday language depends are enormously complicated.

A similar assumption underlies the strategies of modernist poetry. It enables it to appropriate fragments and concepts from other languages and cultures (in its manifold quotations and use of exotic forms, such as the haiku). It also permits its reductive tendencies towards a minimalism regarded as universally valid and comprehensible (in the theory of the apparition in Imagism, for example, and also in Eliot's 'objective correlative' which is, in a way, a structural echo of the former).

The conceptual weaknesses of Wittgenstein's model of purification and the problems of related attempts in modernist poems are also remarkably similar. Both display a blind spot for the subjectivity behind their respective creations. In Wittgenstein, subjectivity is eclipsed by the elementary proposition to which all factual ones can be reduced and from which they are also engendered. Point 5.631 of the Tractatus actually claims 'There is no such thing as the subject that thinks or entertains ideas.' It is telling that Wittgenstein does not come up with an example of one of these smallest elements on which his theory rests. The various modernist attempts at impersonality function in the same way. Always more programmatic than realistic, the frequent calls for impersonality – even in an author whose works abound with depictions of the subject at work, Eliot – hardly manage to conceal that even in the most reduced Imagist fragment (Pound's poem 'Papyrus' is the obvious example) a textual identity remains visibly at work.

The other side of the coin representing the blindness of the purifying endeavour is its simplistic notion of the object. In his sophisticated attempt to show the desperate inadequacy of human expression when faced with objective reality, Wittgenstein naïvely assumes the existence of objects as given. Indeed, he does not even make clear whether they are to be regarded as material or sense-data (Pears 1985: 67). He lacks an underlying theory of knowledge, a reflection about the way in which objects become objects. This corresponds to the weakness of modernism characterised by Wolfgang Hildesheimer as the lack of a theory of cognition. It makes Pound's *res* possible as an object which is simply there without foundations that could be questioned.

In the *Tractatus*, this significant blindness towards cognition can be related to a crucial excluded element in Wittgenstein's reasoning, *Vermitteltheit*, mediation of experience, its shaping through subjectivity with its inevitable metaphoric imprecisions. It invades the basic formulas of the treatise through the back door. In the introductory moves to set up his theory, in section 2 and, more precisely, 2.1 to 3.01, Wittgenstein defines reality in connection with facts, objects and the way in which they are related. Here he reverts to a thinking not unlike Plato's hierarchic one when he claims that 'We picture facts to ourselves' (2.1). Only six steps further he states 'A picture is a fact' (2.141).

The uncertainty about which orders and creates which, the picture the objects or vice versa, projects Wittgenstein's logical reductions back into the metaphoric realm. There, exactly the same process takes place: the metaphor creates while both the poles of its creation and its status remain attached to a pre-existent given, signifiers which are not – or no longer – metaphoric themselves. Otherwise the metaphor would either be a stable sign (if it did not happen 'between') or it would not signify (if the poles between which it happens were as fluid as the metaphoric creation itself).

Even the ascetic logical shape of the *Tractatus* is deeply pervaded by the dialectic observed in Nietzsche's essay on 'Truth and Lying'. The erection of symbolic systems of truth is both generated and eventually undermined by the metaphoric drive characteristic of human intellect. The attempt of the *Tractatus* to suppress this insight is unveiled in little lapses, metaphoric slips in its tightly knit and 'colourless' logical network. Point 2.0232, incidentally, claims 'In a manner of speaking: objects are colourless.' The significance of 'a manner of speaking' in a structure like the *Tractatus* is worth considering. In the final section of the *Tractatus*, especially from clause 6.372 onwards, the treatise is again busy excluding 'nothings', concepts which do not belong in the realm of philosophy.

A collection of late fragments of Wittgenstein's works entitled *Über Gewißheit: On Certainty* shows him still concerned, in an almost manic way, with this exclusion. Fragment 31 reads 'The propositions which one comes back to again and again as if bewitched – these I should like to expunge from philosophical language'. Fragment 33 then brings the matter to a conclusion: 'Thus we expunge the sentences that don't get us any further' (Wittgenstein 1969: 6e).[3] Such propositions are those concerning God, fate, ethics, and, in particular, will. Especially this last and very Nietzschean term crops up repeatedly, as if representing an obstacle not easily integrated or put aside.

Will in the *Tractatus* is indeed similar to the Nietzschean drive towards aesthetic creation. Once unveiled as such, it becomes a borderline of the philosophy of the *Tractatus*, a liminal region where that which shapes the world touches on that which the world means – and which cannot be expressed. First, this speechlessness of the aesthetic appears in a subtle formula:

> 6.421 It is clear that ethics cannot be put into words.
> Ethics is transcendental.
> (Ethics and aesthetics are one and the same.)

The two clauses preceding this inconspicuous equation make clear where this self-limiting insight leads: to a true *reductio ad absurdum* in which the philosophy of the early Wittgenstein condemns itself to silence. In this respect, the final claim of the *Tractatus*, that of the necessary silence in the face of that which cannot be expressed, is more than flippancy. It is a serious structural conclusion. It points in the same direction as the silences that are one of the structural outcomes of modernist poetry. They are the result of the poems' insight into their insurmountable inability to make statements. More than that, silence may be the only means of their survival, either in the attempt to become unchangeable by 'playing dead', as Barthes points out (and it is worth asking whether Wittgenstein's mathematisation of philosophy does not serve a similar purpose), or as a way of fighting death by mimetically depicting it in the most efficient way possible to language.

Death as the most visible barrier of enquiry and as that which hints at the inevitable rupture between subject and object, self and world, suddenly also appears in the *Tractatus* when the treatise attempts its final act of exclusion.

> 6.431 So too at death the world does not alter, but comes to an end.
> 6.4311 Death is not an event in life: we do not live to experience death.
> If we take eternity to mean not infinite temporal duration but timelessness, then eternal life belongs to those who live in the present.
> Our life has no end in just the way in which our visual field has no limits.

The increasing length of the numbers of the subdivisions indicates that statements have shrunk to the status of asides. Even in the formalism of the *Tractatus* lurks the devil of the superfluous, '[a]lways afraid to say more than it meant', to borrow Auden's line (Auden 1977: 25). In Wittgenstein, these asides increasingly mark the transgression into forbidden territory. The treatise is fatally attracted by the very outside it tries to exclude continually. In its final assertion of philosophy's necessary restrictedness (which is simultaneously a pronouncement of its right to exist – in the same way as the purification of modernist poetry tries to make its continuation possible), it also vehemently projects an outside which it calls 'mystical'.

> 6.44 It is not *how* things are in the world that is mystical, but *that* it exists.

The finale of the *Tractatus* shows that inside its cogent argument there hides both an elementary contradiction and an admission of failure. The contradiction is its attempt to distil an elementary truth out of propositions in order to expand its findings into an all-encompassing world-formula in what Pears calls the Tractatus's 'thesis of extensionality': 'all factual propositions are truth-functions of elementary propositions' (Pears 1985: 71). In this way the ultimate reduction eventually manages to bridge the gap between logic and objective reality, things and nothings, sense and non-sense.

Yet at the same time it does not. There remain 'things that cannot be put into words' which can only 'make themselves manifest', the *mystical* (6.522). The defeat of language is complete in the very moment of its victory. And even this minimalist dichotomy of seeing and speaking (which is reminiscent of a related, though different one in psychoanalysis: showing and hiding, i.e. exactly not speaking) retains an ontological problem. None of its sides, neither that of expression or language (speaking) nor that of impression or perception (seeing) can claim authenticity. As little as seeing proves the existence of the perceived objects, speaking – or even refusing to speak, the silence that we will re-encounter in Heidegger – can depict them in other than an arbitrary way (Pears 1985: 60).

The creative potential of the aesthetic as simultaneous origin and ultimate boundary cannot be overcome. Language is both of restricted competence and even within its limited competence ultimately unreliable. The problem of its material therefore pervades language philosophy as much as it does modernist poems. The penultimate statement of the *Tractatus*, the one preceding its advocating of silence, tellingly outlines the problems in images strikingly similar to Yeats's assessment of (his own) poetry in 'The Circus Animals' Desertion'.

> 6.54 My propositions serve as elucidations in the following way: anyone who understands me eventually recognizes them as nonsensical, when he has used them – as steps – to climb up beyond them. (He must, so to speak, throw away the ladder after he has climbed up it.)
>
> He must transcend these propositions, and then will he see the world aright.[4]

Yet Yeats, one could argue, is already a little wiser, not only because he has already lost or got rid of his 'ladder'. His poem rightly sees the abandoning of the potentials of language as a futile endeavour.

4. HEIDEGGER: LANGUAGE AS THE HOUSE OF BEING

Heidegger shares Wittgenstein's suspicion that philosophy has failed in its task. By its concentration on ontology, the question of origins, it has failed to notice man's and its own entanglement in daily practice, the 'ontic', Heidegger's *Dasein*. The question concerning the nature of Being has not been asked correctly throughout the centuries. Its centrality is unveiled in the paradoxical attempt to define it: Being is . . . Any attempt to answer it must have recourse to the actual *Dasein* of the being who can envisage the problem: man (Heidegger 1962: 21–35).

Being and Time, Heidegger's major exploration of the issue published in 1927, summarises the problem in four ways: (1) The nature of *Dasein* is Being-in-the-World (Heidegger 1967: 36–40, 78–86); (2) The nature of Being-in-the-World is care (227, 235–41); (3) The nature of care is temporality manifested in the finality of death (458–64); (4) This temporality is the original time from which all other notions of time (historical, physical, etc.) derive (464–80).

The radicalism of Heidegger's concept and its connection with modernist poetry is first and foremost its farewell to traditional metaphysics. '*Being is the transcendens pure and simple*' (62) is an early statement signalling a farewell even to Kant's idea of an external goal or point of orientation. This inevitably abolishes also the subject–object dichotomy which characterises Western metaphysics from its beginnings. Standing outside *Dasein* is impossible (the special role of death will be discussed below). Although man must assume the availability of things in order to live, this practical relation says nothing about the Being that is both concealed behind the practice and makes it possible. (These things-to-hand are called *Zeug*, 'equipment' in the English translation, but with the connotations of 'stuff' in German, which indicates their reduced value.) It is not viable to talk of a controlling or even creating subject any more either.

Heidegger's attempt to answer the fundamental question of the nature of Being in the analysis of everyday life shows close affinities to T.S. Eliot's poetry. Analogies are the rejection of a transcendental point of view as well as the farewell to a simulated objectivism claiming a special status for man in the realm of *Dasein*. Eliot also explores fundamental issues of what Heidegger calls *Dasein* by depicting it in seemingly banal everyday situations, in Heidegger's words, '*proximally and for the most part* – in its average *everydayness*' (37–8). The dividing line between subject and object becomes fluid for philosopher and poet. This can be noted especially in Eliot's early poems where a continual anthropomorphisation of objects is combined with an often painfully registered reification of human beings. Eliot's early poetry therefore refutes any possible sublimity. It stresses the sordidness of common reality (as, for instance, in 'Preludes') while claiming that this reality is all we have at our disposal.

Behind the appearances, the phenomena of *Dasein*, lies Being, but without being disclosed by them. In a characteristically devious move, Heidegger claims that phenomena simultaneously are referential and yet do not unveil themselves (53–4). He characterises *logos*, the human drive towards understanding, as a mechanism both of disclosure (Plato's *aletheia*) and concealing. In this respect it mirrors the nature of truth (authentic Being) (56–7). This has important implications for the position of language and literature in Heidegger's cosmos. Paul A. Bové rightly claims that '[t]his dualistic definition of *logos* is of crucial importance, because of Heidegger's earlier definition of *logos* as *Rede*, i.e. as speech' (Heidegger 1967: 55–8; Bové 1980: 61). The dialectic of concealing and uncovering is determined by an underlying pattern which is analogous to Pound's notion of *logopoeia*. In Pound's model, *logos* itself structures 'the dance of the intellect among words' (Brooker 1979: 153). This logocentrism pervades the entire modernist 'project'. Its dualism together with the implicit premise that *there is something to conceal or uncover* will become crucial in the evaluation of modernism in Adorno's theory of aesthetics.

The three major characterisations of *Dasein* in *Being and Time*, thrownness (*Geworfenheit*), fallenness (*Verfallenheit*) (Heidegger 1967: 219–24), and that of human action between these poles as a resolute, but eventually ungrounded running towards death (434–9), fit equally well as descriptions of the subject in modernist poems. The origins of this pessimistic concept (which infiltrated French Existentialism) are the disappearance of traditional certainties, the crumbling of established paradigms of ontology, subjectivity and teleology. These encompass the origin, *raison d'être*, constitution and goals of human beings.

The profound disorientation and uncertainty characteristic of modern existence can be found even in poems which seemingly have recourse to traditional models, such as Yeats's earlier ones. They employ traditional narratives, mainly those of Irish folklore. Yet it is evident that they prefer alienated and dislocated protagonists thrown into a hostile environment. It is equally apparent that solutions to their existential impasses are often sought in romantic dissolution, in self-sacrifice and suicidal struggle – Heidegger's running towards death.

Thomas Rentsch links this romantic concept with the rhetoric and experience of the First World War – in which, incidentally, Heidegger never actively took part (Rentsch 1989: 61, 144). It would be worthwhile to pursue this influence on the rhetorical strategies of modernist poems. In some of them, one could argue, it paves the way for fascistic ideas. Heidegger's shifting of nothingness into the centre of attention is clearly analogous to poems of Eliot's middle phase, such as 'Gerontion', 'The Hollow Men', and *Ash-Wednesday*. Pound's *oeuvre*, too, is concerned with endangered existence, although it is more preoccupied with the erection of barricades against the threat than passive suffering. This becomes most obvious in the *Pisan Cantos*, but one can already detect the tendency in the various erections of monuments – to past characters mainly, but also to mere events – in Pound's earlier poetry. It culminates in *Hugh Selwyn Mauberley* where the strategy is analysed and questioned, yet not abandoned.

Pound's pragmatic stress on action also finds its expression in his preference of Confucius, the philosopher of action and order, to Lao-tzu, the prophet of passive suffering. It is paralleled by Heidegger's insistence on action despite lack of orientation and justification. His notion of resoluteness (Heidegger 1962: 434–9) is, as Rentsch argues, based on an uncritical understanding of Truth in *Being and Time* which decides out of itself whether *Dasein* is authentic or not (Rentsch 1989: 166). Furthermore, *Entschlossenheit* (resoluteness) has close affinities with *Erschlossenheit* (uncoveredness) and therefore relates to the observed dialectic of revealing and concealing. Inside the gesture against the transcendental remains an unquestioned and unquestionable authority outside *Dasein* as its very core. This ignorance later blends in with the foregrounding of fate over the individual and forms the link between Heidegger's philosophy and German fascism – which Heidegger actively supported. An echo of this blindness can be detected in Pound's concern for *cheng ming*, correct expression, which also suspiciously lacks exterior norms defining it, but nonetheless becomes the all-encompassing rule of his later works.

Heidegger's emphasis on time as a human concept which is governed by man's existential needs completes the Enlightenment discovery of time as *history*. It removes time from its mythical cyclic origins and its subsequent submission to theological frameworks by making it part of human practice. Yet Heidegger goes even further and removes time from the disposal of the individual altogether. In his stress on existence as an impersonal concept (which later merges with fate again) he shifts time into a mythical realm again. This mirrors the experiments with time schemes in modernist poetry (see the discussion of time in *The Waste Land*) as well as its eventual return to a 'neo-mythical' view of time (as in *Ash-Wednesday, Four Quartets* and *The Cantos*). Heidegger's evaluation, however, is actually capable of discussing the crux that only ever features as a structural impasse in modernist poems: the seemingly paradoxical integration of every new text in a tradition it is designed to overcome and leave behind. In the initial set-up of *Being and Time*, Heidegger discusses the dilemma:

> Dasein 'is' its past in the way of its own Being, which, to put it roughly, 'historizes' (*geschieht*) out of its future on each occasion. Whatever the way of being it may have at the time, and thus with whatever understanding of Being it may possess, Dasein has grown up both into and in a traditional way of interpreting itself: in terms of this it understands itself proximally and, within a certain range, constantly. By this understanding, the possibilities of its Being are disclosed and regulated. Its own past – and this always means the past of its 'generation' – is not something which *follows along after* Dasein, but something which already goes ahead of it.
>
> (41)

The reduced importance of the individual and the mythical idea of destiny are prefigured in Heidegger's shift from *Schicksal*, fate, to *Geschick*, destiny – which is already that of a people in the important paragraph 74 of *Being and Time* (see especially 436). It culminates in Heidegger's famous turn of ideas, his *Kehre*, which he always wanted to be understood as a consequent development, a turning in the path of his thinking, rather than a reversal. It, too, can be linked with the impasses of modernism and its attempts to escape from or solve them. After the elimination of subject and object as distinct poles, Heidegger's stress on human practice as the only legitimate point of orientation is left in a curious vacuum which resembles the locus of the utterance of the modernist poem. Who speaks or acts in the face of what? What has started as a critical enterprise responding to the alienation of the individual in a technological modern world, i.e. what is fundamentally a conservative move (compare the similar paradox of *The Waste Land*), actually destroys the very subjectivity it was meant to rescue from inauthenticity and its alienation from original Being.

The lapse of *Dasein* into inauthenticity, Heidegger's *Verfallenheit*, is always linked with a pronounced distaste for the collective. Just as in modernist poems it is always the individual whose interaction with others is alienated and disturbed, in Heidegger's philosophy it is 'the particular *Dasein*' that becomes the victim of the *Man*, the German grammatical 'one', the faceless human collective into which it disperses ('They' in the English translation: 167).

In this fatal attraction of the collective, the crucial role of language is highlighted. Although present from the introductory moves of Heidegger's concepts, it remains a tool, very much in accord with other 'things-to-hand' or 'stuff' in his terminology. When it comes to scrutinising the mechanisms through which existence loses its authenticity, however, the gap between the authentic and everyday existence opens exactly where the problems of modernist poetry start: in language. Authenticity stands for the connection of original Being and practice and is therefore the very equivalent of signified and signifier in linguistic theory. The crucial proof of lapsing into the inauthentic is the reduction of language to idle talk (*Gerede*), curiosity, and ambiguity (211–24, especially 219).

Bové stresses the connection between idle talk and literature:

> . . . in the context of literature, the idea of idle talk is of most interest. In the immediate context of his discussion of the primordial and derivative senses of truth, Heidegger points out how the authentic use of language to bring about disclosure becomes, through repetition in an assertion, an inauthentic expression of something present-at-hand in which Dasein's disclosedness is covered-up.
>
> (Bové 1980: 59)

In his above summary of Heidegger's concept Bové also outlines the inherent ambivalence of modernism to its outside. Equally important for an evaluation of modernism through Heidegger's ideas is his condemnation of curiosity and ambiguity. While the disqualification of ambiguity is self-evident in a system of thinking that strives towards authenticity, curiosity seems a rather innocent victim of the attack. For is it not, after all, also the generative force behind philosophy? Not exclusively so in Heidegger:

> When curiosity has become free, however, it concerns itself with seeing, not in order to understand what is seen (that is, to come into a Being towards it) but *just* in order to see. . . .
>
> In this kind of seeing, that which is an issue for care does not lie in grasping something and being knowingly in the truth; it lies rather in its possibilities of abandoning itself to the world.
>
> (Heidegger 1967: 216)

This is a shorthand description of self-reflection, the inward turn so central to modernism. An outside is abandoned in favour of introspection, also because internal impasses, lack of foundation, etc. have become evident. Adorno calls this the essential tension between the mimetic and the constructed. In economic terms, a devaluation takes place, an inflationary corruption called usury in Pound's *Cantos*. Language, the shape in which *logos* as human curiosity presents itself, is already the receptacle of true Being in *Being and Time*. When its use detaches it from true Being, this must indeed appear as the ultimate sin. This crucial role of language becomes even more prominent in Heidegger's later works.

In paragraph 17 of *Being and Time*, entitled 'Reference and Signs', the elementary dichotomy within language is analysed with regard to everyday phenomena such as signposts and signals as well as banners and signs of mourning (108). The difference between these signs parallels Peirce's definition of arbitrary signs (which he calls symbols) as opposed to motivated signs (indices). Heidegger defines the distinction as the one between referring and relating: 'Every reference is a relation, but not every relation is a reference. Every 'indication' is a reference, but not every referring is an indicating. This implies at the same time that every 'indication' is a relation, but not every relation is an indicating' (108).

What the convoluted formula describes is again the problematic motivation of the sign, the source also of the structural problems of modernist poetry. It becomes crucial in Heidegger's thinking, because his exclusive orientation in the 'real' confronts him with signs only – out of which he somehow has to extract real Being. This is his attempt to solve the problem: 'Indeed we shall eventually have to show that 'relations' themselves, *because* of their formally general character, have their ontological source in a reference' (108).

The move is analogous to the nominalist upside-down turn of modernism. Signs do not convey meaning because they refer to real things, but reality has its source in the sign.

Heidegger quickly draws a line by claiming that various phenomena must be distinguished from his referential sign. These are traces, residues, commemorative monuments, documents, testimony, symbols, expression, appearances and signification. He disqualifies them because they are subject to interpretation. The exclusion is a safety mechanism against a tendency already encountered in Heidegger's counterpart Wittgenstein: the reduction to absolute factuality procures a universalism. The hotchpotch of excluded phenomena unveils in its logical flaws (traces are certainly indices, and so are residues) that the postulated connection between the inauthentic phenomena of *Dasein* and an authentic Being at their basis is questionable. Heidegger's already mentioned 'turn' eventually overcomes the ambivalence of uncovering and covering-up by succumbing to a universalism which, as a 'positive' result, prepares for his hermeneutic universe, a reality of interpretation (the very mechanism that is still disqualified in *Being and Time*). This eventually and inevitably becomes a linguistic universe.

On the negative side, Heidegger's 'turn' produces results analogous to Nietzsche and Wittgenstein as well as the self-preservation strategies of modernist poems. The individual is wiped out when the linguistic universe takes over in which 'the world worlds'.[5] A system that started as a critique of traditional subject-centred phenomenology (Husserl, its main exponent, was Heidegger's teacher) eventually surmounts individuality altogether. It is arguable that this move, which is analogous to Nietzsche's superman transcending the ordinary individual and Wittgenstein's denial of the subject, is in its facile exclusion as simplistic as phenomenology with its unproblematic notion of subjectivity.

In its inevitability, Heidegger's turn mirrors modernism's attempts at impersonality, one of its ways of closing its eyes to its internal tensions. The effects of the move are also strikingly similar. Once the individual is overcome, two things shift fetish-like into the centre of attention. In his later writings 'The Origin of the Work of Art' and 'The Thing' (Heidegger 1971: 15–87; 163–86), the artistic work and the 'simple things' replace his former interest in human practice. They become substitutes for abandoned transcendental finalities and values. A streamlining and reification has taken place, a reduction of the complexities of existence in *Being and Time* to two petrified poles which the earlier Heidegger would simply have labelled 'stuff'.

This simplification in Heidegger's later philosophy reflects a general tendency within modernism. The interest in 'the simple thing' which merely *is*, despite all knowledge of cognition, interpretation, etc., runs like a thread through the works of the poets discussed in the present study. It eventually culminates in Pound's *res*. The circular move of disqualifying faith and investing art with the task and potentials of former transcendental truths has been outlined in the chapter on economy; as has the resulting need to evoke the powers of these obsolete truths to preserve some paradoxical value for the artistic work and reasons for its existence and continuation. It will be re-encountered below in Adorno's critique of Heidegger's thinking and the stress on the impossibility of reconciliation in Adorno's aesthetic theories.

That underneath the radical destructive attitude of existential philosophy there lurks a tendency to postulate an eventual 'redemption' is demonstrated by Thomas Rentsch in his comparison of traditional Christian dogma and Heidegger's existential analysis. He calls the latter, in accord with Adorno and others, a regressive myth, a theology without God. This is his schema (Rentsch 1989: 150; my translation):

Christian dogma	*Existential analysis*
(1) Protology (teaching of the creation and continuation of the World)	(1) Phenomenology of thrownness (factuality) into a Being-in-the-World
(2) Hamartiology (teaching of Original Sin)	(2) Phenomenology of fallenness; phenomenology of care, anxiety, conscience and guilt; inauthenticity
(3) Soteriology (teaching of redemption; especially Christology, teaching of reconciliation)	(3) Phenomenology of authenticity; disclosure of wholeness through mortal fear and the call of conscience
(4) Pneumatology (teaching of the Holy Ghost)	(4) Phenomenology of the freedom towards death and the fearful determination
(5) Eschatology (teaching of the conclusion, of the end of things and the Last Judgement)	(5) Phenomenology of running towards death

Figure 4

The five aspects of Heidegger's thinking could also act as philosophical descriptions of the poems analysed in the present study. Even texts which are historically, religiously and culturally as distinct as Hopkins's *The Wreck of the Deutschland*, Yeats's 'The Tower', Eliot's *The Waste Land*, and Pound's *The Cantos* (to name but a few major ones) share the same existential premises. These are characterised by radical destabilisation and loss. In Hans-Joachim Höhn's words:

> The process of modernity has unveiled numerous conditions of human life which had previously been regarded as absolute, unchangeable, and necessary to be contingent and thus shifted them into the realm of disposition of human decisions and

> transformations. In the same way, much of that hitherto regarded as uncontrollable, because coincidental, was discovered to be ruled by natural laws and therefore made predictable and calculable. In this bilateral process, both the awareness of contingency was enlarged and the destabilising effects of experienced contingency were removed.
>
> (Höhn 1992: 141–2; my translation)

Rentsch quotes Wilhelm Schapp, Heidegger's contemporary and fellow student under Husserl, who claims retrospectively that of the critical philosophy of the Enlightenment – which culminates in Kant's three postulates of God, freedom and immortality – after Heidegger nothing remains but death (Rentsch 1989: 150–1).

Death, the limit against which modernist poetry has to defend itself both internally and as the macrocosmic enterprise of producing art in the face of inevitable destruction, is turned into a constructive force by Heidegger. To come into existence, man has to learn about his mortality: '*death, as the end of Dasein, is Dasein's ownmost possibility – non-relational, certain and as such indefinite, not to be outstripped. Death is*, as *Dasein's* end, in the Being of this entity *towards* its end' (Heidegger 1967: 303).

'Rational living beings must first *become* mortals', is Heidegger's claim in 'The Thing' (Heidegger 1971: 179), the dark counterpart of Lacan's later dictum 'It is my duty that I come into being, even if I lose myself in the process.' In the face of death, in mortal fear, original Being can still be glimpsed, according to Heidegger.

The modernist project in all its variants is clearly a balancing on the borderlines of its own possibility and destruction. Language supplies both the original source of authentic Being and the means of its decline to inauthenticity. The rift is incurable, and it opens up in the ambiguity, arbitrariness and potential emptiness of the sign itself. It reverberates through the textual structures depending on it where it produces the obscurity, ambiguity and fragmentation so dearly beloved as superficial characterisations of modernism.

The postulation of an original and now lost authenticity, a truth and value inherent in language and now corrupted by it, runs from traditional Christian doctrine through Western metaphysics to the toppling of the latter in Heidegger, Foucault and Derrida. Foucault's claim in *The Order of Things* that the true nature of language is forever removed from human knowledge, yet literature sometimes permits glimpses of it, is the equivalent of Heidegger's concept. Modernist poetry, as has been demonstrated, is based on aesthetic premises which constantly undermine its existence. According to

Paul de Man, this manifestation in spite of an awareness of its own impossibility is the defining mark of modernism. Yet the equilibrium between acknowledging its paradoxical status and creating artistic utterances which, as de Man rightly claims, must strive for duration, is a delicate one.[6]

Adorno criticises Heidegger and a branch of German philosophy following in his tracks of existential analysis which mourns lost authenticity (Karl Jaspers is the main exponent) as producers of an ideologically loaded 'jargon of authenticity' in his book of the same title (Adorno 1973). By merely exposing the discrepancies between an ungraspable true Being and the daily corruption of *Dasein*, this brand of philosophy conveniently ignores the fact that it is itself affected by the corrosion it laments. The reason for this is again its dependence on language: 'The search for meaning as that which something is authentically, and as that which is hidden in it, pushes away, often unnoticed and therefore all the faster, the question as to the right of this something. Analysis of meaning becomes the norm in this demand, not only for the signs, but also for that which they refer to' (Adorno 1973: 41).

In bypassing its own impotence, the philosophical discourse of authenticity sets itself up as authentic. It reifies itself (10) as exempt from societal conditioning – and in its postulation of true Being from both history and personality. Retroactively it thus invests 'fallen' language with some truth too, as a sort of wrapping of an authentic core: 'The nimbus in which the works are being wrapped, like oranges in tissue paper, takes under its own direction the mythology of language, as if the radiant force of the words could not yet quite be trusted' (43).

The analogies to the aesthetics of modernist poetry are evident: out of a total disqualification and devaluation of itself, an insecurity concerning even the smallest elements at its disposal, evolves a universalist model, a machinery that invests itself with value. It sets itself up as a replacement of what it has both wiped aside and actively destroyed – and in a paradoxical counter-move also tried to grasp and retain: truth, reality and subjectivity. Within its own synthetic reality it gains artificial value down to its smallest elements, even though it must employ a constant self-mystification to cover up the simulation strategies which keep its machinery running. The move away from the sign as a constituent of poems to strangely ungrounded 'things', Eliot's 'objective correlative', Pound's *res* and Yeats's concrete artefacts as symbols of art and poetry, his golden nightingale and stone Chinamen, are indications of this strategy.

Yet the setting-up of the immutable, the durable and eternal, whether in the most sophisticated work of art or the 'simple thing', always remains entangled with the complementary forces of dissolution, destruction and death. Heidegger's 'worlding world' in which language constitutes reality and retains an ungraspable essence of true Being (as a closed restrictive economy in Bataille's terms, a perfect narcissistic wholeness in psychoanalytic ones) has its counterpart in the silence of nothingness. 'As the shrine of Nothing, death is the shelter of being' is Heidegger's truly poetic description (Heidegger 1971: 177). The German *Gebirg* contains both *bergen* (to shelter) and *verbergen* (to conceal) in Heidegger's curious etymology, and thus an analogy to Freud's ambiguous *uncanny*: it is reassuring in its familiarity and presence, but simultaneously threatening in its strange mysteriousness. Death mirrors the simultaneously uncovering and concealing nature of Being. Once more, value is to be retained, loss to be prevented. This time the most essential value must be rescued: that of Being itself.

Threatened by its antithesis, death, an inclusion is attempted that puts to shame even the ventures of modernist poems to integrate their own structural impasses. In the same way that death as the negation of existence is declared to make an authentic life as a mortal possible, silence as the negation of language now enters an existential relation with the authentic Being retained by language and the reality constituted by it. Silence therefore gets its share of authenticity and truth as much as its positive twin, language. Indeed, the very symbol of the shrine employed by Heidegger hints at the almost religious significance of its content. Poetry – which represents most clearly the dialectic of speaking and silence – is promoted to an almost messianic representative of truth: 'The nature of art is poetry. The nature of poetry, in turn, is the founding of truth' (Heidegger 1971: 75).

Nothingness cannot be spoilt by *Dasein* in the same way as silence cannot be invaded by the inflationary processes within language. Consequently both entities become even more authentic than the authentic. Here they fall together with what Baudrillard describes in exactly those terms: they become a simulacrum. 'The real does not efface itself in favor of the imaginary: it effaces itself in favor of the more than real: the hyperreal. The truer than true: this is simulation' (Baudrillard 1990: 11). This is what happens in the sophisticated inclusions of death in the structures of modernist poems, in Eliot's *Four Quartets* where death appears as a mere layer in his vertical model of history, and in a more opaque form in the plethora of documents and monuments bringing the past back to life again in *The Cantos*. These are clever acknowledgements of death while simultaneously countering its destructive force by the poems' own act of reconstruction by simulation.

Internally, Heidegger's growing addiction to a symbolically charged language is of course a contradiction of his disqualification of the symbol as inauthentic and incapable of being referential. It merges with his constant attempts to reinvest common language with new meaning by capitalisation, hyphenation and the use of archaic forms (such as *Seyn* for *Sein* in his later writings). This often creates false pathos and even kitsch. In Adorno's biting words: 'the untruth indicts itself by becoming bombastic' (Adorno 1973: 13). In the same way as Wittgenstein's, Heidegger's striving for pure factuality becomes ensnared in the traps of language. While modernist poetry yearns to purify its worn-out material, he tries to create his own vocabulary, a microcosmic endeavour that mirrors his macrocosmic idea that language creates the world. The results of the attempts are similar. In both cases an inflation happens which produces internally the symptoms of the corruption that the utterance (philosophical or poetic) was meant to criticise.

Modernist poetry is caught between the twin attractions of endlessly constituting its synthetic Being along the rails of language and drifting into the authenticity of silence. In a reversal of Heidegger's image, it could therefore be labelled both the manifestation of being in the nothingness of an inauthentic world and the reminder of nothingness in a reality of established certainties. As such, it calls to mind also the limits of existence. It of necessity both constitutes and destroys – certainties, reality and identity. In its affirmation – at least of itself, in its minimal utterance: 'I am a poem' (see *Ash-Wednesday*) – it always also contains its own negation. When Adorno claims that, following Nietzsche's insight, the modernist aesthetic reverses traditional philosophy by postulating that 'truth exists only as a product of historical becoming' (Adorno 1984: 4), he only captures one side of the coin. For this does not automatically liberate it from its 'one-time ignominious relation to magical abracadabra, human servitude and entertainment'. It requires an emphatic view of modernist art to claim that 'it has after all annihilated these tendencies along with the memory of its fall from grace' (4).

The final part of Adorno's statement reveals why. Modernism's necessary work of destruction leaves its traces – and nowhere else but in the artistic works themselves. They become part of the relational tension of existence according to Heidegger. There every affirmation of existence here and now carries with it a wherefrom and whither, an orientation both towards an origin in the past and a goal in the future (Heidegger 1962: 145). This means that artistic works cannot free themselves from past compulsions – such as the search for a hidden truth behind their material. They can only analyse these compulsions in themselves, and this creates the tension of production and destruction described at various points in the present study. Even in lyric poetry, traditionally associated with timelessness and lack of progression, this tension becomes visible (de Man 1983: 166–86). It is no coincidence that in the development of modernism the lyric mode loses its autonomy and becomes increasingly incorporated into larger patterns which, although deriving from a rejection of the epic, drift towards a post- or neo-epic character. The final attempt to rescue the lyric mode as a viable aesthetic model, Imagism, drifts either towards meaninglessness in its inability to make statements – or into silence. Once more, reification or death unveil themselves as alternative limits.

Adorno tries to formulate the impasses of modernism and truth positively in his *Aesthetic Theory:* 'Art works talk like fairies in tales: if you want the absolute, you shall have it, but only in disguise. By contrast, the truth of discursive knowledge, while undisguised, is unattainable' (Adorno 1984: 183).

Art possesses what it strives for, because it cannot gain access to it. In its futile attempt to reach it, however, it unveils it to its percipient – in the form of a riddle. The shape of modernist poetry, the often observed inward turn of self-reflection, is this endeavour to reach beyond its own capacity. This endeavour only ever leads to an insight into its own shortcomings which finds its expression both in silences and gaps and in metonymic fragmentation.

> The enigma of works of art is the fact of their having been broken off. If transcendence were really present in them, they would be mysteries rather than riddles. They are not. They are riddles precisely because they are fragments disclaiming to be wholes, even though wholes is what they really want to be.
>
> (Adorno 1984: 184)

NOTES

1. Published in *Journal of Speculative Philosophy* in the essay 'Questions Concerning Certain Faculties Claimed for Man' (1868) which was followed by two other essays in the same and the following year (Krampen et al. 1981: 32).
2. The law of causality is one of the four basic rules of formal logic. It states that things are as they are, because there is a reason for them being what they are. The sentence has always been the cause of dispute. See Klaus, Buhr 1976, vol. 2: 1089–90.
3. This collections of fragments forms an interesting unity with the *Tractatus* and, apart from shedding some light on various implications of the sometimes cryptic formulas of the much earlier treatise, demonstrates that the claim that Wittgenstein developed two entirely distinct philosophies ignores the recurrence of the same themes and problems both in his early and late stage.
4. The German original abounds with terms that are both physical and metaphysical, such as *Hinausgestiegen* which means to climb on top or over something, but also to transcend, even to become sublime or – in a derogatory sense – over the top.
5. 'World presences by worlding' (Heidegger 1971: 179).
6. 'The ambivalence of writing is such that it can be considered both an act and an interpretative process that follows after an act with which it cannot coincide. As such, it both affirms and denies its own nature or specificity' (de Man 1983: 152).

Defying Conclusions: Opening up Modernism

The truth of modernist poems lies in their continual failure, in their simultaneous constitution and negation of themselves. Their aesthetics are therefore necessarily characterised by paradoxical anti-aesthetic tendencies as well. They try to leave the realm of mere appearances, Thomas Mann's 'sham', behind, but in doing so automatically undermine the premises of their own production and make themselves impossible.

Their relation to the historic, social and political reality in which they manifest themselves is influenced by their internal contradictions. Modernist poems are not mere mimetic depictions, mirror images of an environment that determine their shape and that of their material, language. They are not plaster-casts of society, not even through the psyche of an author living in it. Neither are they completely autonomous, free and unrestricted explorations of possibilities, experiments for experiment's sake. 'While art opposes society, it is incapable of taking up a vantage point beyond it. Art's opposition is thus in part identification with what it opposes' (Adorno 1984: 194). The discussion of modernist poetry reproducing the mechanisms of capitalism in the mystification of its artificial surplus of value has revealed this impasse.

In a complex double bind, modernist poems respond to societal conditions which provide the realm and the stimulus of works as well as their material, but their response dislocates the premises from which they emerge. It destabilises their authority, and questions their validity in a way much later recaptured theoretically in textual deconstruction. To remain within Adorno's imagery: the modernist poem gives answers to the questions of modernity, yet they are always inadequate ones. Inadequate in such a radical way that they undermine even the act of asking questions, i.e. the process of reading and interpretation with its tacit agreements between reader and text. The poem violates the locutionary aspect of discourse by mutilating and obscuring the message until it eventually threatens meaning and interpretation altogether (as in *The Waste Land*). It corrodes the illocutionary aspect, too: the modernist poem makes it increasingly difficult to locate its voice, its identity. It splits it up, disqualifies its fragments as mere quotations or irony, until it eventually unveils the very concept of subjectivity as far from stable.

While obscurity, ambiguity and the problematic 'voice' of modernist poems have received much critical attention, their third and equally radical aspect of destabilisation has often been conveniently neglected: the perlocutionary aspect, the way in which the poems act as reading-instructions, as reader-controlling devices. In this function the shift from a classical readerly work – which presents itself as both approachable and stable, firmly based in a shared code and context with the reader – to a writerly perspective becomes most evident. Modernist poems dislocate both their own position (here, illocutionary and perlocutionary aspect are linked) and that of their percipient. They achieve this destabilisation also by transgressing genre borderlines (both *The Waste Land* and *The Cantos* are lyric *and* epic *and* dramatic) and through fragmentation and montage. Those strategies leave the reader searching for the meaning he expects from a readerly text with an abyss that threatens his very role as reader and turns him into a simultaneous creator and destroyer. This rarely makes modernist poems pleasant reading experiences. They do not reassure us in our settled habits of thinking (or indeed not thinking) about ourselves, but in their act of self-sacrifice highlight the cracks in our concept of ourselves as subjects.

Yet, as the preceding chapters have shown, there is also an equally strong tendency in modernist poems to present themselves as coherent and complete, as works. Even more striking, they display a desire to leave their character as appearance behind and try to overcome internal ruptures by presenting themselves as synthetic wholes, as an artificial consciousness or even a reality of their own. This 'reality' of the modernist poem, far from declaring itself a mere alternative utopian realm (Paul Klee's *Zwischenwelt* or Lyotard's *Nebenwelt*; Lyotard 1989: 202), is – on the contrary – characterised by a continual expansion of its power which has its source in its constructedness. The failure to be mimetic is transformed into a rejection of the mimetic or rather into a massive redistribution of value on to the aspect of construction. This suddenly all-powerful construction (the realm of modernism's complete autonomy, the locus of its 'project') secures its power by exclusion. In Adorno's words, it 'manifests intolerance of all externality and wants to transform itself into a reality *sui generis*' (Adorno 1984: 85). On the level of the smallest constituent of the modernist poem, the sign, the all-too problematic connection between signifier and signified is overcome by a further reduction: now the signifier alone remains and guarantees the absolute control of signification.

This claim for universality is inherent in all facets of modernism and can be detected in their aspiration for unrestricted competence: everything can be interpreted in psychoanalytic or economic terms or those of existential philosophy. And should the object be unwilling to be integrated, it is forcibly excluded as standing for something else or even as something of which we cannot sensibly speak. It is arguable that the claim that literature has no distinct boundaries, that it is concerned with and capable of making statements on everything, is a variant of this universalism. It would be an interesting endeavour to pursue the historic roots of a development which eventually permits the highly specialised discourse called poetry, for instance, to produce a 'poem including history' in the shape of *The Cantos*.

An alternative expression of the totalitarian tendency of modernist poetry, alternative to the ceaseless significatory exertions of a poem like *The Cantos*, is the 'calming' of the material (see Pound's 'Alchemist'), the stabilisation of its processes in once more symbolic shape. Eliot's *Four Quartets* are an example of the seeming reconciliation of the internal contradictions of modernist poems. The recourse to the symbolic helps them overcome their tensions. It creates a oneness, a whole, that – according to de Man's description of modernism as struggle – should no longer be possible. It is, but – as Adorno points out – only in the form of an illusion (Adorno 1984: 425). The illusory harmony of a dubious reconciliation of irreconcilable tensions (between subject and object, work and world, language and truth) is, as Adorno demonstrates, an inward turn within modernism, a retraction of the developments that have brought modernism's negative or anti-aesthetic aesthetics into being. Expression, so Adorno claims, is the result of modernism's insistence on dissonance, its stress on its constructive aspect which clashes with the traditionally mimetic task of art. If this dissonance is overcome, then artistic expression becomes impossible (160–2).

This becomes immediately evident in the problem of the perfect symbol in Yeats which would bring about the end of the poetic utterance. At the opposite end of the spectrum, Vorticism attempts the institutionalisation of a force analogous to Nietzsche's constructive/destructive drive to create metaphors – and therefore the reconciliation of the irreconcilable. Strictly applied, it would remain a theory without application. It is easy to see why: where is the possible abode of a poetic text which must of necessity try to achieve duration, if not permanence, in a concept of perpetual flux? One can only imagine it as the residue left on the walls of the vortex, as deficient and waste from its very conception.

In order to fulfil itself, modernist poetry must keep a precarious balance. It must pursue modernity's tendency (highlighted in Nietzsche) of transforming reality into an aesthetic construct. Yet it must not give in to a complete aestheticisation of reality, to the idea of its own omnipotence in the allure of its simulated reality. For this would, as Wolfgang Welsch convincingly demonstrates, entail the transformation of aesthetics into what he calls anaesthetics. By that he means the equivalent of Adorno's dubious 'more', the reckless adding of a nimbus of truth and authenticity to the results of experiences which are conditioned and conditional, the creation of compulsory norms out of relative insights (Welsch 1990: 25). In this respect, Walter Benjamin's description of fascism as an aestheticisation of history comes to mind (Benjamin 1968: 243–4). Fascism is indeed the most drastic form of complete aestheticisation turning into absolute anaesthesia: of ethics, values and an entire people.

Similar tendencies, albeit on a smaller scale, can be found in extreme examples of modernist poems. *The Cantos* with their aim of selling their own idiosyncratic jumble of fragments as universally valid history have been mentioned several times. But there are other, seemingly more harmless expressions of the same disposition. Eliot's *Four Quartets* represent such an aesthetic reconciliation of tensions, of most existential doubts and impotences. They are indeed capable of creating an enormous beauty out of their desperation. But this is their hook. By laying bare all their impasses, Eliot's *Four Quartets* also cover up their strategy of control. Who could deny the charges of this text? Who could fail to sympathise, indeed to identify with its narcissistic visions of individual failure, and who does not experience relief at the assimilation of these shortcomings into a universal pattern? This seemingly unlimited competence of the poem, its total inclusion of discursive positions towards it, or (which means the same thing) its 'intolerance of all externality', exposes it as an end of modernism, as false according to modernism's own endeavour of relativisation and plurality.

Self-reflection is the key term in modernist poetry's delicate balancing act. It must of necessity constitute itself and even strive to achieve an impossible unity. This is, as Adorno reminds us, the inheritance of myth as an attempt to master the chaos of nature. Yet part of its internal dialectic is also its drive towards dissolution as the acceptance of heterogeneity (Adorno 1984: 266–7). In this modernist poems acknowledge their constructive potential and the tensions created by its interplay with the mimetic. Both the fake unity of their own reification as truth, history and work of art and the unrestrained flow of signification, the dissolution into an endless utterance, are therefore false variants of modernism in poetry. False because they betray the essential character of the modernist work as tension.

> The concept of tension is above the suspicion of being formalistic. Tension highlights dissonant experience and antinomial relations in the artistic object, thus stressing precisely the substantive moment of 'form'. It is through its inner tensions that the art work defines itself as a field of force, even when it has already come to rest, i.e. when it is objectified. A work of art is as much a sum total of relations of tensions as it is an attempt to dissolve them.
>
> (Adorno 1984: 407)

False reconciliation and wholeness as well as unrestricted dissolution break off the modernist dialectic simply because they do not break off the works. The work of art, as has been revealed in the discussion of textual economy, is one of the stumbling blocks of modernist poetry. In Mann's *Doctor Faustus*, it is the devil who not only has the best tunes, but also the best arguments against the concept of the 'work' (he talks about music, but his remarks have general significance):

> The prohibitive difficulties of the work lie deep in the work itself. The historical movement of the musical material has turned against the self-contained work. It shrinks in time, it scorns extension in time, which is the dimension of a musical work, and lets it stand empty. Not out of impotence, not out of incapacity to give form. Rather from a ruthless demand for compression, which taboos the superfluous, negates the phrase, shatters the ornament, stands opposed to any extension of time, which is the life-form of the work. Work, time, and pretence, they are one, and together they fall victim to critique. It no longer tolerates pretence and play, the fiction, the self-glorification of form, which censors the passions and human suffering, divides out the parts, translates into pictures. Only the non-fictional is still permissible, the unplayed, the undisguised

> and untransfigured expression of suffering in its actual moment. Its impotence and extremity are so ingrained that no seeming play with them is any longer allowed.
>
> (Mann 1968: 233–4)

The wrongful continuation of the work in the false reconciliation of its tensions leads to the loss of the riddle, the riddle that Adorno interprets as the only way in which truth can present itself, but also the riddle that Baudrillard regards as the essence of reality itself. Baudrillard calls the productive abstinence from false reconciliation 'seduction'.[1] Seduction is the productive because non-affirmative process (not action, since it is self-determined) which reminds the dubious subject of its object-status. It is indeed the reader-controlling aspect in which the false closure or the true fragmentation of the modernist poem manifest themselves. An open text like *The Waste Land* directs the attention to the problem of interpretation, thus ultimately to the possibility of reading and creating a modernist poem in the best possible sense of Heidegger's definition in *Being and Time*: 'Interpretation [is not] the acquiring of information about what is understood; it is rather the working-out of possibilities projected in understanding' (Heidegger 1962: 188–9).

A closed text like *Four Quartets* convinces and invites to be understood, but does not question and indeed obscures the origins of understanding. It aims at being accepted. In the same way *The Cantos* force their reader to follow their *periplous* of learning, prescribe secondary works without which the text cannot be understood, and spoonfeed their reader their own egotistical canon of underlying material as normative. Out of an organicist notion of the development of signification ('To significations, words accrue'; Heidegger 1967: 204) evolves a work that sells itself as true.[2] Henri Birault characterises the endeavour in emphatic terms (once more in relation to Heidegger): 'To develop a nonaesthetic conception of the work of art and to elaborate a new rule for the dialogue between thinkers and poets . . .' (Kockelmans 1972: 161). Baudrillard interprets this desire in characteristically pragmatic fashion as the artistic work's reaction to the transformation of the aesthetic into a commodity. Its way out, he claims, is the transformation of itself into an 'absolute commodity' (Baudrillard 1990: 116–19), 'absolute' corresponding to Steven Connor's notion of 'the resistance of value' (Connor 1992: 95–9).

The second focus of the end of the modernist poem is the subject. It, too, is in a precarious position. Modernism's tendency to subject both its outside and its inside makes subjectivity immaterial (Adorno

1984: 84–5). This becomes most evident in the various strategies to achieve impersonality. Yet the paradox remains that the greater the impersonality of the poems (as in Imagism or *The Cantos*), the stronger the textual identity at work remains, albeit in concealed form. This is a sign that the poems do not abandon an underlying concept of subjectivity. They endanger it in their identities (as in Eliot's early works culminating in *The Waste Land*) when they unveil its constructedness, but they refuse to give it up – for this would entail their end as works. It would make their discourse one of madness and terminate their message. From a psychoanalytic angle one could argue that even if they wanted to, they could not abandon subjectivity, for this would mean abandoning their ability to return from the symbolic to the imaginary. This way is blocked by consciousness.

All this does not permit the subjectivity expressed in the textual identities of the poems, the *ego scriptor* of a poem like *The Cantos*, an easy victory. Indeed it grants it no victory at all. The inextricable connection of subject and work is also the downfall of the subject. In Adorno's words:

> One reason why works of art are things is that they *qua* autonomous objectification are like an in-itself – a determined and fixed entity which is at rest – patterned after the world of empirical things. Objectification is brought about by the synthetic unity of spirit. Works become spiritual only by being thing-like; their spirit and their thing-likeness are products of their reciprocal relation. Their spirit which serves them as means of transcendence also brings them death. Implicitly, they have had this mortal quality all along but it is the need for reflection that brings it out into the open.
>
> (Adorno 1984: 389–90)

Death is the be-all and end-all of modernist poems. It is the realm in which Adorno's negative utopia of the reconciliation of the irreconcilable is situated.

> Art is left with a single *parti pris*, which is one in favour of death. This allows art to be at once critical and metaphysical. Works of art originate in the world of things: their material as well as their methods are derived from it. In fact, there is nothing in them that does not belong to the world of things also, nothing that does not entail the price of death if it were wrested from that world. Art partakes in reconciliation only because it is deadly, which is why it continues to be enslaved to myth. This is the Egyptian quality that characterizes all art. Wanting to immortalize the transitory – life – art in fact kills it.
>
> The moment of reconciliation in art works has justly been seen to lie in their openness: they alone can heal the wounds that they

> inflict. By forswearing intervention in reality, i.e. by shunning real domination, artistic reason gains a dimension of innocence, although art, the greatest products included, resonates with social repression, and although art becomes culpable precisely because it refuses to intervene – a culpability that is shared by spirit.
>
> (Adorno 1984: 194)

This is the link between modernism's openness, its denial of false reconciliations and the recent dispute about the resurrected notion of the sublime. Wolfgang Welsch stresses the idea of reconciliation as a negative utopia in Adorno and claims that by his insistence on the necessary incompleteness of works, Adorno rejects the possibility of a practical reconciliation although he retains it as a paradoxical goal. This is what makes him an exponent of the idea of the sublime, not the watered-down version which merely designates an empty notion of 'greatness' and 'beauty', but the original idea expressed in Kant that happiness lies only in the human power to bear exposure to art, because it reminds us of the irreconcilable ruptures of our existence (Welsch 1990: 114).

The only atonement of the modernist poem for its existence in spite of its impossibility ('Every work is a "desecration of silence" (Beckett), wishing it were possible to restore that silence'; Adorno 1984: 195) is its death. How this can be achieved in aesthetic terms (a complete negation of the utterance is unthinkable) is a difficult question. It is evident, however, that the modernist dialectic of tensions must be continued and radicalised – until it embraces work and subject. Consequently the 'postmodern' poem is forced to question its own status and refuse a position of authority both to itself and its reader. In Lyotard's characterisation:

> . . . the avant-garde is not concerned with what happens to the 'subject', but with 'Does it happen?', with privation. This is the sense in which it still belongs to the aesthetics of the sublime. In asking the question of the *It happens* that the work of art is, avant-garde art abandons the role of identification that the work previously played in relation to the community of addressees.
>
> (Lyotard 1989: 208)

The work of art could then conform to the most sensible description of postmodernism to date, the one given by Wolfgang Welsch in his seminal study *Unsere postmoderne Moderne* (Our Postmodern Modernism), in which he calls postmodernism the fulfilment of some of the promises inherent in modernism (Welsch 1988: 6, 319–20). The most important of these promises is the one formulated by Adorno as the justice towards heterogeneity (Adorno 1984: 266–7; Welsch 1990: 130). In a negative formulation this means a farewell to totalisations. Under no circumstances must an awareness of the human capacity for speech lead to a world-formula based on nominalist principles as described by Walter Benjamin: 'The conviction that the spiritual essence of a thing consists in its language – this view understood as a hypothesis is the great abyss into which all theory of language threatens to fall, and to sustain itself hovering above it is its very task.' And, in a footnote to the above statement: 'Or is it the temptation to place this hypothesis at the beginning which creates the abyss of all philosophising?' (Benjamin 1988: 10; my translation).

Equally dangerous – and just as much a totalisation – is the opposite of a nominalist world-formula: the setting-up of relativism as norm. Exclusions and assertions will be made and have to be made. It is essential, however, to retain an awareness of these mechanisms and an insight into the – often missing or dubious – premises of one's concepts.

This affects acts of interpretation, too – such as the present study. Adorno stresses the importance of criticism to fight the appearance of unity and the false reification of works of art (Adorno 1984: 267). Yet the nimbus of closure and completeness does not spare interpretations and critical writings either. That makes it necessary to point out at this stage that the present study is *one way* of seeing and evaluating modernist poetry, one approach which of necessity strives towards a relative coherence of its own, but remains partial and must compete in its relative value with possible others. It certainly does not manage to present *the concept of modernism* (this is the only criticism I would aim in the direction of Eysteinsson's excellent book of this title). A closed evaluation would indeed betray its inadequacy concerning its object – if this object is modernism's aesthetics of tension and openness. Yet again, insight into the relativity of one's position must not lead to an institutionalisation of this relativity. Therefore the present study concludes inconclusively with Wittgenstein's warning – which embraces once more the impasses of modernist poetry: 'A doubt that doubted everything would not be a doubt' (Wittgenstein 1969: 59e).

NOTES

1. 'Seduction is not mysterious; it is enigmatic. The enigma, like the secret, is not unintelligible. It is, on the contrary, fully intelligible, but it cannot be said or revealed' (Baudrillard 1990: 107).
2. Heidegger's organicist notion of truth acquiring its own language is discussed in Jan Aler, 'Heidegger's Conception of Language in *Being and Time*' (Kockelmans 1972: 51–2).

Bibliography

HOPKINS

Primary sources

Hopkins G.M. 1953 *Poems and prose* ed. W.H. Gardner. Penguin

Hopkins G.M. 1970 *The poems of Gerard Manley Hopkins* 4th edn 1989, ed. W.H. Gardner, N.H. MacKenzie. Oxford University Press

Hopkins G.M. 1990 *The poetical works of Gerard Manley Hopkins* ed. N.H. MacKenzie. Clarendon Press

Bibliography

Dunne T. 1976 *Gerard Manley Hopkins: a comprehensive bibliography*. Oxford University Press

Secondary sources

Bergonzi B. 1977 *Gerard Manley Hopkins*. Macmillan

Boyle R. 1960 *Metaphor in Hopkins*. University of North Carolina Press, Chapel Hill

Bump J. 1982 *Gerard Manley Hopkins.* Twayne, Boston (Twayne's English Authors Series)

Dilligan R.J., Bender T.K. 1970 *A concordance to the English poetry of Gerard Manley Hopkins.* University of Wisconsin Press, Madison

Downes D.A. 1983 *The great sacrifice: studies in Hopkins.* University Press of America, Lanham

Gardner W.H. 1949 *Gerard Manley Hopkins (1844–1889): a study of poetic idiosyncrasy in relation to poetic tradition* (2 vols). Oxford University Press

Gleason J.B. 1989 The Sexual Underthought in Hopkins' 'The Windhover'. *Victorian Poetry* **27** (2): 201–8

Harris D.A. 1982 *Inspirations unbidden: the 'Terrible Sonnets' of Gerard Manley Hopkins.* University of California Press, Berkeley

Heuser A. 1958 *The shaping vision of Gerard Manley Hopkins.* Oxford University Press

Hopkins G.M. 1980 *Selected prose* ed. G. Roberts. Oxford University Press

Johnson W.S. 1968 *Gerard Manley Hopkins: the poet as Victorian.* Cornell University Press, Ithaca

Johnson W.S. 1976 Sexuality and Inscape. *Hopkins Quarterly* **3** (2): 59–65

Kapitułka K. 1976 *Structural principles of Gerard Manley Hopkins' poetry.* Panstwowe Wydawnictwo Naukowe, Warsaw

Kenyon Critics 1975 *Gerard Manley Hopkins: a critical symposium.* Burns and Oates

Kitchen P. 1978 *Gerard Manley Hopkins.* Hamish Hamilton

Korg J. 1977 Hopkins' Linguistic Deviations. *PMLA* **92** (5): 977–86

Loomis J.B. 1988 *Dayspring in darkness: sacrament in Hopkins.* Bucknell University Press, Lewisburg

MacKenzie N.H. 1981 *A reader's guide to Gerard Manley Hopkins.* Thames & Hudson

Milroy J. 1977 *The language of Gerard Manley Hopkins.* André Deutsch

Ong W.J. 1986 *Hopkins, the self, and God.* University of Toronto Press, Toronto (The Alexander Lectures)

Peters W.A.M. 1948 *Gerard Manley Hopkins: a critical essay towards the understanding of his poetry.* Oxford University Press

Robinson J. 1978 *In extremity: a study of Gerard Manley Hopkins.* Cambridge University Press

Sprinker M. 1980 *'A counterpoint of dissonance': the aesthetics and poetry of Gerard Manley Hopkins.* Johns Hopkins University Press, Baltimore

Sutton M.K. 1975 Selving as individuation in Hopkins: a Jungian reading. *Hopkins Quarterly* **2** (3): 119–30

Thornton R.K.R. 1973 *Gerard Manley Hopkins: the poems*. Edward Arnold

van Noppen L.M. 1980 Gerard Manley Hopkins: *The Wreck of the Deutschland* (dissertation). Groningen

Weyand N. 1949 (ed.) *Immortal Diamond: Studies in Gerard Manley Hopkins*. Sheed and Ward

Yadugire M.A. 1984 Linguistic Deviations in Hopkins' Poetry. *Hopkins Quarterly* **1/2**: 3–30

YEATS

Primary sources

Yeats W.B. 1937 *A vision*. Macmillan

Yeats W.B. 1950 *The collected poems of William Butler Yeats*. Macmillan

Yeats W.B. 1955 *Autobiographies*. Macmillan

Yeats W.B. 1983 *The poems: a new edition* ed. R.J. Finneran. Gill and Macmillan

Bibliography

Jochum K.P.S. 1978 *W.B. Yeats: a classified bibliography of criticism*. University of Illinois Press, Chicago

Wade A. 1951 *A Bibliography of the Writings of W.B. Yeats*. Rupert Hart-Davis

Secondary sources

Albright D. 1972 *The myth against myth: a study of Yeats's imagination in old age*. Oxford University Press

Bell M. 1973 The assimilation of doubt in Yeats's visionary poems. *Queen's Quarterly* **80** (3): 383–97

Berrman C. 1967 *W.B. Yeats: design of opposites.* Exposition Press, New York

Bloom H. 1970 *Yeats.* Oxford University Press, New York

Bruch H. 1975 *W.B. Yeats: Dichterische Tradition zwischen Isolation und Integration.* Peter Lang, Frankfurt am Main

Donoghue D. (ed.) 1964 *The integrity of Yeats* Mercier Press, Cork (The Thomas Davis Lecture)

Donoghue D. 1971 *Yeats.* Fontana/Collins (Fontana Modern Masters)

Donoghue D., Mulryne J.R. (eds) 1965 *An honoured guest: new essays on W.B. Yeats.* Edward Arnold

Driscoll R.O. 1975 *Symbolism and some implications of the symbolic approach: W.B. Yeats during the eighteen-nineties.* Dolmen Press, Dublin (New Yeats Papers)

Ellmann R. 1954 *The identity of Yeats.* Faber & Faber

Ellmann R. 1961 *Yeats: the man and the masks.* Faber & Faber

Engelberg E. 1964 *The vast design: patterns in W.B. Yeats' aesthetics.* University of Toronto Press, Toronto

Garab A.M. 1969 *Beyond Byzantium: the last phase of Yeats's career.* Northern Illinois University Press, De Kalb

Hahn H.J. 1971 *Die Krisis des Lyrischen in den Gedichten von W.B. Yeats und W.H. Auden.* Alfred Kümmerle, Göttingen

Hessenberger E. 1986 *Metapoesie und Metasprache in der Lyrik von W.B. Yeats.* Andreas Haller, Passau

Hirschberg S. 1979 *At the top of the tower: Yeats's poetry explored through 'A Vision'.* Carl Winter, Heidelberg

Hone J. 1971 *W.B. Yeats.* Pelican

Jeffares A.N. 1949 *W.B. Yeats: man and poet.* Yale University Press, New Haven.

Jeffares A.N. 1950 Notes on Yeats's 'Lapis Lazuli'. *Modern Language Notes* 65 (75): 488–91

Jeffares A.N. 1961 *The poetry of W.B. Yeats.* Edward Arnold

Jeffares A.N. 1968 *A commentary on the collected poems of W.B. Yeats.* Macmillan

Jeffares A.N. 1970 *The circus animals: essays on W.B. Yeats.* Macmillan

Jeffares A.N. 1971 *W.B. Yeats.* Routledge & Kegan Paul

Jeffares A.N. 1984 *A new commentary on the collected poems of W.B. Yeats.* Macmillan

Jeffares A.N., Cross K.G.W. (eds) 1965 *In excited revery: a centenary tribute to W.B. Yeats.* Macmillan

Keane P.J. (ed.) 1963 *William Butler Yeats: a collection of criticism.* McGraw-Hill, New York

Kleinstück J. 1963 *W.B. Yeats oder Der Dichter in der modernen Welt.* Leibniz, Hamburg

Klimek T. 1967 *Symbol und Wirklichkeit bei W.B. Yeats.* Bouvier, Bonn (Abhandlungen zur Kunst-, Musik- und Literaturwissenschaft)

Komesu O. 1984 *The double perspective of Yeats's aesthetics.* Colin Smythe, Gerrards Cross (Irish Literary Studies)

Kremen K.R. 1972 *The imagination of the resurrection: the poetic continuity of a religious motif in Donne, Blake, and Yeats.* Bucknell University Press, Lewisburg

Lander J. 1967 *W.B. Yeats: Die Bildersprache seiner Lyrik.* Kohlhammer, Stuttgart (Sprache und Literatur)

Latimer D.R. 1972 *Problems of the symbol: a theory and the application in the poetry of Valéry, Rilke, and Yeats* (thesis). University of Michigan

Levine B. 1970 *The dissolving image: the spiritual–esthetic development of W.B. Yeats.* Wayne State University Press, Detroit

Mac Liammóir M., Boland E. 1971 *W.B. Yeats.* Thames & Hudson (Literary Lives)

Maxwell D.E.S., Bushrui, S.B. (eds) 1965 *W.B. Yeats: centenary essays on the art of W.B. Yeats.* Ibadan University Press, Ibadan

Melchiori G. 1960 *The whole mystery of art: pattern into poetry in the works of W.B. Yeats.* Routledge & Kegan Paul

Miller L. (ed.) 1965–68 *The Dolmen Press Yeats centenary papers.* Dolmen Press, Dublin

Olney J. 1980 *The rhizome and the flower: the perennial philosophy – Yeats and Jung.* University of California Press, Berkeley

Parkinson T. 1964 *W.B. Yeats: the later poetry.* University of California Press, Berkeley

Regueiro H. 1976 *The limits of imagination: Wordsworth, Yeats, and Stevens.* Cornell University Press, Ithaca

Rosenthal M.L. 1978 *Sailing into the unknown: Yeats, Pound and Eliot.* Oxford University Press

Saul G.B. 1966 The winged image: a note on birds in Yeats's poems. In Miller, L. (ed.) *In . . . Luminous Wind.* Dolmen Press, Dublin (Yeats Centenary Papers)

Seiden M.I. 1962 *William Butler Yeats: the poet as a mythmaker.* Michigan University Press, Michigan

Shaw P.W. 1964 *Rilke, Valéry and Yeats: the domain of the self.* Rutgers University Press, New Brunswick

Snukal R.M. 1973 *High talk: the philosophical poetry of W.B. Yeats.* Cambridge University Press

Stauffer D.A. 1949 *The golden nightingale: essays on some principles of poetry in the lyrics of W.B. Yeats.* Hafner, New York

Tindall W.Y. 1966 *W.B. Yeats.* Columbia University Press, New York

Tuohy F. 1976 *Yeats.* Macmillan

Unterecker J. (ed.) 1963 *Yeats: a collection of critical essays.* Prentice-Hall, Englewood Cliffs

Webster B. 1974 *Yeats: a psychoanalytic study.* Macmillan

Whitacker T.R. 1959 *Swan and shadow: Yeats's dialogue with history.* University of North Carolina Press, Chapel Hill

Wilson F.A.C. 1958 *W.B. Yeats and tradition.* Macmillan

Wilson F.A.C. 1960 *Yeats's iconography.* Victor Gollancz

Zwerdling A. 1965 *Yeats and the heroic ideal.* New York University Press, New York

ELIOT

Primary sources

Eliot T.S. 1957 *On poetry and poets.* Faber & Faber

Eliot T.S. 1974 *Collected poems 1909–1962.* Faber & Faber

Eliot T.S. 1975 *Selected prose of T.S. Eliot* ed. F. Kermode. Faber & Faber

Bibliography

Ricks B. 1974 *T.S. Eliot: a bibliography of secondary works.* Scarecrow Press, Metuchen

Secondary sources

Allen M. 1974 *T.S. Eliot's impersonal theory of poetry.* Bucknell University Press, Lewisburg

Austin A. 1962 T.S. Eliot's theory of dissociation. *College English* **23** (4): 309–12

Austin F.O. 1982 'Ing' form in *Four Quartets*. *English Studies* **63**: 23–31

Bay-Petersen O. 1985 T.S. Eliot and Einstein: the fourth dimension in the *Four Quartets*. *English Studies* **66** (2): 143–55

Bedient C. 1986 *He do the police in different voices: 'The Waste Land' and its protagonists*. University of Chicago Press, Chicago

Beehler Michael 1987 *T.S. Eliot, Wallace Stevens, and the discourse of difference*. Indiana State University Press, Baton Rouge

Chandran K.N. 1988 Ṣhantih in *The Waste Land*. *American Literature* **61** (4): 681–3

Childs D.J. 1991 T.S. Eliot's rhapsody of matter and memory. *American Literature* **63** (3): 474–88

Davidson H. 1985 *T.S. Eliot and hermeneutics: absence and interpretation in 'The Waste Land'*. Louisiana State University Press, Baton Rouge

Ellmann M. 1987 *The poetics of impersonality: T.S. Eliot and Ezra Pound*. Harvester Press

Hildesheimer W. 1974 Die Wirklichkeit der Reaktionäre: Über T.S. Eliot und Ezra Pound. *Merkur*: 630–47

Johnson A.L. 1985 'Broken images': discursive fragmentation and paradigmatic integrity in the poetry of T.S. Eliot. *Poetics Today* **6** (3): 399–416

Kenner H. 1965 *The invisible poet: T.S. Eliot*. Methuen

Kermode F. 1957 Dissociation of sensibility. *Kenyon Review* **19**: 169–94

Kirk R. 1974 Personality and medium in Eliot and Pound. *Sewanee Review* **82**: 698–704

Matthiessen F.O. 1935 *The achievement of T.S. Eliot: an essay on the nature of poetry*. Oxford University Press

Nevo R. 1982 *The Waste Land*: ur-text of deconstruction. *New Literary History* **13**: 453–61

Patterson G. 1971 *T.S. Eliot: poems in the making*. Manchester University Press

Pinkney T.A. 1984 *Women in the poetry of T.S. Eliot: a psychoanalytic approach*. Macmillan

Preston P. 1959 A Note on T.S. Eliot and Sherlock Holmes. *Modern Language Review*, **54**: 397–9

Rajan B. 1976 *The overwhelming question: a study of the poetry of T.S. Eliot*. University of Toronto Press, Toronto

Roth S. 1993 Eliot comforted: the Yeatsian presence in *Four Quartets*. *Journal of Modern Literature*, **18**(4): 407–16

Schmidt A.V.C. 1983 Eliot and the dialect of the tribe. *Essays in Criticism* **33**: 36–48
Schmidt A.V.C. 1991 The integrity of Eliot. *Essays in Criticism* **41** (3): 222–39
Smith G. 1974 *T.S. Eliot's poetry and plays: a study in sources and meaning* 2nd edn. University of Chicago Press, Chicago
Southam B.C. 1968 *A student's guide to the Selected Poems of T.S. Eliot.* Faber & Faber
Unger L. 1966 T.S. Eliot's images of awareness. *Sewanee Review* **74** (1): 197–224

POUND

Primary sources

Pound E. 1910 *The spirit of romance.* Dent
Pound E. 1938 *Guide to Kulchur.* Faber & Faber
Pound E. 1954 *The literary essays of Ezra Pound* ed. T.S. Eliot. Faber & Faber
Pound E. 1968 *Collected shorter poems.* Faber & Faber
Pound E. 1973 *Selected prose* ed. W. Cookson. Faber & Faber
Pound E. 1987 *The Cantos.* Faber & Faber

Bibliography

Ricks B. 1986 *Ezra Pound: a bibliography of secondary works.* Scarecrow Press, Metuchen

Secondary sources

Ackroyd P. 1981 *Ezra Pound.* Thames & Hudson (Literary Lives)
Alexander M. 1979 *The poetic achievement of Ezra Pound.* Faber & Faber

Bell T.A. 1988 *The hero Polumetis: a new interpretation of 'The Cantos' of Ezra Pound* (thesis). Oxford

Brooker P. 1979 *A student's guide to the Selected Poems of Ezra Pound.* Faber & Faber

Carpenter H. 1988 *A serious character: the life of Ezra Pound.* Houghton Mifflin, Boston

Cookson W. 1985 *A guide to 'The Cantos' of Ezra Pound.* Croom Helm, Sidney

Davenport G. 1983 *Cities on hills.* UMI Research Press, Ann Arbor

Davie D. 1964 *Ezra Pound: poet as sculptor.* Oxford University Press

Davie D. 1975 *Ezra Pound.* University of Chicago Press, Chicago

Durant A. 1981 *Ezra Pound: identity in crisis.* Harvester Press

Ellmann M. 1979 Floating the Pound: the circulation of the subject in Pound's *The Cantos. Oxford Literary Review* **3** (3): 16–27

Harmon W. 1977 *Time in Ezra Pound's work.* University of North Carolina Press, Chapel Hill

Hesse E. (ed.) 1969 *New approaches to Ezra Pound: a co-ordinated investigation of Pound's poetry and ideas.* Faber & Faber

Homberger E. (ed.) 1972 *Ezra Pound: the critical heritage.* Routledge & Kegan Paul (Critical Heritage Series)

Jung H.Y. 1984 Misreading the ideogram: from Fenollosa to Derrida and McLuhan. *Paideuma* **13** (1): 211–27

Kearns G. 1980 *Guide to Ezra Pound's 'Selected Cantos'.* Dawson, Folkestone

Kearns G. 1989 *Ezra Pound: The Cantos.* Cambridge University Press (Landmarks of World Literature)

Kenner H. 1972 *The Pound era.* Faber & Faber

Kenner H. 1974 *The poetry of Ezra Pound.* Kraus Reprint Co., Milwood

Link F. 1984 *Ezra Pound.* Artemis, Munich and Zurich (Artemis Einführungen)

Longenbach J. 1988 *Stone cottage: Pound, Yeats and modernism.* Oxford University Press

Makin P. 1985 *Pound's Cantos.* Allen & Unwin (Unwin Critical Library)

Moody A.D. 1982 The Pisan Cantos: making cosmos in the wreckage of Europe. *Paideuma* **12** (1): 135–46

Nänny M. 1973 *Ezra Pound: poetics for an electric age.* Francke, Bern

Nicholls P. 1984 *Ezra Pound: politics, economics and writing – a study of 'The Cantos'.* Macmillan (Macmillan Studies in American Literature)

North M. 1983 The architecture of memory: Pound and the Tempio Malatestiano. *American Literature* 55 (3): 367–87

Rabaté J.-M. 1986 *Language, sexuality and ideology in Ezra Pound's 'Cantos'*. New York State University Press, Albany

Ruthven K.K. 1969 *A guide to Ezra Pound's 'Personae' (1926)*. University of California Press, Berkeley

Smith M., Ulmer W.A. (eds) 1988 *Ezra Pound: the legacy of Kulchur.* University of Alabama Press, Tuscaloosa

Smith P. 1983 *Pound revised.* Croom Helm

PSYCHOANALYSIS

Abraham N., Torok M. 1986 *The Wolf Man's magic word: a cryptonymy* trans. Rand N. University of Minnesota Press, Minneapolis (Theory and History of Literature)

Bersani L. 1986 *The Freudian body: psychoanalysis and art.* Columbia University Press, New York

Collier P., Davies J. (eds) 1990 *Modernism and the European unconscious.* Polity Press

Deleuze G., Guattari F. 1984 *Anti-Oedipus: capitalism and schizophrenia* trans. Hurley R., Seem M., Lane H.R. Athlone

Felman S. (ed.) 1982 *Literature and psychoanalysis: the question of reading: otherwise.* Johns Hopkins University Press, Baltimore

Freud S. 1973–86 *The Pelican Freud library* ed. Richards A., Dickson A. (15 vols). Pelican

Hartmann G. 1978 *Psychoanalysis and the question of the text.* Johns Hopkins University Press, Baltimore (Selected Papers from the English Institute, 1976–77, New Series, 2)

Jung C.G. 1959 *The collected works of Carl G. Jung* trans. Hull R.F.C., ed. Read M., Fordham M., Adler G. (20 vols + 4 unnumbered vols). Routledge & Kegan Paul

Kristeva J. 1984 *Revolution in poetic language* trans. Waller M. Columbia University Press, New York

Lacan J. 1977a *Ecrits: a selection* trans. Sheridan A. Tavistock

Lacan J. 1977b *The four fundamental concepts of psychoanalysis* trans. Sheridan A., ed. Miller J.-A. Hogarth (The International Psychoanalytical Library)

Lyotard J.-F. 1974 *Économie libidinale.* Editions de Minuit, Paris (Collection 'Critique')

Oxford Literary Review 1990 *Psychoanalysis and Literature: New Work.* 12 (1-2)

Rogers R. 1978 *Metaphor: a psychoanalytic view.* University of California Press, Berkeley

ECONOMY

Bataille G. 1967 *La part maudite: précédé de La Notion de dépense.* Edition de Minuit, Paris (Collection 'Critique')

Bataille G. 1988 *The accursed share: an essay on general economy* trans. Hurley R. Zone Books, New York

Baudrillard J. 1972 *Pour une critique de l'économie politique du signe.* Gallimard, Paris (Les Essais)

Baudrillard J. 1976 *L'Echange symbolique et la mort.* Gallimard, Paris (Bibliothèque des Sciences humaines)

Baudrillard J. 1987 *L'Autre par lui-même: habilitation.* Editions Galilée, Paris (Collection Débats)

Baudrillard J. 1988 *Selected writings* ed. Poster M. Polity Press

Baudrillard J. 1900 *Fatal strategies* trans. Beitchman P., Niesluchowski W.C.J., ed. Fleming J. Pluto Press

Connor S. 1992 *Theory and cultural value.* Blackwell

Knapp J.F. 1988 *Literary modernism and the transformation of work.* Northwestern University Press, Evanston

Marx K. 1976 *Capital: a critique of political economy* trans. Fowkes B. (3 vols). Penguin

Tawney R.H. 1926 *Religion and the rise of capitalism.* Penguin

Weber M. 1930 *The Protestant ethic and the spirit of capitalism* trans. Parsons T. Allen & Unwin

PHILOSOPHY

Adorno T.W. 1973 *The jargon of authenticity* trans. Tarnowski K., Will F. Routledge & Kegan Paul

Adorno T.W. 1984 *Aesthetic theory* trans. Lenhardt C., ed. Adorno G., Tiedemann R. Routledge (The International Library of Phenomenology and Moral Sciences)

Adorno T.W., Horkheimer M. 1979 *Dialectic of Enlightenment* trans. Cummings J. Verso

Aristotle 1920 *On the art of poetry* trans. Bywater I. Oxford University Press

Bové P.A. 1980 *Destructive poetics: Heidegger and modern American poetry*. Columbia University Press, New York

Deleuze G. 1986 *Foucault*. Editions de Minuit, Paris

Derrida J. 1976 *Of grammatology* trans. Spivak G.C. Johns Hopkins University Press, Baltimore

Derrida J. 1978 *Writing and difference* trans. Bass A. Routledge & Kegan Paul

Derrida J. 1982 *Margins of philosophy* trans. Bass A. Routledge & Kegan Paul

Foucault M. 1963a Préface à la transgression *Critique* **19** (195–6): 751–69

Foucault M. 1963b Le langage a l'infini. *Tel Quel* **15**: 44–53

Foucault M. 1970 *The order of things*. trans. from the French. Tavistock (World of Man)

Foucault M. 1972 *The archaeology of knowledge* trans. Sheridan Smith A.M. Tavistock (World of Man)

Griffiths A.P. (ed.) 1984 *Philosophy and literature*. Cambridge University Press (Royal Institute of Philosophy Lecture Series)

Habermas J. 1987 *The philosophical discourse of modernity: twelve lectures*, trans. Lawrence F.G. Polity (Studies in Contemporary German Social Thought)

Heidegger M. 1962 *Being and time* trans. Macquarrie J., Robinson E. Blackwell

Heidegger M. 1971 *Poetry, language, thought* trans. Hofstadter A. Harper & Row, New York

Höhn H.-J. (ed.) 1992 *Theologie, die an der Zeit ist*. Schöningh, Paderborn

Jaspers K. 1964 Umgang mit dem Mythos. *Merkur* **191**: 1–13

Jay M. 1984 *Adorno*. Fontana (Fontana Modern Masters)

Kearney R. 1991 *Poetics of imagining: from Husserl to Lyotard.* HarperCollins (Problems of Modern European Thought)

Klaus G., Buhr M. (eds.) 1976 *Philosophisches Wörterbuch* (2 vols). Verlag das europäische Buch, Berlin

Kockelmans J.J. (ed.) 1972 *On Heidegger and language.* Northwestern University Press, Evanston (Northwestern Studies in Phenomenology and Existential Philosophy)

Lyotard J.-F. 1989 *The Lyotard reader* ed. Benjamin A. Blackwell

Marquard O. 1989 *Farewell to matters of principle: philosophical studies* trans. Wallace R.M. Oxford University Press (Odéon)

Nietzsche F. 1980 *Sämtliche Werke: Kritische Studienausgabe* ed. Colli G., Montinari M. (15 vols). Deutscher Taschenbuch Verlag, Munich

Nietzsche F. 1989 *Friedrich Nietzsche on rhetoric and language* trans. and ed. Gilman S.L., Blair C., Parent D.J. Oxford University Press

Norris C. 1987 *Derrida.* Fontana (Fontana Modern Masters)

Pears D. 1971 *Wittgenstein.* Fontana (Fontana Modern Masters)

Plato 1935 *The republic* with an English translation by Shorey P. (2 vols). Heinemann

Rentsch T. 1989 *Martin Heidegger – Das Sein und der Tod: Eine kritische Einführung.* Piper, Munich and Zurich (Serie Piper)

Ries W. 1982 *Nietzsche zur Einführung.* SOAK, Hanover (SOAK-Einführungen)

Sprinker M. 1987 *Imaginary relations: aesthetics and ideology in the theory of historical materialism.* Verso

Welsch W. 1988 *Unsere postmoderne Moderne* 2nd edn. VCH, Weinheim (Acta humaniora)

Welsch W. 1990 *Ästhetisches Denken.* Reclam, Stuttgart

White D.A. 1978 *Heidegger and the language of poetry.* University of Nebraska Press, Lincoln

Wittgenstein L. 1961 *Tractatus logico-philosophicus: the German text of Ludwig Wittgenstein's Logisch-philosophische Abhandlung with a new translation* trans. Pears D.F., MacGuinness B.F. Routledge & Kegan Paul (International Library of Philosophy and Scientific Method)

Wittgenstein L. 1969 *Über Gewißheit: on certainty* trans. Paul D., Anscombe G.E.M., ed. Anscombe G.E.M. von Wright G.M. Blackwell

THEORIES OF LANGUAGE AND LITERATURE

Attridge D. 1981 The language of poetry: materiality and meaning. *Essays in Criticism* **31**: 228–45

Bakhtin M.M. 1984 *Rabelais and his world* trans. Iswolsky H. Indiana State University Press, Bloomington

Barthes R. 1967a *Writing degree zero* trans. Lavers A., Smith C. Cape (Cape Editions)

Barthes R. 1967b *Elements of semiology* trans. Lavers A., Smith C. Cape (Cape Editions)

Barthes R. 1973 *Mythologies* trans. Lavers A. Paladin

Barthes R. 1974 *S/Z* trans. Miller R. Hill and Wang, New York

Barthes R. 1975 *The pleasure of the text* trans. Miller R. Farrar, Straus and Giroux, New York

Bloom H. 1973 *The anxiety of influence: a theory of poetry*. Oxford University Press

Collier P., Geyer-Ryan H. (eds) 1990 *Literary theory today*. Polity Press

Cooper D.A. 1986 *Metaphor*. Blackwell (Aristotelian Society Series)

de Man P. 1983 *Blindness and insight: essays in the rhetoric of contemporary criticism* 2nd edn. University of Minnesota Press, Minneapolis (Theory and History of Literature)

de Saussure F. 1960 *Cours de linguistique générale* ed. Bally C., Sechehaye A., Riedlinger A. Payot, Paris (Bibliothèque Scientifique)

de Saussure F. 1983 *Course in general linguistics* trans. Harris R. Duckworth

Eagleton T. 1986 *Literary theory: an introduction*. Blackwell

Eco U. 1972 *Einführung in die Semiotik* trans. Trabant J. Fink, Munich

Emig R. 1991 Text–literature–text: self-reflection and self-destruction as two related features of textual systems. *Warwick Work in Progress* **1**: 1–7

Frye N. 1970 *The stubborn structure: essays on criticism and society*. Methuen

Holenstein E. 1976 *Roman Jakobson's approach to language: phenomenological structuralism* trans. Schelbert C., Schelbert T. Indiana State University Press, Bloomington

Jakobson R. 1971 *Word and language*. Mouton, The Hague (Selected Writings)

Jakobson R. 1979 *Poetik: Ausgewählte Aufsätze 1921–1971* ed. Holenstein E., Schelbert T. Suhrkamp, Frankfurt am Main

Jakobson R. 1987 *Language in literature* ed. Pomorska K., Rudy S. The Belknap Press, Cambridge (Mass.)

Jefferson A., Robey D. (eds.) 1982 *Modern literary theory: a comparative introduction*. Batsford

Jolles A. 1930 *Einfache Formen: Legende, Sage, Mythe, Rätsel, Spruch, Kasus, Memorabile, Märchen, Witz*. Niemeyer, Tübingen (Konzepte der Sprach- und Literaturwissenschaft)

Kittay E.F. 1987 *Metaphor: its cognitive force and linguistic structure*. Clarendon Press (Clarendon Library of Logic and Philosophy)

Krampen M. et al. (eds) 1981 *Die Welt als Zeichen: Klassiker der modernen Semiotik*. Severin & Siedler, Berlin

Lévi-Strauss C. 1963 *Structural anthropology* trans. Jacobson C., Schoepf B. G. Basic Books, New York and London

Link J. 1974 *Literaturwissenschaftliche Grundbegriffe: Eine programmierte Einführung auf strukturalistischer Basis*. Fink, Munich

Lodge D. (ed.) 1972 *Twentieth-century literary criticism: a reader*. Longman

Lotman Y. 1976 *Analysis of the poetic text* trans. Johnson D.B. Ardis, Ann Arbor

Miles J. 1983 Poetic Space. *Poetica* **14**: 22–35

Müller M., Sottong H.J. 1991 Äusserung, Simulation, Realität: Typen der Referenz auf 'Wirkliches'. *Zeitschrift für Semiotik* **13** (1–2): 149–64

Rice P., Waugh P. (eds.) 1989 *Modern literary theory: a reader*. Edward Arnold

Ricoeur P. 1976 *Interpretation theory: discourse and the surplus of meaning*. Texas Christian University Press, Fort Worth

Riffaterre M. 1978 *Semiotics of poetry*. Indiana State University Press, Bloomington (Advances in Semiotics)

Riffaterre M. 1983 *Text production* trans. Lyons T. Columbia University Press, New York

Sacks S. (ed.) 1979 *On metaphor*. University of Chicago Press, Chicago

MODERNITY, MODERNISM, POSTMODERNISM

Bell M. (ed.) 1980 *1900–1930.* Methuen (The Context of English Literature)

Bell M. (forthcoming) Odysseus Bound: Joyce, Nietzsche and the Myth of Modernism. In Bell M. (ed.) *Modernism and mythopoeia: belief in the twentieth century*. Cambridge University Press

Benjamin W. 1968 *Illuminations* trans. Zohn H., ed. Arendt H. Harcourt, Brace and World, New York

Benjamin W. 1988 *Angelus Novus.* Suhrkamp, Frankfurt am Main (Ausgewählte Schriften)

Blumenberg H. 1979 *Arbeit am Mythos.* Suhrkamp, Frankfurt am Main

Bradbury M., McFarlane J. (eds) 1976 *Modernism: 1890–1930.* Penguin

Brooker P. 1992 *Modernism/Postmodernism.* Longman

Bürger P. 1984 *Theory of the avant-garde* trans. Shaw M. University of Minnesota Press, Minneapolis (Theory and History of Literature)

Donoghue D. 1968 *The ordinary universe: soundings in modern literature.* Faber & Faber

Evans B.I. 1948 *English literature between the wars.* Methuen

Eysteinsson A. 1990 *The concept of modernism.* Cornell University Press, Ithaca

Faulkner P. 1977 *Modernism.* Methuen (The Critical Idiom)

Fokkema D.W. 1984 *Literary history, modernism, and postmodernism.* John Benjamin, Amsterdam and Philadelphia (Utrecht Publications in General and Comparative Literature)

Foster H. (ed.) 1985 *Postmodern culture.* Pluto Press

Hermans T. 1982 *The structure of modernist poetry.* Croom Helm, London and Canberra

Iser W. 1966 *Immanente Aesthetik, ästhetische Reflexion: Lyrik als Paradigma der Moderne.* Fink, Munich (Poetik und Hermeneutik)

Jones P. (ed.) 1972 *Imagist poetry.* Penguin

Langbaum R. 1970 *The modern spirit: essays on the continuity of nineteenth- and twentieth-century literature.* Oxford University Press

Langbaum R. 1977 *The mysteries of identity: a theme in modern literature.* Oxford University Press

Larrissy E. 1990 *Reading twentieth-century poetry: the language of gender and objects.* Blackwell

Levenson M.H. 1984 *A genealogy of modernism: a study of English literary doctrine 1908–1922.* Cambridge University Press

Lyotard J.-F. 1984 *The post-modern condition: a report on knowledge* trans. Bennington G., Masumi B. Manchester University Press (Theory and History of Literature)

McLuhan H.M. 1967 *The mechanical bride: folklore of industrial man.* Routledge & Kegan Paul

Robinson A. 1985 *Poetry, painting and ideas 1885–1914.* Macmillan

Schwartz S. 1985 *The matrix of modernism: Pound, Eliot, and early twentieth-century thought.* Princeton University Press, Princeton

Smith S. 1994 *The origins of modernism: Eliot, Pound, Yeats and the rhetorics of renewal.* Harvester Wheatsheaf

Wilson E. 1961 *Axel's Castle: a study in the imaginative literature of 1870–1930.* Collins (The Fontana Library)

MISCELLANEOUS

Auden W.H. 1977 *The English Auden: poems, essays and dramatic writings 1927–1929* ed. Mendelson E. Faber & Faber

Carpenter H. 1981 *W.H. Auden: a biography.* Houghton Mifflin, Boston

de Vries L., van Amstel I. 1973 *History as hot news 1865–1897: the late nineteenth century as seen through the eyes of 'The Illustrated London News' and 'The Graphic'.* John Murray

Frisch M. 1964 *Mein Name sei Gantenbein.* Suhrkamp, Frankfurt am Main

Mann T. 1968 *Doctor Faustus: the life of the German composer Adrian Leverkühn as told by a friend* trans. Lowe-Porter H.T. Penguin

Tuchel H.G. 1942 (ed.) *Die Trobadors.* Dieterich'sche Verlagsbuchhandlung, Leipzig (Sammlung Dieterich)

Index